INCARNATION AND IMAGINATION

INCARNATION AND IMAGINATION

A Christian Ethic of Ingenuity

Darby Kathleen Ray

FORTRESS PRESS
MINNEAPOLIS

INCARNATION AND IMAGINATION
A Christian Ethic of Ingenuity

Cover image: Microscopic view of the planktonic diatom actinoptychus. Ca. 1900. Copyright © Adoc-photos / Art Resource, NY. Used by permission.
Cover design: Danielle Carnito
Book design: Michelle L. N. Cook

Library of Congress Cataloging-in-Publication Data
Ray, Darby Kathleen, 1964–
  Incarnation and imagination: a Christian ethic of ingenuity / Darby Kathleen Ray.
    p. cm.
  Includes bibliographical references and index.
  ISBN 978–0–8006–6315–5 (alk. paper)
  1. Christian ethics. 2. Imagination—Religious aspects—Christianity. I. Title.
  BJ1275.R39 2008
  241—dc22   2008016363

12   11   10   09   08   1   2   3   4   5   6   7   8   9   10

CONTENTS

For Chandler and Elena,

whose ingenious play and passion for justice

are daily inspirations

PREFACE

ow can we live responsibly and faithfully in today's morally complex and ambiguous world? When our religious and political leaders use moral language cavalierly—for example, assigning the "evil" label easily to others, with nary a self-critical impulse—do they threaten the language and enterprise of ethics itself? In our varied contexts today, what is meant by moral language such as "good" and "evil"? If we Christians find that we have divergent, perhaps even conflicting interpretations of moral language, are we in danger of losing our way in the world? How are ethics and power related to each other? If moral language is at least to some degree the product of the will to power, then do the powerless have their own language, their own ethic? If so, what wisdom or prophetic truth might it have to offer the dominant classes?

In this book, I acknowledge the diversity of moral languages that we speak and hear in today's world, but instead of decrying this diversity as the babble of moral relativism or the battle cry of spiritual warfare, I take a moment instead to listen to some of the voices that I ordinarily do not hear. I invite my reader to join me in attending especially to voices from the margins of social, political, and economic power—to children, women, and people of color. What moral language is being spoken at the edges of power, on the underside of privilege, and what might it have to teach Christians about responsible, faithful living in the twenty-first century?

In addition to familiar experiences, themes, doctrines, and convictions—we are, after all, shorn from the same human fabric—I hear strange, disconcerting things when I am attuned to the margins . . . things that call my own moral language, assumptions, and certainties into question, that require me to stretch my notion of the ethical to uncomfortable proportions. The discomfort does not subside. However, alongside it come fresh insights, surprising revelations, new ways of thinking about what it means to love God and neighbor, to be followers of Jesus the Christ, and to live a "good" life.

In relation to the dominant moral paradigm, ethics from the edge is edgy indeed. Dispositions, behaviors, and choices discounted by the dominant paradigm as problematic, deviant, or immoral are shown to have genuine moral value. In particular, an array of behaviors I collect into the trope of "ingenuity" requires a revaluation of values, a rethinking of Christian ethics. When understood within their proper context, these "deviant" choices and behaviors are without a doubt morally worthy responses to the very real evils of misogyny, slavery, poverty, and racism. They are powerfully imaginative and daringly liberative. They are also, I propose, profoundly Christian. An ethic of ingenuity has its roots in the Incarnation—in God's audacious becoming-of-body in the midst of a body-fearing culture; in God's mind-boggling embodiment of finitude and vulnerability despite the irrefutable assumption that divinity is impassible and infinite; in God's scandalous affirmations of those whom society despises, humiliates, or ignores; in God's unbelievable choice of empathy over empire, mercy over might, persuasion over force. Becoming these things, choosing these things, God risks, God dares, God reveals Godself as the Ingenious Divine.

This book identifies traces of an ethic of ingenuity in Christian history— moments in the past when men and women seeking to live responsibly and faithfully found themselves embracing a deviant morality, an edgy ethic. They did so not to make a statement or stand out as different, not to create a rival moral discourse or a new moral philosophy, but simply to survive with dignity in extraordinarily difficult times. Their ethic of ingenuity did not displace the dominant moral paradigm, nor was it intended to do so, but its very existence stands as an implicit contestation of the dominating power and authority of that paradigm, articulating its excesses, blind spots, and destructive effects, and proving that alternatives are possible.

In addition to tracing the trope of ingenuity in Christian history, this book asks about the potential legitimacy of an ethic of ingenuity in our own day, and not simply for those at the margins but also for those who would be in solidarity with them. What difference might a little "incarnational" creativity make if directed toward today's most daunting challenges? What can we learn from the "christic" imagination of our Christian forebears that might help us respond more courageously and effectively to poverty, terrorism, domestic violence, global warming, imperiled public education, and racism? Troubling the moral waters may well imbalance the powers that be, but given their impotence in the face of many of today's moral challenges, perhaps it is time to rock the ethics boat just a bit.

The book begins with a rather unusual combination as children's stories are put into conversation with what some might call high theory. (Who knew that children's author Leo Lionni and poststructuralist philosopher Judith Butler had so much in common?) The querying of ethics with a liminal sensibility—with an eye on the margins—raises discomfiting questions about the moral authority of ethics itself. Moving from center to periphery, we see the outlines of a moral minority report in which ingenuity, imagination, wit, and cunning are strategically important and communally efficacious. In chapter 1, the *theological* warrants for an ethic of ingenuity are presented. With guidance from a handful of early church fathers, we meet God as the Ingenious Divine, Jesus as Ingenuity Incarnate, and the Spirit as the ongoing vitality and proleptic lure of the Way-Making God who was and is and will be forever. To flesh out the theological vision and test out its ethical implications, I present two extended case studies of an ethic of ingenuity in Christian history. Chapter 2 focuses on medieval women and their curiously body-centered religiosity, while chapter 3 explores a wide range of insights and practices from African-American history and culture. In the book's final chapter, I ask about the possibilities for an incarnation-inspired and -guided ethic of ingenuity for our own day, arguing that such an ethic has enormous potential to enliven Christian communities and redefine discipleship for the twenty-first century.

The thought experiment that eventuated in this book endured its own turbulent journey—a much longer one than anticipated. It began in Nashville with an intriguing comment by Saint Augustine and unexpected support from Gene TeSelle, and worked its way into a theology-focused volume written in upstate New York and published a full decade ago. That volume immediately demanded ethical reflection. The heart of that reflection took place when my oldest daughter, now ten, was but a toddler. Four editors, two presses, a move from New York to Missisippi, a second child, a couple of health scares, a few failed job searches, and several crises of confidence later, this book is a reality at last.

Along this journey, my spirit and confidence have been buoyed by the support of many, many people, only some of whom I can remember at this point. My Millsaps College students and colleagues have shared with me what may well be the most collegial work environment in academe—a gift of a place to work. In particular, I am grateful to students who took my courses, "Discourses of Desire: Spirit and Matter in the Medieval World" and "(G)race Matters: Race, Religion, and Contemporary Black America," in which we tested the ideas explored in chapters 2 and 3. And I raise a glass of gratitude to Millsaps colleagues who offered comment on one part or another of the manuscript: Steve Smith, James Bowley, Kristen Tegtmeier Oertel, Kristen Brown, Sandy Zale, Amy Forbes, Elise Smith, Cory Conover, Brent Fogt, and Laura Franey. Others who provided vital moral, emotional, and/or intellectual support along the way include Jon Berquist, Richard Smith, John Thatamanil, Holly Sypniewski, Bill Danaher, Joerg Rieger, Dwight Hopkins, Sallie McFague, Peter Hodgson, John Kellogg, Louise Hetrick, John Conway, Chip and Melba Bowman, Victoria Krebs, Angie Loflin, Bob and Sharon Clothier, my sister Amy, and my father Jeff Ray. A huge thank you is also due to Michael West, who came to the rescue at the crucial moment, and his great colleagues at Fortress Press. My partner in life and father extraordinaire, Raymond Clothier, helped me carve out the time and generate the will to persist when both were scarce, and he maintained a sense of humor through it all. Finally, the project would not have come to fruition without the unflagging prayers, emotional support, and theological camaraderie of my mother, Pamela Brown Ray.

INTRODUCTION: CHILD'S PLAY?

Children's Stories and an Ethic of Ingenuity

Many of my earliest memories involve books and reading. My mother, who taught pre-school for thirty years, took me along on hot summer mornings as she conducted "story hour" at a public library in my small Florida hometown. The library was a satellite branch—the one on the east side of town. As the paved roads turned to bumpy dirt, our trusty station wagon stirred up thick clouds of yellow-brown sediment that stuck to everything in its path, mixing with the moisture of the dog day air to produce a palpably thick humidity. I remember how proud I felt sitting beside my mom as she skillfully transported us out of the heat and into far-flung universes of cool possibility. Some thirty years later, I find myself reading each week to Mrs. Barnes's kindergarten class at a miserably "under-resourced" public school in Jackson, Mississippi. I reach deep into time to pull out my mother's vocal gymnastics and animated expressions in hopes of pulling one or two of those children into the world of books, a realm of hope and possibility where crack houses and kitchen rats needn't exist and where brave little boys and girls have a genuine shot at adventure and accomplishment regardless of skin color and family income.

THE MORALITY OF TRICKERY AND DECEPTION

One thing has caught my interest. So many of the books I read to those children—the same ones my mother and father read to me and that I now read to my two young daughters—involve trickery or deception. Again and again in children's literature, the weak outwit the strong, the needy one finds some resourceful way to feed herself or find shelter against all odds, the wily one lures the powerful one into making a mistake and hence giving up some bit of mastery or control. And *we as readers are invited to applaud such behavior.* What an odd concept to swallow for fine, upstanding adult citizens of a law-and-order society! Why am I, as a willing reader of these tall tales, encouraging such shenanigans? Why do so many children's books contain themes of cunning, surprise, and ingenious resourcefulness?

Could it be that children's relative social and political powerlessness makes their subversive maneuvering appear harmless or quaint? Are these stories the repository of adults' subconscious desire for deviance and rebellion? Exactly what is going on here? From my vantage point as a Christian theologian interested in the flourishing of all God's creatures and, consequently, the overcoming of unjust, oppressive attitudes, actions, institutions, and discursive regimes, I offer this suggestion: Perhaps children are so fascinated by stories of transgression and subversion because they live in a world largely defined and bound by others, a world in which the rules and regulations are always already there—inexplicable, irrefutable, and often arbitrary—a world of big and little, strong and weak, fast and slow. In such a world, border-crossing must be an intriguing fantasy. The poor, hungry boy who uses a mere stone and a mighty imagination to trick a propertied old woman into giving him a magnificent feast is worthy of admiration: "fancy that!"[1] The little woman who uses the limited resources at hand—a baking pan, a quick wit, and a powerful male's assumption that she is nothing but a harmless wife and mother—defeats a giant and saves her home and husband from destruction. Hooray![2] These acts of moral deviance are also acts of political defiance. This is class-crashing and gender-bending at its best.

So why is an ethic of ingenuity or cunning permissible, even predictable, in children's literature? Why don't we ban such tales as incendiary or subversive? *Because children don't have any real power anyway.* Their games of subterfuge and deception are only games—imaginary play that offers opportunities for the development of a healthy sense of agency, power, and self;[3] narratives that help children learn that "might doesn't make right," that resistance to unjust domination is appropriate and even laudable. Not all children's stories contain this lesson, of course. As William Bennett and other interpreters have shown, this literature is replete with moral teachings aimed at instilling "mainstream" virtues and values such as honesty and loyalty.[4] Still, there is no denying that the moral of many children's stories is at odds with the mainstream morality that Bennett and company promote. Ingenuity, wit, and cunning are portrayed *positively* in these texts. This portrayal causes me to wonder, why aren't such lessons appropriate for *all* of us? Why are subversion, cunning, and scrappy resourcefulness generally considered morally suspect or corrupt? Don't we *all* need to question the rights and rites of the mighty and feel empowered to resist injustice in imaginative ways?

A GENUINE ETHIC OF INGENUITY?

What would it mean to recognize an ethic of ingenuity as a genuine and authentic moral posture? Would such recognition lead to utter chaos? moral relativism? cynical nihilism? Or might it be possible to articulate this posture as one piece of a complex, multilayered, and constantly re-worked mosaic of ethical tradition and moral reasoning? If we were to view an ethic of ingenuity within certain historical, political, materialist contexts, then it might emerge as appropriate rather than aberrant, prophetic rather than pathological. The attitudes and actions of its proponents might be rendered intelligible, worthy of study and evaluation, instead of being dismissed as curious oddities or moral abominations. Then, perhaps, this ethical tradition or stance would merit consideration by scholars and students of moral philosophy and theological ethics.

My purpose in writing this book is to foreground and thematize a strand of moral reasoning that has more often than not been deemed *un*reasonable. In pushing against the constraints and proprieties of ethics as usually conceived, my goal is not so much to discredit previous attempts to frame and evaluate moral discourse as to make room for new considerations, new voices, and fresh hearings of old voices. I argue that the "household" of Christian ethics needs to be expanded—or perhaps renovated—to make room for a larger, more diverse family. Traditional conceptions of ethics and the ethical simply cannot account for the myriad ways in which Christian people forge lives of meaning and responsibility.

In particular, I am interested in one such "way"—a way forged from the underside of power, from the attempts of the oppressed to survive with dignity, agency, and stubborn hope in the face of dehumanization, terror, and moral absurdity. Dominant conceptions of good and evil, right and wrong, and responsible and irresponsible simply cannot account for the experiences of many of those at the margins of social, political, and economic power. More often than not, the complex moral universe of the oppressed is either not really seen at all, or else is dismissed as incomprehensible or immoral. Taking the time to *see* this world reveals the clear presence of what I am calling an ethic of ingenuity—a moral posture that employs imagination, wit, courage, and gritty resourcefulness as morally worthy strategies in the search for and construction of individual and communal flourishing. Admittedly, the epistemology and logic informing and undergirding an ethic of ingenuity may be foreign to many people. Still, I argue it is an ethic with distinctive and identifiable motivations, contours, and criteria. It is an ethic, moreover, without which the larger body of Christian ethics is incomplete, despite the tensions an ethic of ingenuity creates.

This ethic recognizes ingenuity, imagination, cunning, surprise, and parody as appropriate and responsible responses to certain contexts and quandaries. Yet, it also imposes limits on these responses so that it is not an embrace of subversion for subversion's sake. In the two cases I address most thoroughly in this book, the imposition of limits seems to be motivated and shaped by particular interpretations of Christian tradition and discipleship. Thus, these communities' embrace of "christic" or Christ-like imagination results in their embodiment of an ethic of incarnation and ingenuity. Their moral posture can be seen as growing out of their Christian formation and commitment, imbuing their resistance and cunning with the power and danger of the sacred, and offering theological criteria for negotiating that tension.

WIDENING THE BOUNDARIES OF CHRISTIAN ETHICS

In this book, I want to ponder whether the boundaries of Christian ethics have been drawn too narrowly and policed too vigilantly. Perhaps such tight boundaries, regardless of their intentions, function to blind the relatively privileged among us to difficult truths—truths about what it is like to try to live and move and have one's being with integrity and courage in the face of brutal constrictions and dehumanizing dynamics. What difference might it make if we were the tortoise instead of the hare—the one presumed to be slow, dense, and perennially behind rather than the quick one, the sharp one, the one always on the cutting edge? Would we see things differently? Would we *value* things differently? What if we were the poor young man with nothing to eat? Might we consider tricking the old lady into a meal "fit for a king"? What if the forces of the strong and powerful were arrayed unjustly against us? Would we be justified in using wit and deception to upend them? If so, what limits should be placed on our subversion?

These are complex questions, to be sure—questions not fully answered here. However, I believe such questions are worth pondering, worth chewing on for a good while, because they emerge with surprising regularity in the lives of marginalized folk and pose interesting and important challenges to dominant moral traditions and their beneficiaries. From where I sit as a well-educated, upper-middle-class, white North American, questions such as these are more than a bit unsettling. It is decidedly *not* to my advantage to have the dominant definitions of right and wrong, ethical and unethical, called into question. People like me benefit daily from these definitions, and so will our children. Nevertheless, having found myself standing, as it were, face to face with Christian communities that have apparently embraced very different ethical models than I am accustomed to, I cannot help but wonder: What is going on here? Are these people who appear in other respects to be living lives of Christian discipleship and moral integrity really engaged in morally aberrant behavior when they embrace deception, for instance, as a modus operandi in the face of their oppressor? Do they warrant correction, denunciation, pity? Or might there be an eye-opening, mind-stretching lesson for me and my kind here? Having stumbled upon what looks to me like a pattern of non-traditional yet codifiable moral postures among Christian communities very different from my own, my instinct is not to ignore but to explore, not to denounce but to announce. Hence here is this book, this modest attempt to delve into these "non-normative" stances to see what I can see.

At the very least, what I see is an intriguing set of choices—choices that do not always make sense to me, at least at first blush. These choices can seem ill-conceived and ineffective. They can appear to stem from some kind of group pathology rather than a concerted effort at moral existence. At the same time, they are choices that share a family resemblance and that, when viewed from the vantage point of this resemblance, *do* make sense. It is precisely the relative *un*intelligibility of these choices—their lack of fit within the parameters of ethics as traditionally conceived, their *non*sensical nature from the perspective of the dominant class—that piques my interest. Insofar as these choices belong to a "family" of choices and hence constitute a pattern or model of moral thinking, and insofar as this model is embraced or articulated by those "outside" the halls of power and influence, then what we have here might be an outsider's ethic, a way of negotiating moral agency from the outskirts. Perhaps if we insiders could "see" the pattern and appreciate the marriage of form and function it represents, then we could also see and appreciate more fully the resourcefulness, intelligence, and humanity of its practitioners.

THE LIMITS OF AN ETHIC OF INGENUITY

Beyond the goal of increased understanding, I find myself pulled also toward an explicitly theological task. My encounter with this surprising family of choices, this ethic of ingenuity, is shot through with theological valences that cry out for recognition and thematization. As I recount in this book, the choice for cunning or indirection in the face of extreme and systematic delimitation sometimes involves *religious* motivation or confirmation. In this book, we encounter religiously serious women and men who engage in practices of deception or ingenuity and who consider these practices to be moral. We might assume that they are misunderstanding or misusing their religion. But I am intrigued by the possibility that these people have it right—that their religion, in this case Christianity, genuinely empowers them to embrace a non-normative or "immoral" morality. I am convinced that there is something about Christianity—an identifiable strand of narrative or tradition—that permits this embrace. Few Christians today are familiar with this narrative, and yet it was once a vibrant tradition, a respectable gloss on the gospel. Once we become aware of this Christian "minority report" on who God is and what the Incarnation is all about, then certain strands of Christian history that appeared to be patently *un*Christian and *im*moral suddenly look different. Instead of standing easily outside the pale of acceptability, they beg for reconsideration. In the process, they challenge our assumptions about what counts as Christian and as ethical.

Even as this non-normative morality calls traditional notions of Christian truth and ethics into question, the tradition "talks back," insisting that the proverbial baby not be thrown out with the bath water. Christian thought may well include within its parameters a minority moral tradition that can legitimately be used to criticize the dominant moral tradition. However, that minority tradition is not without its own boundaries and limits. An ethic of ingenuity that is rooted in Christian tradition is not a free-for-all but includes its own set of guiding principles and aims. The theo-logic explored in this book asks us to consider that authentic moral agency may vary depending on the specific context under consideration, but it does not lead to the unbounded relativism of what was once known as "situation ethics." Even those forced to negotiate moral existence from contexts of severe restriction and hence with sometimes unorthodox means must nevertheless scrutinize their motives and their aims. In the case of a *Christian* ethic of ingenuity, it is the Incarnation that mentors and guides the imagination; it is the Incarnation that motivates, tutors, and judges moral action. As we will see, the Incarnation constitutes an ethical plumb line that offers both greater moral flexibility than we might have imagined possible within Christian tradition, *and* deep grounding in the familiar. It frees us to recognize the moral legitimacy of previously maligned or misunderstood behaviors in Christian history *and* to see and evaluate their excesses and perversions. An ethic of incarnation and ingenuity pushes in new and, at least for the powerful, discomfiting directions, but it also reiterates ancient convictions and familiar traditions.

AN UNLIKELY WISDOM TRADITION

This combination of familiarity and novelty, of routine and surprise, is the hallmark of a good theology. It is also the key to a good children's book. In *Stone Soup*, that fanciful tale about a poor young man who responds to the evils of poverty and hunger not with despair or resentment but with wit and cunning, we see this mix in action.[5] The reader is comforted by well-known sights and sounds of meal preparation and everyday ingredients, as well as by the reiterated incantation, "Soup from a stone—fancy that!" These familiar refrains prepare the reader's palate for the surprising reality the story dishes out: A penniless boy begins with nothing but a stone gleaned from the street, but thanks to his audacious ingenuity, he winds up enjoying a feast "fit for a king." When a propertied old woman refuses him the hospitality of a simple meal, he uses his wits to con her into an extravagant feast. However, this is not a tale of simple reversal; instead of the rich being made low and the poor raised high, *both* enjoy the plenitude and pleasure of the banquet. The boy's good-natured trick elicits genuine hospitality from the old woman, pulling her out of her miserly world of self-concern and into an open space of shared play and mutual concern.

In *The Five Chinese Brothers*, we have the story of a mother and her five identical sons, each of whom has an extraordinary talent—one can swallow the sea, one is resistant to fire, one's neck can stretch and stretch, and so on.[6] When one of the brothers is unfairly convicted of murder and sentenced to death, the others use their gifts to deceive the murderous authorities. With each new day, the townspeople gather in the town square—appetites stoked by the smell of retributive justice—to witness the scheduled execution. And each day, their bloodlust is confounded by the brothers' shenanigans. Finally, townspeople and authorities alike tire of the boys' game and announce clemency. Their hunger for violence is not sated by the blood of a victim but is instead neutralized by the tenacity of courageous play nurtured round home's maternal hearth.

Leo Lionni's *Swimmy* is another story of the weak outwitting the strong.[7] In this tale, the tiny but resourceful fish named Swimmy finds himself all alone after the rest of his school is devoured by a ferocious tuna. Sad, lonely, and scared, Swimmy finds solace in the marvels of the vast underwater world—shapes, colors, creatures, and movements so magnificent they buoy the little fish's spirits and renew his zest for life. When Swimmy happens upon a school of fish like his own, he is delighted at the prospect of playmates and friends. But alas, these fish are paralyzed by fear of the bigger fish and spend their time in hiding. After much thought, Swimmy comes up with an ingenious plan. He teaches the little fish to swim in a tight formation, creating the shape of a big fish. Their insignificance camouflaged by the guise of size, the little fish swim free once again, no longer captive to a politics of fear.

Again, in *The Bigger Giant* the smallest actor saves the day—not through might or dominance but through the use of intellect and surprise.[8] Fin McCool's wife is not even given a name in the tale, but her courageous use of culinary cunning teaches the predatory giant Cucullan a sobering lesson. Cucullan is not only the biggest, meanest giant around, but he has the additional advantage of a magic finger that increases his strength when needed. When he decides to give Fin McCool a beating, the smaller giant confides in his wife that he is terrified. She assures Fin that she will take care of Cucullan and sets about baking some cakes, putting a rock in the middle of all but one of the cakes. As Cucullan's thunderous footsteps are heard in the distance, she puts her skeptical husband in the baby bed and waits. When Cucullan arrives, the tiny woman tells him her husband is away but invites him to have a cake anyway. Two broken teeth and pained yelps later, Cucullan is amazed to witness Fin's "baby boy" eating one of the cakes without incident. Accepting the mother's invitation to look more closely at her baby's fine teeth, Cucullan puts his magic finger in the baby's mouth, whereupon Fin bites it off. Cucullan, the bigger giant, limps away, never to return, leaving Fin and his witty wife to live in peace.

Then there are the trickster tales from African-American traditions. The best known are the Brer Rabbit stories. Rabbit is depicted alternately as arrogant and compassionate, mischievous and brave, but always as resourceful, creative, and gutsy. Often, his ingenious adventures involve the unsettling of the powerful. In an encounter with Bear, who lives a life of selfish lethargy thanks to the land and money he inherited from his father, Rabbit uses wit and cunning to eke out a survival for himself and his family.[9] He proposes what looks like a sweetheart deal for Bear: If Bear will let Rabbit and his family work one of his fields, he can continue to sleep the days away and Rabbit will give him half the yield. Bear greedily concurs. Cunningly, Rabbit gives Bear the choice of yielding either the tops or the bottoms of the harvested crops. After Bear chooses the top half, Rabbit and his family get to work planting and cultivating a robust yield of carrots, radishes, and beets. As promised, they deliver the top half to Bear and keep the bottom half for themselves. Angry that Rabbit got the best parts of the harvest while he got only leaves and stems, Bear pronounces that he wants the bottom half of the yield the next season. He slumbers while Rabbit and his family plant and harvest a bumper crop of lettuce, broccoli, and celery. When he wakes to see his pile of inedible roots, he is enraged and insists that in the upcoming season, he get both tops and bottoms. Back to sleep he goes as

Rabbit and company work the field, this time planting corn. For the third time, Rabbit gets the choice yield—bright yellow ears of corn—while Bear is left with roots and tassels. Fed up with Rabbit's tricks, Bear ends the business deal, announcing that he will work his own fields from now on. Meanwhile, Rabbit and his family buy their own land with the profit from the three seasons.

Whether the hero(ine) is a poor boy, a little woman, a tiny fish, or a scrawny rabbit, children's literature is filled with tales of the small and disenfranchised outwitting the strong and advantaged. Again and again, the underling takes what is at hand—a stone, a cake, a mighty imagination—and uses it with creativity and cunning to unseat the powerful. These everyday insurrections rely on the time-honored truth that those in power tend to have insatiable appetites, voracious egos, and predictable minds. The privileged seek constantly to shore up and expand their power and assets. As a result, they often do not notice or take seriously the small subversions and petty plotting of the weak. They tend to assume that those at the margins are there because they are dumb, lazy, or otherwise incapable. The mighty know that the poor and the small have few material resources, and so they rest assured that whatever disgruntlement exists will be innocuously expressed.

What we learn from so many children's stories is that the weak can exploit these very blind spots and assumptions. They represent points of vulnerability, small but potentially significant chinks in the armor of the strong. Fin McCool's wife is able to fool the bigger giant precisely *because* she is small and female and is thus assumed to be harmless. True, she has neither great physical size or strength, nor impressive material resources with which to mount an offensive; instead, she has her mind, her domestic wares, and her opponent's assumptions about his own superiority and her impotence. Together, these are enough to send the oppressor packing. Similarly, Rabbit has no land, no money, and no track record of success, but he *does* have a nimble imagination, a willingness to work hard, and both Bear's underestimation of Rabbit's intellect and Bear's assumption that others should work while he luxuriates. In each case, the crucial combination of the courage and cunning of the "weak"—plus the myopic assumptions and predilections of the "strong"—opens the door to resistance and transformation.

DIVINE DECEPTION AND CONTEMPORARY RECEPTION

As my weekly encounter with children's literature in Mrs. Barnes's kindergarten class kept the trickery trope fresh in my mind, I was putting the finishing touches on a book about an early Christian interpretation of the person and work of Christ in which redemption from evil involves the divine use of stealth and ingenuity.[10] Working on that book caused me to wonder why the idea of divine deception, popular in the first centuries of Christianity, fell so quickly and dramatically into disrepute, particularly among the educated elite. What had changed? Why did the motif seem to express some truth about God for the earliest generations of Christians but not for later ones? Was it simply a matter of maturation, of an internal impetus away from the mythological, from theological "child's play," or was there something else?

My suspicion was (and is) that the church abandoned the idea of divine ingenuity when it shifted from being a marginal religious sect to being the religion of the powerful. The affirmation of trickery and subversion is fine when one is the underdog, but once one has power, subversion is the enemy. Those who benefit from the status quo want stasis, not change; they want to remain in power and have their power respected, affirmed, and reiterated by their powerful peers as well as by the relatively powerless. Anything that might rock the boat of their privilege is anathema. Not coincidentally, the early church's trickster christology fell out of official favor just as Christianity became the religion of the Roman Empire and a bulwark of Western civilization. Once it had acquired credibility, authority, and wealth, Christian theology had no time for play, parody, and the like. Such activities are useless at best and treacherous at worst. Trickery and play, we learn, are the stuff of children's stories, not of Christian ethics.

But what if Christian ethics were reconceived as more pliable, as able to hold more together than we might have imagined? This book performs this rethinking. It uses methodological insights culled from feminist, cultural, and postcolonial theory to consider the complex moral lives of Christian communities at the margins of social, political, economic, and ecclesial power. Lifting up early Christian traditions of divine cunning, it claims theological and ethical credibility for these lives. Ultimately, this book challenges readers to consider ingenuity as a moral virtue in our own day, one that merits further reflection and even exploratory enactment, especially for those interested in disabling systems of hierarchical power and imperial desire. Perhaps part of what it means to be a Christian is to live creatively and courageously, using "christic imagination" to confront evil in ingenious, unexpected ways. In situations of ethical dilemma or conflict, the "right" or "good" response may well be one that circumvents or even defies the dominant morality. The profoundly paradoxical character of some medieval Christian women's religiosity and the consistent embrace of cunning and ingenuity by African-American women and men serve in this book as powerful articulations of such a "non-normative" or "deviant" morality. Their evocations of christic imagination are provocative in the questions they posed to the dominant systems of meaning in their own time and in the novel possibilities they suggest for ours. What if we were to embrace an ethic of ingenuity? What would it look like, and what would be its purpose and limits?

RECONSIDERING DOMINANT DEFINITIONS OF MORALITY

Ethics is the study of human morality. It is the aim of ethicists, or moral philosophers, to help us understand our behavior and choices better, to be more thoughtful and consistent in our moral judging, and to be able to deal with new problems that come our way. In theory, the ethicist does not create or impose moral law but helps moral agents clarify and reflect on the meaning, application, and consequences of that law. In practice, the ethicist's rendering of moral judgments and laws is itself a constructing of the law. In other words, ethics is not merely descriptive but prescriptive as well: It reflects on a moral universe and, in so doing, constructs one as well. *positive + normative*

Interestingly, the constructive nature of moral philosophy has usually been at least partially obfuscated, intentionally or not, by those undertaking the task. The common assumption of a pure core of moral knowledge that "the" moral agent taps into is, contends ethicist Margaret Walker, utterly contrary to "the commonplace reality [of] *different moral identities in differentiated moral-social worlds.*"[11] Because few ethicists have recognized their own imprint on that which they name morality, they have assumed that what is moral in their own eyes and in the eyes of those like them is morality itself rather than one (contestable) version of morality. If we are truthful about the matter, argues Garth Kasimu Baker-Fletcher, then we must admit that ambiguity lies at the heart of ethics. We live in a complex world characterized by competing versions of the good, diverse aims, and hotly contested common ground. In such a world, says Baker-Fletcher, we inevitably act with "dirty hands"—hands that grapple with the nitty-gritty realities of everyday existence instead of with some ideal sphere of moral purity and unanimity. Ethical reflection is "the serious work of getting dirty hands, even as we aspire to lift up 'holy hands.'"[12]

The vast majority of ethical tradition has ignored the reality of moral ambiguity—the messiness of moral particularity, multiplicity, and contestation. Ethics in this dominant key has been presented and understood as what ethics *is*, as ethics itself, while other moral postures have been viewed, by definition,

social construct

as unethical, as beyond the pale of the ethical. But if all moral philosophy is inevitably limited by the moral-social specificity of its articulators—in other words, if there is no access to an unmediated core of moral knowledge—then who is to say that the dominant tradition's construal of the ethical is credible, worthwhile, or sufficiently complete? And why should its depiction of the unethical be privileged or trusted? In this book I explore a moral posture assumed by the dominant tradition to be unethical, immoral. I call this posture an ethic of ingenuity. I contend that the moral worth of this ethic of ingenuity merits consideration. I do not herald it as "the" ethical; rather, I seek to understand its shape and logic, to gain some insight into why it seems to have been embraced by community after community throughout history. The fact is, this posture has and does function as a morality—not usually as a discrete, self-sufficient one, but as a valid and fruitful dimension of a larger moral whole. Yet, it has, generally speaking, been dismissed or maligned as not at all moral, as decisively immoral.

Could this dismissal of an ethic of ingenuity be linked to the fact that its proponents tend *not* to be "the" moral agent—the autonomous, enfranchised one whom moral philosophers, looking in the mirror, assume to be the quintessential human? Rather, those who embrace this alternate morality are usually those whom theologian Gustavo Gutierrez calls "the nonperson"— "the human being who is not recognized as such by the prevailing social order."[13] Is it any wonder that the "nonperson," when viewed from the perspective of the dominant tradition, embraces a "non-morality"? What happens, I wonder, when the "nonperson" is finally seen as the full human being s/he has always been? Is the "non-morality" s/he affirms also valorized?

This book attempts to take this latter question seriously from within a Christian context. In particular, I want to explore the possibility that practices of ingenuity, wit, and cunning constitute a moral language that is true for certain communities. Entertaining this possibility means viewing the moral language of ingenuity as the result of what ethicist Jeffrey Stout calls a process of moral *bricolage*—a process grounded in a particular time and place and in response to that locale's material realities and conceptual traditions. It means recognizing that like all moral languages, this one represents "the best that [can] be done under the circumstances."[14] As part of a moral system emerging from a particular epistemic context, I propose that the language of ingenuity makes sense. It offers persuasive explanations of and rational guidance for events and behaviors and, hence, is recognized by those within that moral system as "true" and "good." It is by no means immune to critique, either from those within the system or outside of it; but in the absence of a God's-eye view of all moral systems or a facile assumption that there is only one moral language, neither can it be easily dismissed as unethical by those not fully grasped by its truth. When such dismissal comes from privileged locations, we should perhaps be particularly alert to the power plays involved.

My main task is not so much to assess the validity of the moral language of ingenuity as to identify it *as* a moral language and to try to understand its internal logic from specific locations where its truth is recognized or embodied. The very process of taking this language seriously as a moral language necessarily expands our vision: We see things we did not see before. We recognize the existence of something that was before now unrecognizable except as perversion. In addition to a fresh focus and an expanded vision, I am also in this book engaging in evaluative or prescriptive work because I am proposing that the language of ingenuity is sometimes vocalized in a Christian key. In other words, I am suggesting that one way of making sense of the practices of ingenuity of certain marginalized groups is to interpret them as exercises in "christic imagination," as embodiments of incarnational creativity.

While I do not in this book engage in a thoroughgoing evaluation of ingenuity as a moral language, I do treat that language with respect, putting it into conversation with Christian theology and articulating the points of correspondence I see between a theology of incarnation and the language of ingenuity. Ultimately, I find these correspondences to be compelling—that is, I hear a deep resonance between a particular strand of Christian tradition and the moral language of ingenuity. Once distinguished, the soft but distinctive echo of recognition between these two discourses reverberates through each, changing our hearing of them. When this happens, we recognize not only the harmonies between the moral languages of ingenuity and Christianity but also their melodic dissonances—the ways in which they clash with and self-correct each other. Thus even while I am interested in turning up the volume on the resonances so we can hear what has been muted or indistinguishable, I do not want to turn a deaf ear to the differences and dissonances. Instead, I propose that it is only when we attend to both dimensions that we can fully appreciate the ways in which the languages of incarnation and ingenuity simultaneously illuminate and interrogate each other. The result is a deepening of our understanding of certain marginalized communities in Christian history as well as a new appreciation of Christianity's breadth and flexibility, of its ability to embrace experiences and choices assumed to be anathema.

MIMICRY, HYPERBOLE, AND HYBRIDITY

So what, exactly, *is* this "non-normative" morality, this ethic of ingenuity? What practices, strategies, and insights does it involve? What does it hope to accomplish, and why does it tend to be dismissed or ignored by most versions of theological ethics? Put simply, *an ethic of ingenuity is a way of living in the world in which imagination, courage, and scrappy resourcefulness function as primary positive goods, as life-protecting, world-sustaining strategies for thinking and living.* This ethic does not occur in a vacuum; it is not appropriate to all times and circumstances, and thus it has no pretensions of universality. But within certain contexts—specifically those characterized by severe or entrenched power inequities—this ethic can save lives, preserve dignity, foster hope, and in so doing, make the world a little more humane. Where John Caputo argues for a turn away from concepts of agency and autonomy in order to account for the moral lives of "those who are laid low by the cruelty of events," I am suggesting that we not overlook the subtle ways in which even these ravaged ones find ways of being moral actors. I agree with Caputo's critique of ethics as privileging the realities of the dominant, as being preoccupied with "strong or healthy people, with autonomous agents and aggressive freedoms." At the same time, I urge that we not go too far in the other direction by assuming that victims are not also survivors, creators, and moral agents.[15] My perspective here is indebted to feminist, cultural, and postcolonial theories, particularly their insights into the possibilities for liberative moral agency under conditions of profound agential constraint.

The question of how people whose lives are dramatically overdetermined by the power of others can nevertheless experience genuine moral agency— that is, freedom to define and determine their own selves and lives—is a difficult and complex one. None of us, after all, are thoroughly or even primarily self-determined. We are co-defined in every moment by other people, institutions, and systems of meaning (for example, biological, cultural, technological, theological systems). And yet, the extent to which others define our lives and the degree to which we experience ourselves as moral agents vary widely. In situations of entrenched and systemic inequality typical of tyranny, slavery, misogyny, extreme poverty, and domestic violence, for example, the space for genuine moral agency may be minute. Compared to other contexts, the victims of such situations may appear to have no freedom at all. Or if they *do* have some freedom, it can appear to be too little, too isolated, or too sporadic to make any real difference.

Feminist theorists have developed compelling explanations for how master narratives like patriarchy have been able to create and sustain their dominance by promulgating assumptions of their universality and totality and, by extension, discrediting or excluding alternate versions of reality.[16] This exclusionary dynamic makes it difficult even to recognize the dominating discourse *as* a discourse, as a language *about* reality instead of as reality itself. What defines a master narrative is precisely its mastery—not only its *claim* to authority but also its ability to elicit acquiescence to that claim, its ability to produce conformity to the norm among those who are actually disadvantaged *by* that norm. Capitalism "masters" us when, as is increasingly the case, we cannot even imagine, much less materialize, viable alternatives to it. It "dominates" us when we cannot effectively think outside its (big) box, even when we are the ones dispossessed by its script of productivity, consumption, and profit.[17] It is this kind of seductive dynamic that characterizes dominant discourses or master narratives. So pervasive and persuasive are they that it is difficult to imagine any alternative, to construct a different language or script for one's existence. When one's reality is overdetermined by a master narrative, real moral agency in relation to that narrative is difficult to conceive, much less enact. The more masterful the narrative, the less viable the agency.

Feminists like Luce Irigaray and Judith Butler acknowledge that while it *is* possible to resist totalizing systems of meaning and power, postures and acts of resistance cannot actually escape the grasp or imprint of these systems. For example, I cannot wake up in the United States one morning and simply choose to be free from capitalism. Similarly, medieval Christian women had as little freedom to "escape" from patriarchy as African Americans in the seventeenth century had of living in a world without slavery. The scope and impress of master narratives or systems of meaning are formidable. Simply put, they set the terms for thinking and living.

The good news is that even given such thoroughgoing constraints, resistance *is* possible. Irigaray's interpretation of "mimesis" and Butler's rendering of "performativity" suggest that the key to moral agency within situations of extreme constraint is a kind of subversive creativity. Those on the underside of power may not be able to write their own script for living, but they can perform the script they are given disloyally, refusing to allow its intentions or caricatures to be fully defining.[18] The very fact that we can mimic or hyperbolically perform the master narrative—poke fun at its absurd pretensions to know and define us fully—indicates that we are not, in fact, fully mastered by it. Our being, our "who-ness," is not fully captured but remains "elsewhere," says Irigaray, constituting a "disruptive excess" that defies the mastering intentions of the dominant discourse.[19]

In truth, most of us play our socially prescribed roles and speak our culturally scripted lines most of the time (for example, intentionally or not, most women "perform" their culture's norms of femininity, most Americans "perform" the role of consumer, and most young people "perform" their generation's script of youth.) But it is also possible to practice mimesis/imitation/performance with critical intentionality. In the very performance of the norm, says Butler, lies the possibility for *hyperbolic* repetition, "the parodic inhabiting of conformity."[20] Such disloyal performances of cultural norms push the script or ritual beyond its intended meaning and eke out a space for genuine freedom, real agency. Extended examples of such disloyal reiterations are presented in chapters 2 and 3 of this book. They demonstrate feminist theorist Rosi Braidotti's contention that mimesis or subversive performativity can be used by those whose lives are overdetermined by the power of others as a tool to effect real change. These practices of subversive creativity clear out a space for the development and expression of an alternative political consciousness, an embodied awareness of the self as an agent, an actor in the world in one's own right.[21] In sum, those at the margins of power may not be able to escape master narratives, but they *can* become intentional about how they reiterate them, doing so in ways that foster what Julian Wolfreys calls "dissonant identities" that demonstrate not only the limits of these narratives but also one's own relative freedom in relation to them.[22]

In his discussion of *doxa*, orthodoxy, and heterodoxy, sociologist Pierre Bourdieu makes a point complementary to those summarized above by feminist theorists.[23] Orthodoxy, or the dominant discourse, says Bourdieu, equates "the good" and "the moral" with the normative and defines the different as "immoral," "deviant," and "evil." According to Bourdieu, orthodoxy's "misrecognition" is shattered in times of crisis when its myth of self-evidence is uncovered and discredited. In such times, it is possible (though not probable) for minority discourses to emerge. Such heterodox discourses "bring the undiscussed into discussion, the unformulated into formulation," and allow the subjugated to reject "the definition of the real that was imposed upon them."[24] In rare cases, a politics of heterodoxy involving concrete practices of subversion and resistance can develop. Like Irigaray and Butler, Bourdieu contends that those on the underside of dominating power cannot confront that power directly but must instead use indirection and cunning to insert a wrinkle of contestation into the apparently smooth fabric of mastery. Occasionally, these theorists aver, the subjugated succeed in reshaping the prevailing discourse toward openness and participation.

In reflecting on how the oppressed or "subaltern" subject is at the same time both victim and agent, both inscribed by the dominant discourse and able in small but significant ways to resist that inscription, postcolonial theorists employ the concept of "hybridity."[25] Hybridity refers to the colonized subject's grafting together of two different realities or subject positions: the experience of the colonizer and that of the colonized.[26] To engage in hybridity, says Botswanian theologian Musa Dube, is pragmatically to take from each reality what is useful to one's own effort to construct a new postcolonial identity. Hybridity, then, is "the right to reap from both fields, from that of the colonized as well as the colonizer, and use whatever [is found] life affirming."[27] The display of hybridity, says Homi Bhabha, "intervenes in the exercise of authority" in order to reveal the discriminatory forces at work in that authority and to "turn the gaze of the discriminated back upon the eye of power." Thus, he continues, the enactment of hybridity by the marginalized or disavowed—the colonized, the poor, the disenfranchised— "terrorizes authority with the *ruse* of recognition, its mimicry, its mockery" and hence discredits its pretensions to mastery. The disloyal reiteration of the norm becomes "a form of defensive warfare," an act of "civil disobedience within the discipline of civility."[28] The notion of hybridity put forth by postcolonial theory involves a kind of scrappy resourcefulness in pursuit of freedom and dignity that often includes a strategically duplicitous complicity with the regime of dominating power. In full awareness of the limited choices available to them, the colonized scour that very regime for subversive or liberative possibilities. Such possibilities are then grafted onto indigenous cultural practices and knowledge to produce a new moral language and political practice.

SUBTLE SABOTAGE: AN INFRAPOLITICS OF INGENUITY

To understand what strategies of hybridity, hyperbole, or heterodoxy might actually *look* like, we can consider the work of cultural theorist James C. Scott.[29] Scott's interest in the question of how victims of structural oppression respond to their victimization led him first to the village of Sedaka in Malaysia to study the moral language of poor peasants and then to a compelling inquiry into the structural similarities in practices of resistance among those subordinated by slavery, serfdom, and caste.[30] What Scott discovered among the Malay peasants was a moral arsenal that had been largely ignored, misunderstood, or assumed by political scientists and cultural anthropologists not to exist. Scott's thematization of peasants' "politics of resistance" bears a clear family resemblance to categories of mimesis, performance, hybridity, and heterodoxy and provides strong evidence of the reality and vitality of what I am calling an ethic of ingenuity.

The lives of the Malay peasants whom Scott studied were defined at almost every turn by the brutal realities of exploitation and poverty—by what he calls the "symbolic straightjacket" of the ruling class with its myth of absolute power. Nevertheless, these peasants somehow found ways to embody resistance, to evade total domination.[31] Indeed, they developed a sophisticated array of "guerilla" tactics—behaviors and attitudes so subtle or ambiguous as to be undetected by the ruling elites and, interestingly, by most scholars of peasant society and resistance.[32] By adopting practices such as pilfering, foot dragging, and arson, peasants registered their displeasure with their own exploitation while frustrating the desired outcome of the ruling class.

Such everyday forms of resistance are rarely coordinated efforts intended to debunk an oppressive system, admits Scott. Rather, their immediate aim is survival—something to eat, a moment's rest—and perhaps a modicum of dignity in the face of crushing oppression. Yet, history reveals that "such Brechtian modes of resistance are not trivial" but can constitute effective challenges to unjust power relations and economic arrangements.[33] Consider, for example, the role played by "silent and undeclared defections" in the demise of the Confederacy in the U. S. Civil War, where nearly a quarter million eligible white soldiers avoided conscription or deserted their units.[34] Similar stories can be told of France, East Africa, Southeast Asia, and numerous Third World countries, where again and again, we see the very real results of what Scott identifies as "a social avalanche of petty acts of insubordination."[35] The fact is that in situations of dramatic or systemic inequality, direct defiance of the powerful would in most cases be a death-wish, yet it is generally only these fatal acts of bravery that are noted by historiography. Left unremarked are the countless small, subtle acts of resistance to domination that comprise the "weapons of the weak." As Scott notes, such acts "make no headlines. Just as millions of anthozoan polyps create, willy-nilly, a coral reef, so do thousands upon thousands of individual acts of insubordination and evasion create a political or economic barrier reef of their own."[36]

Scott's comparative study of situations of tyranny and persecution led him to conclude that the subtle arts of resistance employed by the Malay peasants whom he observed were not isolated phenomena. Rather, they are part of a structure or pattern of behavior demonstrated by any number of subjugated groups. These groups employ two distinct though related moral languages— what Scott refers to as public and hidden transcripts. The public transcript is the dominant language of a society. Although it presents itself as objective history, it tells the story of reality from the perspective of the ruling class. It is their "self-portrait . . . designed to be impressive, to affirm and naturalize the power of dominant elites, and to conceal or euphemize the dirty linen of their rule."[37] The public transcript includes a mythology that justifies and sustains the prevailing social, political, and symbolic order, as well as elaborate rituals such as inaugurations and parades that continually re-authorize this mythology by dramatizing social roles and unity and encouraging public acts of deference among the subjugated.

The "hidden transcript" articulates a very different construal of the real and the good. Hidden transcripts are expressed by subordinate groups to protest their persecution, to search out survival strategies, and to witness to the contingency of the master narrative—its inability, ultimately, to narrate the whole picture, to gain total mastery. Hidden transcripts are proof that brutality births not only suffering and despair but also steely resolve and creative defiance. This discourse is hidden but by no means private. The songs, gestures, folk tales, rumors, and jokes that comprise the hidden transcript—the clandestine critique of power—occur most often in the public arena, in the presence of the elite, yet they go undetected or unaddressed by the powerful because they cloak themselves in the conventions of the public transcript. Whether by feigning ignorance and stupidity, donning the smile of naïve acquiescence, or assuming a temporary stance of productivity when the master is at hand, subordinates wear masks of compliance, façades of passivity, and hence escape notice and scrutiny. They "lean into" dominant assumptions of their own inferiority in order to express a presumably non-existent self-respect, autonomy, and creativity.

Thus, despite the best-laid plans of the powerful, those at the periphery of power are nevertheless able to construct what Scott identifies as an "infrapolitics of the powerless." This is a pastiche of everyday insubordinations and double meanings that, taken together, constitute a shared critique of domination and a viable alternative moral landscape and language. Gossip, rumor, euphemism, and strategic grumbling are examples of such behaviors, all of which conceal the identity or culpability of the actor while allowing her or him opportunities for critique and self-expression. More elaborate forms of camouflaged resistance include trickster narratives, world-upside-down drawings, and carnival. Taken together, the "everyday resistances" of individuals and groups can have a marked impact on the production and maintenance of power inequities.

Admittedly, such petty acts *can* function as little more than inconsequential outlets for individual anger and despair, but Scott argues persuasively that they also often do much more than that. These apparently insignificant behaviors belong to a larger pattern, and as such, they constitute a significant and verifiable arena of political action. Scott calls this arena an "infrapolitics" to signal its unobtrusive or invisible character. Far from being a substitute for or hindrance to "real" political action, he suggests that it be understood as the condition for the possibility of more overt resistance. An infrapolitics of resistance prepares the soil, so to speak, for further dissent. It marries a keen political awareness of the constraints imposed by the dominant discourse to a savvy and courageous creative spirit. The result is a low-profile but surprisingly effective strategy for acting in and on the world. Its subtle practices, says Scott, "aim at an unobtrusive renegotiation of power relations" and can have "dramatic economic and political effects."[38]

What Scott, Irigaray, Butler, Bourdieu, Bhaba, and others help us to see is that there is among the subjugated a pattern of moral existence that includes a consistent valuation of subversive imagination—an ethic of ingenuity that informs the attitudes and actions of many marginalized people, reflecting and supporting their struggles for self-respect and self-determination and fueling their opposition to their own subordination. What this book contributes to the discussion is a *Christian* articulation of this ethic. I argue that for men and women whose lives are characterized by deep and sustained inequalities of power, ingenuity may well be an appropriate moral posture. God's Incarnation in Jesus helps Christians determine the relative suitability of this ethic.

MORAL WISDOM FOR A NEW DAY

In this book, then, I trace the lineage of a non-normative Christian moral tradition—not scientifically or exhaustively but with broad strokes—in order to identify the tradition *as* a tradition; to see and appreciate its motivating concerns and unifying themes; and to consider its implications for the ethical realities of our own day. Paying attention to this moral minority report throws into relief the *dominance* of the dominant moral traditions and summons their proponents to move toward new ways of seeing, being, and valuing.

Looking anew at sites of non-normative morality among Christian communities also sheds light on the theo-logic at work there—what I am calling christic imagination. This involves a sensibility rooted in the recognition that God in Christ moves in mysterious and *heterodox* ways to confront and unseat evil. I propose that this "theo-logic" enhances Christian ethics in four ways:

- It functions as a helpful interpretive tool in relation to Christian history, offering a lens through which heretofore inexplicable behaviors can become intelligible.
- It reveals that some of what the dominant ethical tradition has defined as "aberrant," "irrational," and "illogical" may instead be seen to have a coherent logic that has characterized multiple groups, movements, and ways of being.
- It offers a precedent from deep within Christian tradition for recognizing and valuing these non-normative ethical stances.
- It articulates a theological imperative for those who take seriously God's confrontation of evil in the person of Jesus the Christ. Thus, it calls us toward a new vision of ethics and challenges us to develop new traditions of moral wisdom for our own day.

THE PERILS AND PROMISE OF AN ETHIC OF INGENUITY

To entertain the idea that trickery, cunning, and indirection ought to be given a place of legitimacy within the matrix of Christian ethics is to raise the ire of many and the eyebrows of most.[39] Some will see it as yet another move in the direction of moral relativism, a sign of the breakdown of standards and values that is fast discrediting mainstream Christianity. Others will decry it as the (il-) logical outcome of liberal attempts to pander to minorities and glorify victims. Still others will find it interesting at an intellectual level but frightening in its implications at a practical level. None of these concerns is without some merit. Nevertheless, I am convinced that the "moral minority" whose lives are defined both by extreme delimitation of choice and opportunity *and* by courageous attempts at creative resistance deserve careful consideration. If their deadly serious play takes us by surprise or offends our sense of propriety, perhaps it is because we have been defining the rules of the game for too long. Opening our minds to new strategies, different players, and unexpected moves may be part of a faithful response to our contemporary situation.

Given the complexity and ambiguity of that situation—the sheer magnitude of human and ecological suffering our world reflects despite all the wealth and technological advances some of us boast—a healthy dose of christic imagination may be exactly what is needed. Indeed, I believe it is. This intuition, this proposed ethic, this book . . . these are wagers rather than certainties. They stem from my own experience as a "progressive" Christian whose attempts to live out my religious convictions are in constant need of inspiration and accompaniment. This book is part of my search for fresh ideas with which to meet the trials and tribulations of my life, my church, my public school system, my empire-building nation. I write from the poorest state in the union. It is a state where we mobilize heroically to respond to the high drama of a mighty hurricane but where the more subtle and insidious forces of poverty, underemployment, substandard housing, unaffordable health care, and unsupported public schools wreak far more damage than even the most horrific storm surge and yet motivate far less concern. What good news, I wonder, does my Christian religion have to offer to *this* situation?

In these tumultuous times, the idea of an ethic of incarnation and ingenuity is more intriguing than ever. What inspiration and direction might it offer? What new interpretations of Christian history, identity, community, and praxis might it foster? In this book I engage these questions by directing our attention to the (im)moral margins. I draw us into imaginative conversation with those whose moral wisdom has been dubbed foolish, grotesque, or dangerous, and I challenge us to listen to their logic and consider how it might illumine our own struggles and responsibilities, how it might spark our own imaginations. Who knows what the encounter may yield? Like the propertied old woman whose inhospitality was transformed by a quick wit and a round stone, we may just find ourselves celebrating a new kind of communion with those whose strangeness redeems us from our sameness. Fancy that!

1. THE THEO-LOGIC
OF AN ETHIC OF INGENUITY

Any theological ethics deserving of the name biblical has to honor

what we call the incarnational perspective. . . . The Incarnation

becomes the clue for understanding all of God's dealings

with human history and with the whole of world reality.

—José Míguez Bonino[1]

ome may wonder why an ethic of ingenuity should be inserted into the discourse of Christian ethics. The simple answer is that it does not need to be inserted because it has been there from the beginning, but it *does* need to be recognized and reflected on. Toward that end, in this chapter I go back in time to the early centuries following Jesus' death, a time when the religious and *Christian* valences of ingenuity were relatively commonplace.[2] Between the second and sixth centuries of the common era, many Christians believed one central piece of "good news" to which they were to attest was the message that God had defeated the devil—that the powers of evil had been definitively overcome through God's presence and activity in the person and work of Jesus the Christ. This confrontation of evil was believed to have hinged on God's use of creativity or cunning. More specifically, it was believed that salvation was wrought through God's "deception" of the devil.

God the deceiver? To modern ears this idea is likely to arouse surprise and dismay.[3] What were those ancients *thinking*? How could they, and why *would* they, make such an outrageous claim? Most importantly, why can't we just forget about this unfortunate idea? Why resurrect it now?

As I argued in *Deceiving the Devil*, the reason contemporary Christians ought to engage the deception of the devil motif is that it offers a way of understanding God's atoning work in the person of Jesus that avoids many of the major pitfalls of other atonement theories while preserving their best insights.

Without rehearsing my argument about atonement, I present here the main contours of the divine deception trope because it is my current contention that its presence and vitality among biblical texts and, even more markedly, in the life and thought of the early church constitutes a theological warrant for its serious consideration today. In other words, I propose that an ethic of ingenuity is not only not *un*Christian but was, in fact, an important feature of the construction of Christian theology and identity in the first place and, hence, is arguably *constitutively* Christian. At the very least, I contend that contemporary Christian people should be aware of the divine deception narrative because it witnesses to the relative elasticity of the early church on the question of what constitutes ethical norms and moral existence. Moreover, it can be used today as an interpretive tool for making sense of certain behaviors and choices whose meaning and logic have been obfuscated by the assumptions of the dominant moral language.

SIFTING THROUGH THE PAST

It is probably news to most contemporary Christians that the motif of divine deception was employed by many of our earliest forebears as a way of understanding God's role in confronting the forces of evil, known collectively as Satan or the devil.[4] Many on today's theological left are likely to dismiss the idea out of hand because of its reliance on devil language. For these Christians, talk of Satan smacks of a primitive supernaturalism or a metaphorical imagination gone wild. Worse yet, it is thought to signal an oversimplifying, dualistic worldview that divides the world easily into good and bad, with all things bad being "of the devil" and strictly anathema. Such a dualistic mentality is believed by many liberal and progressive Christians to fuel fear and contempt toward people and behaviors that are different or strange, as well as an insular self-righteousness that eschews critical thinking and openness to change.[5] On the theological right, by contrast, it is not the language of the demonic that is troubling about certain early Christian ideas but rather the apparent affirmation of deception as a strategy for dealing with evil. It is the *devil*, after all, who is the great deceiver. To think of *God* as using surreptitious indirection muddies the waters by questioning the radical difference between good and evil and impugning the absolute moral purity of the Divine.

　　Even as both sets of concerns strike me as legitimate, I want to press my colleagues on each end of the theological spectrum to entertain the possibility that our early Christian forebears were on to something important when they warmed to the idea that God outsmarted Satan. On the one hand, theological reflection on "the devil" need not bring with it a dualistic metaphysic or an "us versus them" mentality. On the other hand, entertaining the idea that evil is so complex as to require imaginative response need not be the first step down a slippery slope to moral nihilism. Theology has always involved the careful sifting-through of tradition in search of insights for present-day situations and challenges. Surely, our day, with its complex convergence of sophisticated technologies, global markets, transnational corporations, and extraordinary concentrations of wealth and power, calls for continual sifting of texts and traditions. We need creative appropriations of images and traditions that may have been overlooked or dismissed. Ideas that were deemed offensive, dangerous, or irrelevant in one context may merit new consideration in another. Indeed, it is my contention that the motif of divine deception is precisely such an idea. To be sure, it is an idea that *is* offensive and dangerous, but it is so primarily to those whose status and power are supported by the categories and judgments of the dominant morality. For those whose moral agency is all but destroyed by the dominant discourse, and for those who wish to be allies of such victims, I hold up the motif of divine deception as an idea whose time has come (again). It is an idea with the potential to shake up the theological house, pry open its doors and windows, and usher in new winds of understanding and respect for those locked out or kept waiting for far too long.

DECEPTION AND DIVINITY IN EARLY CHRISTIAN IMAGINATION

At the heart of this offensive and dangerous—but definitely not irrelevant—early Christian motif was the belief that by becoming incarnate in Jesus of Nazareth, God fooled Satan into overreaching his power and, hence, into causing his own defeat. The logic behind this conviction is interesting to consider.

According to the early Christian imagination, God and Satan, representing the forces of good and evil, justice and injustice, were locked in battle. At the epicenter of this cosmic struggle were the life, death, and resurrection of Jesus. Human beings were also in the thick of the drama because human sin caused the ruckus in the first place. It was thought that in turning away from God, humans turned *toward* Satan, or evil. As Augustine put it, instead of directing our desire toward God, the highest good, we humans tend to focus it on "lesser goods" or "lower beauties" —material pleasures, worldly status, and the like. This choice is not exactly a choice for evil per se because these lesser realities are part of God's good creation.[6] However, when we love them inordinately—in place of God or as more important than God, in practice if not in principle—then our love becomes perverted and our will swerves away from its proper focus.[7] This swerving of the will away from God and toward lesser realities is what Augustine calls evil.[8] At first, he admits, our desire for lesser goods may be innocuous enough—after all, we are desiring things that are, of themselves, good. But over time, these choices have a kind of cumulative effect so that we find ourselves with a bad habit of sinning. This habit becomes, before long, a full-blown addiction. Thus, we find ourselves, says Augustine, incapable of not sinning, incapable of proper orientation to God and the world. What starts out as a small series of indiscretions rooted in freedom turns into a kind of self-imposed bondage from which we cannot liberate ourselves.[9]

To say that humans are enslaved to sin or held captive by the devil is not necessarily, then, to discount human freedom. Neither is it an endorsement of the idea of a rapacious force or being named Satan who preys on innocent (or not so innocent) victims and sucks them into some kind of cruel universe at the middle of the earth. Instead, the language of bondage to sin or the devil can point to the very real dynamic by which human freedom becomes distorted and disabled, the very real process by which love becomes destructive and destruction becomes addictive. I do not have to believe in the existence of a creature called Satan to recognize that my will is susceptible to swerving away from God and that, in reality, such disorientation is probably inevitable. To experience my own impotence in the face of such addictive swerving—to have my everyday life defined, for instance, by the impulse to consume/acquire/ buy/produce—is to feel deep in my bones the compelling nature of the language of demonic possession or bondage to evil. This language may not be the kind that I normally employ in my workaday world, but if and when I am confronted with the complex layers and profound pull of my own disorientation, my own unhinging from the good, it is this kind of metaphorical language that comes closest to expressing my reality. Like most of my middle-class peers in North America, my life is so powerfully shaped by habits of consumption and addictions to social and economic power that I can barely even *see* the habits and addictions, much less curb or reject them. For me, for us, the language of demonic possession and bondage to evil may sound jarringly unfamiliar or inappropriately hyperbolic, but these are words we need to hear, words that hit home, indicting our lifestyles, decrying our inertia and acquiescence, narrating our self-imposed impotence.

Similarly, one need not believe in the reality of an otherworldly duel between God and the devil to feel the force of the struggle in one's own daily existence of good and evil, mercy and mastery, justice and injustice. While the language of cosmic battles and supernatural enemies can certainly be adopted to serve a dualistic, other-effacing worldview, there is no reason why this very powerful language *must* be used toward that end. My own appropriation of the language is undertaken in order to get at some of the insights into the nature of evil and of God's response to it that lie within the folds of this multivalent discourse. These insights are, I contend, simply too intriguing and promising to ignore.

RANSOM AND THE OVERSTEPPING OF AUTHORITY

Returning, then, to an explanation of the divine deception motif as found in early Christianity, we understand that human beings were commonly thought to be held captive by sin and evil and thus in need of being saved or "ransomed." Patristic theologians found in Christian scriptures ample evidence to support the theory that Jesus' life served as a ransom, or release fee of sorts, paid to free humankind from bondage to evil. In the gospels, they drew on passages such as Matt. 20:28, in which Jesus claims that "the Son of Man came . . . to give his life as a ransom for many"; on John, where the cross is presented as a victory over the powers of darkness and death; and on the countless "tyrants" who oppose Jesus, from Herod, to the Pharisees, to the devil himself. Pauline imagery, rich with references to redemption as victory over the demons, offered additional fodder for the ransom interpretation.

However, there was much disagreement about what should comprise the ransom and to whom it should be paid. Despite considerable debate, a consensus gradually emerged that Christ was the ransom who was paid to the devil in order to purchase humanity's freedom. As Origen of Alexandria argued in the third century, "We were doubtless bought from the one whose servants we were. . . . He held us until the ransom for us, even the soul of Jesus, was paid to him."[10]

According to this view of salvation, the devil was understood to have certain rights over human beings. The fact of original sin meant that the devil had some sort of hold over human beings that the justice of God would not ignore. Moreover, human decisions to turn against God in various ways constituted a rejection of the good and a kind of allegiance to the powers of evil. As a result of human sin, therefore, the devil was thought to have a significant degree of legitimate authority in the world. It was consequently thought that the ransom presented to the devil was given in accordance with the rules of "fair play," for humanity was understood to be justly held by the devil and hence subject to death instead of life eternal.

Unlike other human beings, Jesus was believed to be completely without sin and, hence, not under the devil's authority nor subject to death. In other words, while the rest of humanity had become enthralled to sin—or in Augustinian terms had allowed the will to swerve habitually toward lesser goods and away from God and, hence, had become enslaved or addicted to sin—Jesus had not done so. Unlike the rest of us, Jesus had throughout his life maintained a proper balance between his passion for God and his desire for lesser goods, never allowing the latter to obscure or diminish the former. As a result, Jesus' will was not enslaved to evil, which meant to the metaphorical imagination that he was not held captive by the devil and was not subject to death. Early Christians assumed that death was the result of sin. It was, to use our contemporary parlance, the inevitable consequence of lifelong addiction or, to use their language, the devil's ultimate act of enslavement. There was thought to be, then, a kind of justice at work in the death of humans. After all, we had turned away from God, "the Life of lives, Livingness itself," in order to turn toward other loves. Because those loves were merely finite, their satisfying light would inevitably die out, taking our misdirected and disappointed love with them.[11]

In stark contrast to our own death, the death of Jesus was clearly a grave injustice. His murder could by no means be rationalized as the result of sin or as a rightful capture. It was a horrible breach of justice, a fatal mistake. Was it also, one had to wonder, a triumph for the forces of evil? Early Christians agreed that it was not. So far from a victory for the devil, they interpreted Jesus' unjust death as a decisive defeat of evil. In killing this sinless one over whom he had no rights, the devil was said to have made a terrible blunder. He overstepped the bounds of his authority and overreached his power. It was believed that this "tragic overstepping or *hamartia*" caused the devil's defeat by revealing the illegitimacy of his claim to Jesus' life and, consequently, undermining any further claims to power he might make.[12] It was thought that because of his fateful error, the devil had to forfeit his right to the souls of those who follow Christ. Thus, it was the devil's hubris and avarice–his desire to have it all, his refusal to live within limits–that led to humanity's liberation from sin and evil. And it was Jesus' own life of genuine love—his refusal to love lesser goods more than God and neighbor—that stood in stark contrast to evil as love perverted.

GOD'S ROLE IN THE DRAMA OF REDEMPTION

The ideas of ransom and the overreaching of authority helped early Christians understand the nature and consequences of evil, personified as the devil, but it was the motif of the "deception of the devil" that enabled them to grasp *God's* role in the drama of redemption. The central piece in this rationale was God's incarnation in the person Jesus. By becoming incarnate, it was argued, God fooled Satan into thinking that Jesus was just another human being, sinful and subject to death. Popular images that conveyed this pattern of deceit were often quite vivid, and they tend to be alienating to contemporary audiences. However, the divine deception trope employed a plot line and details that would have been familiar to early Christians and, therefore, were effective in addressing questions of great import and urgency during that time. Because of this efficacy, the deception motif became quite popular by the fourth century and continued to claim notable proponents for centuries to come, including Athanasius, Gregory of Nyssa, John Chrysostom, Augustine, John of Damascus, and Maximus the Confessor. Despite the fact that it was relegated to the margins by scholastic theology, the divine deception trope nevertheless continued to be enormously influential in folk religion throughout the Middle Ages.[13]

THE PROBLEM OF JESUS

One pressing question with which early Christians had to contend was what to do about the suffering and anguish of Jesus, a fact that the four gospel accounts are unanimous in emphasizing and yet that conflicted mightily with the reigning decorum of the day.[14] According to Roman etiquette, pain should be endured stoically, passively, in proper masculine fashion. To cry out loudly and beg that suffering be removed was clearly ignoble, effeminate behavior and was cited by anti-Christian philosophers like Celsus as evidence of Christian wrongheadedness. If Jesus were truly divine, argued Celsus, "he would have never uttered loud laments and wailings, nor prayed to avoid the fear of death, saying something like: 'Oh Father, let this cup pass from me' (Matt. 26:39)."[15] In addition to the problem of how to defend Jesus' divinity and masculinity in spite of his anguished suffering, early Christians also had to contend with the challenge posed by Arianism, a popular fourth-century theology. This perspective saw in Jesus' suffering—particularly in his "cowardly performance in the garden of Gethsemane"—a compelling reason for arguing that Christ could not be identical to God, who was, above all else, impassible, impervious to change.[16] Arians proposed, instead, that Christ was subordinate to the Father, a sub-divinity, so to speak.

In response to challenges to Jesus' full divinity and masculinity, the divine deception motif was articulated by early Christian leaders to explain why the ineffable, impassible Divine would have taken on human existence and, furthermore, experienced a full range of human emotions and fears. Put simply, it was proposed that God did these things in order to outwit evil. In other words, what appeared to be shameful cowardice and effeminacy, nothing but "shame and folly," was, in fact, when properly understood, an expression of the "'secret and hidden wisdom of God' (1 Cor. 2:7)."[17]

The idea of deception as a strategy of the Divine strikes a cacophonous chord in our contemporary context, creating discomfort and dissonance vis-à-vis the dominant moral paradigm. In early Christian times, by contrast, no such disharmony would have been heard. This was a context saturated by Platonic assumptions of the essential untrustworthiness of the earthly realm. Because of its inherent changeability and instability, the empirical world was seen as inevitably ambiguous—constantly shifting in form, impossible to pin down. As Nicholas Constas concludes, "It was, in a word, deceptive, and any figure incarnate in that world was just as likely to conceal the truth as to reveal it."[18] Add to this common sense assumption the theological conviction that God is ultimately unknowable and mysterious, at some level utterly hidden from human view and comprehension, and the idea that God might use deception or concealment as a modus operandi becomes increasingly intelligible. Adding even more weight to the argument was the commonplace assumption in antiquity that deception was, says Constas, "an acceptable pedagogical, strategic, and therapeutic device. . . . For example, deception was permissible for fathers who thereby concealed their affection for their children in order to discipline them. So too for physicians, who were expected to sugar their bitter pills and conceal their sharpened scalpels beneath the surface of a sponge." Plato even argues, via a debate about whether Achilles or Odysseus was the greatest Homeric hero, that it is the wily Odysseus rather than the "true and simple" Achilles who is greater. Thus, concludes Constas, the category of deception in early Christian times rested on "a broad cultural foundation" and could boast "a distinguished literary and philosophical lineage."[19]

The most popular image for making this point portrayed Jesus in all his humanity and vulnerability as the bait that lured the devil onto a hook, ensnaring Satan in his attempt to catch another sinner. While this image may strike contemporary readers as starkly discontinuous with biblical and Christian tradition, it was actually derived from what Constas characterizes as "a theologically consistent conflation of several biblical passages, including Job 40-41; Ps. 104:26; and Isa. 27:1, all of which are concerned with mocking the cosmic dragon and dragging him up from the depths of the sea on a fishhook."[20] Other images used to express the incarnation-as-deception idea included a mousetrap and a snare. All were metaphorical attempts to express the conviction that things are not always what they seem—that God moves in ingenious ways; that the powers of evil were defeated at the very point of their apparent victory; and that, paradoxically, Christ was triumphant at the moment of his "defeat" on the cross.

IRENAEUS: "A GOD OF COUNSEL"

What enabled this triumph was the ingenuity of the Divine. According to Irenaeus, the premier Christian thinker of the second century, it was God's power of persuasion and creative wisdom that undid Satan. Instead of using force or violence to confront Satan, God employed an indirect method, surprising and disarming the opponent. Rather than squash evil by means of a frontal approach, God chose to become human, to abdicate omnipotence in favor of "weakness" and "humility." By becoming incarnate, God entered the contested arena discreetly and surreptitiously, communicating in a camouflaged language. God created a hidden transcript of parable and paradox with which the powerful were confused and confounded.

The result of this undercover work, says Irenaeus, is that God "baffled His adversary" and "exhausted the force" of his attack.[21] Whereas the devil had "obtained dominion" over humans by "insatiably snatch[ing] away what was not its own" and "tyranniz[ing] over us unjustly," Irenaeus notes that God responded "not by violent means" but "by means of persuasion." In the Incarnation, therefore, God is revealed as "a God of counsel"—that is, a God of intellect and ingenuity, a God who uses unexpected but ultimately wise and effective means for confronting the adversary.[22]

In Irenaeus's mind, God *could* have chosen to use "violent means to obtain what He desires."[23] In other words, God could have countered the devil's display of power with an even greater one, for "God is neither devoid of power nor of justice."[24] As the more powerful one in the contest, the predictable response would be simply to obliterate one's opponent. But instead of flexing the divine muscles with a frontal assault, suggests Irenaeus, God orchestrates an ambush. God captures the capturer (Satan) and liberates the captive (human being) by striking a perfect balance between power and justice. This path to victory is more circuitous and less remarkable than forceful obliteration, but it is also infinitely more interesting *and* just.

JUSTICE, POWER, AND ENFLESHED VULNERABILITY

For Irenaeus, the issue of divine justice is paramount. The key to understanding his endorsement of the divine deception idea lies in his recognition that in using force against Jesus, the powers of evil acted unjustly. Their violent response to Jesus lay bare the essence of evil as the abuse of power. In the crucifixion, we see evil defined, quintessentially, as power used destructively and without limit.[25] Here, evil is portrayed in terms of an insatiable appetite—an intention to acquire the object of one's desire at all costs or to destroy one's adversary. Given this portrait of evil as a kind of violent acquisitiveness, it is no wonder Irenaeus eschewed the notion of triumph over evil by means of divine overpowering or consumption, gravitating instead to the idea of divine persuasion and counsel.

According to this reading, God is the One who confounds evil instead of crushing it. The Incarnation becomes not only the definitive expression of divine love but also the exemplary approach to evil. Indeed, the exemplary approach to evil *is* love, ferocious and deep.[26] Confronted with evil, God becomes one of evil's victims. The Divine Self abdicates power and literally enfleshes vulnerability. With this logic-defying move, Christians affirm, God actually *becomes God* by becoming the suffering other, by identifying completely with the fragility and "murderability" of the other.[27] God, for Christians, is always already the incarnate one, the other(ed) one whose own vulnerability reveals the Godhead in the mode of infinite concern and responsibility. Jewish philosopher Immanuel Levinas argues that this experience of deep identification with or "proximity" to the *human* other is the moment of humanization because it marks the emergence of the ethical. Christians, by extension, think of the Incarnation as the moment of both humanization *and* divinization ("fully human, fully divine") because it marks the manifestation of the Divine *as* other, as mercy in the face of vulnerability, even as it constitutes the human as the one made possible *by* mercy. God's ingenious embrace of compassion ("feeling with") is both abdication and assumption: God relinquishes power as domination and enfleshes power as solidarity and mercy. This abdication of mastery is no retreat, however, but the strategic praxis of what Ireneaus recognized as "wise counsel." This is kenosis with real kinesis!—more like the fierce resistance and fiery creativity of the freedom fighter than the predictable force of an unjust law and order.

For Christians, God's active, ingenious, nonviolent resistance to evil—actualized via the Incarnation—becomes the model for discipleship: Faithful responses to evil begin with the experience of proximity to the vulnerable other. They involve a radical move into solidarity with the suffering one(s).

They elicit kinetic kenosis—a courageous emptying of power and ego in the face of the other and the vivifying embodiment of resistance to evil in the mode of relentless compassion and audacious creativity.

GREGORY OF NYSSA: "THE DISEASE OF THE LOVE OF RULE"

Writing two centuries after Ireneaus, Gregory of Nyssa reiterated the divine ingenuity motif as he attempted to understand why God, "that incomprehensible, inconceivable, and ineffable reality, transcending all glory of greatness," deigned to "wrap Himself up in the base covering of humanity."[28] To appreciate Gregory's question, it helps to recall that his early Christian context was powerfully shaped by a Greco-Roman worldview that looked askance at bodily existence. Neoplatonic philosophical assumptions formed the "common sense" of the day. According to them, human bodies were part of the earthly, material realm—the realm of reality that is subject to the forces of change, corruption, decay, and death. To be a body was, first and foremost, to be subject to change. It was continually to be losing oneself to decay and disease. It was to have one's identity constantly threatened by the certainty of death, perhaps by violent dismemberment at the hands of wild animals or by the excruciatingly slow march of a simple infection in a world without antibiotics. To be a body in Gregory's day was, ultimately, to be unceasingly vulnerable, perpetually at risk, dramatically out of control, in ways it is difficult for the contemporary imagination to appreciate.[29]

No wonder, then, that this realm of unstoppable change and uncontrollable decay was contrasted with a very different realm—the spiritual or conceptual sphere of ideas. Unlike the bodily world, this is the sphere of the eternal, of things that are not subject to the laws of change and corruption. The *idea* of beauty will last forever, long after any given temporal beauty has passed away. So also would love, justice, and friendship. In Gregory's day, it was simply common sense to assume that this realm of the eternal, unchanging idea or spirit was what was really real. *It* was the seat of genuine worth. By contrast, the temporal realm of bodies and other material things was merely a shadow of the real—a faint and imperfect likeness, a distortion, a cheap imitation.

THE INCONCEIVABILITY OF THE INCARNATION

To claim as the early Christians did that God became incarnate in the person Jesus defied logic and sound reason. The divine become human? Nonsense! The unchanging and eternal become change and death? Preposterous! Why in the world would God—"that incomprehensible, inconceivable, and ineffable reality, transcending all glory of greatness"—abdicate the purity and certainty of eternality and spirituality for the filth and vulnerability of bodily existence? Why, Gregory implored, would the Divine choose to "wrap Himself up in the base covering of humanity, so that His sublime operations as well are debased by this admixture with the grovelling earth"? Why give up the masterpiece for the cheap imitation? What could be more preposterous, more incredible, more thoroughly confounding? As a man of his time, Gregory certainly felt the weight of these questions, admitting that "our faith is staggered" by the idea that God would "descend to such humiliation."[30]

Steeped though he was in the common sense mentality of his day, Gregory and other early Christians nevertheless held firm to the conviction that God underwent this mind-boggling "othering," becoming incarnate—carnal, flesh, body.[31] The radical action of incarnation was necessary, Gregory concluded, in order to deal effectively with evil. Evil, he understood, is enormously complex and compelling. To confront it effectively is no simple task. For this, special tactics and energies are required. For this, unprecedented risks must be taken. For this, reality as we know it must be stretched and redefined. For this, finally, divine and human must come together.

LOVE PERVERTED, LOVE REDEEMED

What is the nature of this evil for which reality as we know it is forever redefined? And why is incarnation the only effective response to its searing presence? The deceptively simple answer to both questions is the same: love. Love perverted and love redeemed. Love perverted can be redeemed only by love redirected, love recentered. Love diseased can give way to love healed. As Augustine thematized so memorably in his *Confessions*, we humans are most fundamentally lovers. We are creatures of desire, restless seekers of satisfaction, and that character trait is both our downfall and the key to our salvation.

For his part, Gregory presents us with a convincing evocation of the perversion of love. Evil, he writes, is "the disease of the love of rule."[32] Evil is love gone bad, love twisted into lust, love in the service of self-aggrandizement and mastery. Like a disease, it may be unrecognizable at first—a small and apparently innocent blemish or preference. However, over time it gathers force, often slowly and imperceptibly—lying undetected for years, subtly gathering strength for the kill; but sometimes lightning quick and with decisive, deadly force. Eventually, whether slow or fast, with stealth or great drama, the ravaging force is undeniable, its invasive power unrelenting. This is evil, "the disease of the love of rule." It is this love perverted, love corrupted, love misdirected and untamed, says Gregory, that is the "primary and fundamental cause of propension to the bad and the mother, so to speak, of all wickedness that follows."[33] The impulse to relate to the other not in the mode of hospitality or mutuality but in the mode of mastery, if left unchecked and allowed to gather steam, is the fount of all evils. Like an untreated disease, it will surely destroy its host.

Having arrived at clarity about the nature of evil, Gregory moves on to reflect on the character of God's response. What shape might healing take in the face of such disease? Gregory reasons that if mastery or the love of rule(s) is the essence of evil, and if God's response to evil is to be "consonant with justice" and, hence, not itself evil, then the divine response cannot be a violent one. It cannot be an imposition of force or rule. A different way must be found. This way, of course, is the Incarnation. Divinity-become-humanity is the indirect path, the different way, the abdication of force and the redefining of power. By becoming incarnate in the man Jesus, says Gregory, God responds to evil not "by tearing us away by a violent exercise of force from [evil's] hold, thus leaving some colour for a just complaint," but by peaceful negotiation.[34] God chooses to reject the way of force and the imposition of rule, entering instead into the "humiliation" of earthiness (from the Latin, *humus*) and the humility of humanity. God abdicates force in order to respond to *our* embrace of the love of rule, our rejection of *humus* in its multiple meanings—an embrace that deforms our nature, infecting and ravaging our very essence as lovers of God and the good. Wisely, given the nature of the disease, God enacts divinity not in the mode of mastery but, insists Gregory, in the mode of healing: "Here is the reason for which you are in search, here is the cause of the presence of God among men. Our diseased nature needed a healer. Man in his fall needed one to set him upright. He who had lost the gift of life stood in need of a life-giver, and he who had dropped away from his fellowship with good wanted one who would lead him back to good."[35] Or, using the language of the ransom theory of atonement, Gregory says, "The captive sought for a ransomer, the fettered prisoner for someone to take his part, and for a deliverer he who was held in the bondage of slavery."[36]

DIVINE STEALTH

Gregory uses a fishing image to portray the liberative strategy of divine stealth and wisdom in the face of evil's avarice. According to this image, what happened in the Incarnation is that God disguised the Divine Self "under the veil of our nature"—that is, became human—"that so, as with ravenous fish, the hook

of the Deity might be gulped down along with the bait of flesh."[37] Evil, depicted
here as insatiable appetite, is "caught" by divine ingenuity. Not expecting divinity to present itself in any form other than magnificent power and grandeur, the
devil assumes the simple-living carpenter from Nazareth is merely human. He
is taken by surprise when the human one turns out also to be divine. Interestingly, Gregory implies that despite the devil's ignorance about Jesus' divinity,
he nevertheless knew that Jesus was someone special. Perhaps he could recognize a wholehearted commitment to mercy and justice when he saw it. Whatever the content of the devil's recognition, Gregory suggests that God's choice
to become human in the particular way that Jesus was human—a human whose
love never swerved from God and neighbor—was an intentional strategy on
God's part to force the devil to make a misstep. The prospect of conquering
such a human as Jesus—so genuinely disinterested in the love of rule yet so
abundantly filled with personal power—must have whetted the devil's appetite
mightily. Indeed, says Gregory, God's choice to become that kind of person was
an intentional appeal to the devil's "own special passion of pride," luring him
into taking the "bait"—luring him, that is, into desiring mastery over this one
so badly that he fails to see the true nature of the opponent and the impossibility of conquering him.[38] His love of rule is so all-consuming, so addicting, that
the devil can do nothing else but reach for mastery over this One who cannot
be mastered.

In making that reach and grasping for ever more power—power divorced
from mercy and justice—the devil finally goes too far. Thus, according to
Gregory's analysis, evil is "hooked" by a combination of two things:

- the destructive dynamic of evil itself—the seductive, addictive pull of
  acquisitive power that drives it to consume and consume, with no concern for the consequence to self or other;
- the strategic "baiting" of evil—the ingenious luring of the ravenous one
  into excess, into swallowing what cannot be chewed and choking at the
  very moment of anticipated satisfaction.

What Gregory insightfully personifies with the bait and hook imagery is
the character of evil as destructive appetite *and* the way in which that appetite can become its own undoing. God's role in the drama is to expose the
true nature of evil, to direct attention to the violent overreaching of power
or overstepping of boundaries, to the perversion of love that constitutes evil.
By becoming incarnate in the person Jesus, God signals that it is not worldly

power or possession that matters—indeed, love of each ultimately destroys by the force of its own consumptive dynamic. Rather, it is the choice to curb one's appetite, to live within limits, to allow oneself to be moved to obligation by the vulnerability of the other that defines moral existence. According to the drama of incarnation, it is, ultimately, the power of love in the mode of courageous compassion that saves the day. God chooses this uncommon path by abdicating force in favor of negotiation, totalizing authority in favor of infinite responsibility. Thus, what strikes contemporary readers as *ir*responsible—deception, cunning, ingenuity—is exactly the mode of being chosen by God.

SUPREME WISDOM

Could God have chosen a different response to the complexity and pervasiveness of evil? Gregory certainly thinks so, and yet he is equally convinced that God's choice to confront mastery with the ingenuity of incarnation represents the moral high ground and "a manifestation of supreme wisdom."[39] Moreover, it constitutes a redefining of power: "That the omnipotence of the Divine nature should have had strength to descend to the humiliation of humanity, furnishes a clearer proof of that omnipotence than even the greatness and supernatural character of the miracles."[40] To be omnipotent means, Gregory learns, to use power wisely—with the aim of healing, reconciling, giving life. *This* constitutes "a kind of superabundant exercise of power," a kind of power that is dramatically non-normative, as jarring to convention as would be the sight of fire "stream[ing] downwards" instead of abiding by its normal tendency to move upwards.[41]

While it was God's embrace of *humus* that struck Gregory's peers as staggeringly inappropriate, given their assumptions about the morally impure nature of earthly existence and the revoltingly effeminate character of anguished suffering and death, it is the Divine embrace of *deception* that is more unsettling to contemporary Christians. Gregory offers this acknowledgment of such discomfort:

> A person is, perhaps, induced to entertain the thought that it was by means of a certain amount of deceit that God carried out his scheme on our behalf. For that not by pure Deity alone, but by Deity veiled in human nature, God, without the knowledge of His enemy, got within the lines of him who had man in his power, is in some measure a fraud and a surprise; seeing that it is the peculiar way with those who want to deceive to divert in another direction the expectations of their intended

victims, and then to effect something quite different from what these latter expected.[42]

In response to this concern about God's deployment of deceit as a strategy for confronting evil, Gregory argues that this strategy was, in fact, both just and wise. The essence of justice, he says, is "to give every one according to his due," while it is the proper role of wisdom to ensure that "the benevolent aim of the love of mankind" is not dissociated from "the verdict of justice." Justice, then, must always serve the end of "kindness, not swerving from the aim of that love of man."[43]

Using justice and wisdom as criteria for judging the moral viability of God's decision to outwit evil with guile and imagination, Gregory concludes that the devil did, indeed, get his just desserts since his murder of the innocent one, his overreaching of power, caused him to be stripped of power.[44] Moreover, the strategy of divine deception had as its sole aim the liberation and healing of those enslaved by the tyranny of evil. Just as "two persons may both mix poison with food, one with the design of taking life, the other with the design of saving that life; the one using it as a poison, the other only as an antidote to poison," so it is that both God and Satan can employ deception, but toward quite opposite ends.[45] Where the devil deceives in order to enslave and gain mastery, God deceives in order to liberate and empower. To Gregory's mind, deception used to confront evil on behalf of the victims of evil and in the service of justice is not at all incommensurate with divine wisdom and, hence, does not impugn the moral character of divinity. In fact, it reflects the "superabundant" justice and wisdom of God that God is able to disarm evil without employing the violence of mastery and, in so doing, to enact and hence endorse a totally different form of power and way of being. To those who fear that linking God with deception—even if it is understood as a temporary strategy aimed at undermining evil—abrogates God's moral authority and hence destroys the very essence of divinity, Gregory offers this reassurance: "One thing there is that is not beneath the dignity of God, and that is, to do good to him that needed it. If we confess, then, that where the disease was, there the healing power attended, what is there in this belief which is foreign to the proper conception of the Deity?"[46]

AUGUSTINE: "THE MOST EXCELLENT WISDOM OF GOD"

What we have seen in the writings of early church thinkers Ireneaus and Gregory of Nyssa, we find also in the thought of the enormously influential

Augustine of Hippo, who wrote at the turn of the fourth century in the twilight years of the Roman Empire. Like Ireneaus and Gregory, Augustine found
the notion of divine deception compelling. Like them, he employed the motif
in an attempt to understand the character of evil, personified as the devil, as
well as the divine response to it.[47] Sounding a now-familiar theme, Augustine
characterized the devil as "a lover of power" and, consequently, "a deserter and
assailant of justice." It was the devil's "perversion" of desire—his inordinate and
misplaced desire—that was his "essential flaw."[48] Instead of loving God and the
good, he craved worldly power. Instead of being content with some power and
possession, he wanted it all. Evil, suggests Augustine, begins harmlessly enough
as misplaced desire, and, yet, as that desire is stoked through the force of habit,
its appetite overrides all else, consuming even its subject. Eventually, nothing else matters but the feeding, the consuming, the acquiring of power and
possession. All too easily, Augustine admits, we humans become infected with
the same "perversity" of desire, setting our "hearts on power, to the neglect or
even hatred of righteousness."[49] The dynamic is so dramatic, moving inexorably
from freedom in relation to evil to complete bondage to evil, that mythological
personification (that is, devil-talk) seems to Augustine and other church fathers
to be warranted. What happens to the devil (and to us) is a sad but familiar tale,
they agree: He is consumed by the fire of his own inordinate desire.

As Augustine points out, this eventual consumption is brought about by
divine ingenuity. Echoing Ireneaus and Gregory, he expresses his conviction
that while God *could* have chosen different means for overcoming evil, "there
was," nevertheless, "no other more suitable way of freeing man from the misery
of mortality than the Incarnation of the Word." The choice for ingenuity instead
of force is manifest in the very embrace of incarnation as divine modality—in
the embrace of humanity, finitude, vulnerability. In the culture of early Christianity, such a choice would have signaled a dramatic, nearly incomprehensible
rejection of the common sense mentality with its strong loathing of bodily
existence and concomitant exaltation of disembodied, spiritual, or conceptual reality. God-become-human would not have evoked romantic notions of
a quaint, divine-human mutuality but rather an instinctive recoiling from a
dangerous mixing of pure and impure, spiritual and material. Yet, it would have
been precisely this new creation of the Incarnation—love enfleshed, transcendence made immanent, mastery become vulnerability—that made all the difference in the world. In a world ruled by the love of rule, a world contaminated
by the contagion of empire, and a world saturated with the perversity of power,
the folly of love in the mode of courageous compassion stands as a stubborn

witness to the dehumanizing effects of love misdirected and as a summons to a very different way of being and a very different kind of love.

AUGUSTINE'S CONTEMPORARY RELEVANCE

A contemporary probing of Augustine's long-ago ruminations on the character of evil and of God's response to it yields several conclusions. First, evil is, in essence, love perverted. Augustine's version of this proposal is that the source of evil, or its defining shape, is the orienting of love away from God, the misdirecting of desire toward lesser goods, and the confusion of priorities such that these lesser goods take the place or obscure recognition of higher goods, the highest of which is God. Gregory's analysis of evil fits easily into this Augustinian paradigm: For Gregory, as we have seen, it is explicitly the love of rule— the forsaking of humility, mercy, and mutuality in favor of mastery—that is the fount of evil. This way of defining the problem is certainly applicable to most contemporary North American Christians, who participate to one degree or another in the economic and political domination of the rest of the world. For most of us, the lives we live—the way we spend our time and money, cast or don't cast our votes, and relate to those who differ from us—*do* reflect pretensions to mastery, whether over the possibility of economic scarcity, over other nations, religions, races, or classes, or over the nonhuman world. Thus, Gregory's indictment of the love of rule as the essence of evil hits home for many millions of contemporary Americans.

Different versions of Augustine's definition of evil as love unhinged are also possible—versions that may sound antithetical to Gregory's. For example, Augustine's thesis that evil is, at heart, a matter *of* the heart, a matter of love become disoriented and misdirected, can be seen not only in the destructive dynamics of self-arrogation but *also* in the death-dealing realities of self-abnegation and self-hatred. Here, the "lower beauty" of the self is assumed to be so low as to be unlovable, not at all beautiful or worthy of defense, protection, or flourishing. Such self-effacement points, ironically, to the same shape as does the mastery impulse, and that is the shape of misdirected love. In the case of self-loathing or radical self-doubt, love is erroneously directed always and only *away* from the self, as if the self is not one of God's good and beautiful creations—as if, in Augustine's language, the self is "deprived of all goodness," thoroughly corrupted.[50] Yet, such a thing would be, Augustine argues, no thing at all, for everything that exists does so by virtue of its participation in being, of which God is the source and perfect fulfillment. Insofar as something has being or exists, then, it is related to God. It points with its being toward the source and perfection of being (God) and is, therefore, good, lovable, and beautiful. Augustine's analysis of evil in terms of misdirected love speaks this word to the one who experiences herself as fundamentally unworthy: "All finite things are in you, [O God]: but in a different manner, being in You not as in a place, but because You are and hold all things in the hand of your Truth, and all things are true inasmuch as they are."[51]

In addition to his compelling insights into the character of evil as misdirected love, Augustine's writings reiterate the nature of God's response to evil, emphasizing God's surprising, yet wise and just rejection of the logic of mastery. "The devil was to be overcome," insists Augustine, "not by the power of God, but by his righteousness," and it is this same response that is commended to us humans:

> Since the devil, by the fault of his own perversity, was made a lover of power, and a forsaker and assailant of righteousness—for thus also men imitate him so much the more in proportion as they set their hearts on power, to the neglect or even hatred of righteousness, and as they either rejoice in the attainment of power, or are inflamed by the lust of it—it pleased God, that in order to [rescue] man from the grasp of the devil, the devil should be conquered, not by power, but by righteousness; and that so also men, imitating Christ, should seek to conquer the devil by righteousness, not by power.[52]

Augustine does not have in mind the total abdication of all power but rather the subjection of power to the discipline of justice and mercy. When power is loved inordinately, it can take one over, assaulting and overpowering other characteristics or values that could limit and correct the desire for power. He suggests that power is a dangerous thing to desire and that perhaps, as such, it ought not to be sought at all but left "to immortals." If and when power *is* embraced by mortals, Augustine admonishes that one ought to seek power only "against himself for himself"—that is, one should desire the power of self-constraint, the power to abdicate power for one's own sake and the sake of others.[53] Such self-emptying is precisely what God embraces by becoming incarnate, and it is the defining shape of Jesus' life and death as well.

This embrace is not only an enactment of God's character, but it is also the revelation and performance of genuine moral existence. By becoming incarnate, God abdicates the power of mastery and adopts the surprisingly potent "un-power" of vulnerability. The result of God's performance of ingenuity for the sake of justice is that evil's performance of violence and destruction—of power undisciplined by righteousness—finally becomes visible, irrefutably recognizable. No longer can there be any doubt about the destructive consequences of love's perversion. This revelation of the true nature of evil is prompted by God's ingenious evocation of that truth. It signals a new moral horizon, a new definition of the ethical. The strategy of intentionally becoming flesh in a flesh-fearing world and of exalting vulnerability and mercy in the long shadow of empire is the epitome of non-normativity, a surprising and audacious departure from the expected. Yet, insists Augustine, "there neither was nor need have been any other mode more appropriate for curing our misery."[54] Eschewing violence and force, God nevertheless triumphs over evil with courageous creativity. Demonstrating that "the devil should be conquered, not by power, but by righteousness," God deftly uses the devil's lust for power against him, luring him with the bait of mastery until he eventually grasps for more than he can chew.[55] The "bait" here is the incarnate God—the one who becomes vulnerable and, hence, the one whom the devil assumes is an easy prey. Yet, enfleshed within that vulnerability is an indomitable spirit and an unflagging justice. These, the devil learns, cannot be consumed or destroyed; they live on in the commitment and praxis of those who come after Jesus and recognize him as Christ.

This redemptive recognition of Jesus as the Christ is the result not of divine fiat or acclamation, nor of a supernatural display of power or authority. Rather, it is a response to absolute moral clarity—to the moment in which the true character of evil is definitively revealed, and the options for response laid bare. Jesus' death reveals in dramatic fashion what his life's praxis and teachings iterate more subtly: Evil is that which murders hope, exploits vulnerability, ignores suffering, undermines justice, and lusts after power. In his life, Jesus' consistent rejection of such dispositions causes him to be reviled and eventually executed by the power brokers of his day. It is their very contempt for his way of being—his courageous self-emptying, active compassion, and thoroughgoing solidarity with the vulnerable—that, once taken to its logical conclusion of death-dealing violence, causes their public discrediting. Just as they flex the muscles of their power and authority, acting decisively to eliminate one whose praxis defies their dominating regime, the ugly underside of that regime comes into sharp, irrefutable focus. Such clarity ignites moral indignation, eliciting a new will to resist the temptation of mastery and to follow Jesus in a new way of being. Thus, says Augustine, "the devil was conquered when he thought himself to have conquered."[56]

With the pre-meditated murder of mercy—the state-sponsored execution of compassion—everything changes. Suddenly, and no doubt fleetingly, there is absolute clarity about right and wrong, good and evil. Jesus should *not* have been killed. A terrible mistake was made. The crucifixion of such a one discredits the entire logic of empire. At the same time, ironically, it breathes life into the il-logic of Jesus' way. Now, perhaps for the first time, it is plain to see that empathy, not empire, defines genuine power. What a revelation! What an uncovering! What an incredible challenge! A kingdom built around this revelation would be unlike any the world has ever known. Indeed, it would not be a "king-dom" but a "kin-dom." It would establish a new moral language, and the dominant trope of this language would be what God articulated in Jesus—the trope of incarnation and imagination.

THE MORAL LANGUAGE OF INCARNATION

What would it be like to speak the language of incarnation? What sound would this moral language make? The revelation of God in Jesus proclaims that to speak the Incarnation is to enflesh courageous compassion and kinetic kenosis. It is to be a conduit for divine mercy and a testimony to justice. Scriptural accounts, the reflections of church fathers such as Ireneaus, Gregory of Nyssa, and Augustine, and the testimony of Christian tradition through the ages agree that among the many things to be said about God, perhaps the most significant is that God is an *incarnate* God. Out of the deepest imaginable regard for creation, God became part *of* creation, not as an exercise in self-aggrandizing power or arbitrary play but as the profoundest kind of self-expression—the expression of the Divine Self's deep desire for whole-making relationship, connection, and intimacy. Moved by this desire, God fashioned and sustains creation, vivifying it, caring for it, and calling it toward fulfillment. Also moved by this desire, God bemoans the multitude of ways in which the divine intention for creation's flourishing is thwarted, defied, or ignored.

While it is easy for Christians to assume that God-become-flesh is an exclusively Christian notion, it is important to note that we are not alone in experiencing the astounding mystery of divine incarnation. Hindu tradition, for instance, is filled with bodily manifestations of divine reality. Closer to home, the Hebrew scriptures (or "Old Testament") offer numerous accounts of the conviction that God was from the beginning an embodied God. As biblical scholar Jon Berquist notes, "God's body lingers throughout the text"—sometimes in narratives of God's physical presence and, more often, in powerful memories of those times when God was tangibly present to the people of

Israel.[57] Berquist cites numerous examples from Hebrew scripture of God's embodied reality. In the opening pages of Genesis, we encounter the "gigantic body" of the Creator, who stands "big enough to straddle worlds and separate out the land from the seas." In the following chapter, the more human-scale God creates with the divine hands—attentive craftsman—and strolls through the Garden of Eden at dusk. Throughout the Jewish Bible, we meet an irrefutably embodied God.[58] The memory of this tangible presence remains long after physicality has gone, powerfully shaping Israel's self-understanding and theological imagination, as for instance in the striking image of the mothering Divine of the book of Hosea, who coddles the child Ephraim (that is, God's people), teaches him how to walk, and nurses him at the divine breast. As Berquist notes, "We cannot imagine a God more embodied and more incarnate than this."[59] Such vivid depictions and memories of divine incarnation undergird Israel's hope for the future as well when, according to Ezekiel, God will be tangibly present once again, living in our midst and accessible to all.

To recognize God's embodied presence in pre-Christian or non-Christian places need not negate or neutralize the good news of God's incarnation in the person Jesus. Such testimonies can be seen instead as compelling reiterations of a profound, and profoundly surprising, truth: God—Creator of all, utterly ineffable and uncontrollable—becomes a body in order to relate to creation, in order to establish meaningful, even redemptive, connection to the myriad and diverse bodies God has so wondrously created.[60]

Christians claim that a decisive moment in the drama of divine creating, embodying, and redeeming is God's incarnation in the person Jesus. In this watershed moment, God deepens—radically, exponentially, incomprehensibly—the compassionate self-expression begun in creation. God bodies forth the limitless love and justice of the Divine in the flesh and blood person of Jesus of Nazareth. In so doing, God chooses to entrust the Divine desire for whole-making self-actualization to the warp and woof of the finite realm. That is what *incarnation* in Christian parlance means—God's becoming carnal, finite, flesh and blood; God's becoming vibrantly present, astonishingly intimate. What Christians experience and then proclaim—confidently, robustly, faithfully—is that "there is a sense in which God is more visible in Jesus than anywhere else."[61] God as bodied forth in Jesus is made known to Christians in a way more tangible, more persuasive, more *real* than any other manifestation of divine reality.

This claim is so familiar to Christian people, forming the very foundation of our distinctive worldview, that it is easy to lose sight of its profound il-logic.

The choice to become finite makes no sense at all if God's godness is all about power, authority, and mastery. The decision to become body is unintelligible if God's primary aim is to establish and rule over a spiritual world, a heavenly kingdom. Only if God's main concern is love does the Incarnation make sense. Only if God is a God whose primary aim is whole-making relationship does this strange move of incarnation become intelligible. When one loves with infinite depth and divine ferocity, one cannot keep such feeling to oneself. One is compelled by the force of love itself to express it, to reach out to the other, and hence to risk rejection or misunderstanding. This is precisely what God does in Jesus. God reaches out to the world in love, becomes vulnerable to rejection and misunderstanding. God does not remain aloof or immune to the pain and struggle of finite existence but enters fully into it, experiencing the good and the evil, the ecstasy and the agony, that are part of real living.

When Christians affirm the incarnate God, the God made flesh, we are not presuming to know God's full being or to see God face to face. However, we *are* claiming, in faith, that the Incarnation tells us at least two crucial things about God. First, we learn from the Incarnation *what God values* or cares about. God values creation, bodily existence, flesh, matter, earth—enough to become it, to dwell in and with and for it. God also values relationship, connection, and the responsibility, caring, and risking that genuine relationship requires. A second thing we learn from the Incarnation is *how God values* what God values. Looking at the life and death of Jesus reveals that God values us by relating to us in modes of deep caring—drawing near to us, becoming vulnerable, dwelling and suffering alongside us, desiring our healing and well-being, respecting our freedom, challenging us to reorient our lives, relationships, and institutions. And God relates to us in modes of creativity—often going against the grain of common sense, defying the prevailing logic and circumventing ethical norms, opting for persuasion instead of coercion, vulnerability rather than domination, foolishness instead of pride. God's incarnation in Jesus tells us not only that we are valued and loved by the source and sustainer of all, but also that God's love takes unconventional, unexpected shapes and directions. In a world defined primarily by self-interest and dreams of mastery, the message of love as compassion, solidarity, and just relations is unorthodox indeed. No wonder, then, that this message is delivered via the atypical means of incarnation and ingenuity.

CHRISTIC IMAGINATION AND AN ETHIC OF INGENUITY

In Jesus' own life as depicted in scripture, we find convincing evidence of an ethic of ingenuity. Again and again, Jesus surprises his adversaries and allies alike

by responding to questions and situations in unexpected ways and by expressing a way of being and seeing—even of speaking—that is anything but orthodox.[62] For example, reflecting on the cultural norm of mimetic violence—"an
eye for an eye and a tooth for a tooth"—Jesus encourages his listeners to reject
the norm by refusing to retaliate against violence with still more violence. As
Walter Wink points out, many translations of the crucial "turn the other cheek"
passage of Matt. 5:38-41 interpret Jesus' words as an affirmation of passivity in
the face of evil. In actuality, his use of the Greek term, *antist nai*, is best translated not as "resist not" evil but as "resist or oppose or be firmly against violent
rebellion or armed revolt" as a *response* to evil. Thus, in stark contrast to the
common assumption that the only two options when faced with the destruction of evil are passive submission and violent resistance—flight or fight—Jesus
endorses a third way, what Wink calls a position of "militant non-violence" and
what I name an ethic of ingenuity.[63] Wink reminds us that Jesus is speaking here
not to the powerful elite but to the victims of their oppressive policies—to
those who were "forced to stifle their inner outrage at the dehumanizing treatment meted out to them by the hierarchical system of caste and class, race
and gender, age and status, and as a result of imperial occupation."[64] In other
words, Jesus directs this advice to those for whom violent revolt would mean
certain death and, hence, to those whose only apparent option is submission. To
these, Jesus counsels that if they are hit by a "superior" in an attempt to admon-
ish or insult them, the best response is to take the moral high ground, refusing
to cower or slink away in humiliation but standing tall and offering the other
cheek to the oppressor, effectively stripping him of the power to humiliate.[65] In
this situation of radically differentiated power, Wink suggests that "the person
who turns the other cheek is saying, in effect, 'Try again. Your first blow failed
to achieve its intended effect. . . . You cannot demean me.'"[66] Such a response
takes the powerful one by surprise, pulls him out of his game, so to speak. It
also amplifies the injustice of his act, his dehumanizing intention, and hence
undermines his public credibility.

Similarly, when Jesus advises those who are sued for their outer garment
to respond by giving up also their cloak, or inner garment, he is not advocating
passive acceptance of an exploitative legal system but is, instead, articulating
a strategy of ingenious resistance. As Wink explains by using Deuteronomy 24
to understand the context within which one would be sued for one's outer
garment, "only the poorest of the poor would have nothing but an outer garment to give as collateral for a loan."[67] So Jesus is advising such ones that if they
are sued for their outer garment because they are unable to pay off their debt

burden—most likely caused or exacerbated by the Roman empire-building system of taxation—they should respond by offering not only the outer garment as demanded in the suit, but the inner garment as well, leaving them completely naked.

This move takes the oppressive logic of mastery and pushes it to its breaking point. When the debtor removes that inner garment, he takes control of the situation. He signals a refusal to submit passively to humiliation and destitution and forces the ruthless creditor to endure the considerable shame of having caused and viewed the nakedness of another.[68] With this ingenious turning of the tables, the powerless one does not abolish the Roman imperial system or even win the lawsuit, but she does expose the naked truth of that system—its raw will to power and devastating effects—and she refuses to be dehumanized by its death-dealing machinations. The underdog pushes the envelope of the normative morality, embracing a cultural taboo (nakedness) as a strategy of resistance against an economic, legal, and social system built on the backs of widespread landlessness and destitution. In doing so, he not only finds a way to express a personal agency or power that his social position would deny him, but he also uncovers for others to see the corrupt character of the dominant regime and its authorizing morality. Embodying the il-logic of an ethic of ingenuity, the powerless one uses the assumptions and demands of the logic of the empire to expose and indict *its* "logic." The powerless one is not completely powerless after all, we see, although she opts for the power of ingenuity and nonviolence rather than the power of domination, refusing to play the oppressor's game and, hence, gesturing toward the moral bankruptcy of that very game.

If we are honest with ourselves, we must admit that this choice of a different way of being and valuing, this rejection of the goal of mastery, is difficult to get one's head around. Perhaps it is possible for the few heroic ones—the prophets and martyrs—but in reality, it is simply too unorthodox to be taken seriously as an ethic for the masses. But then what do we make of the Incarnation, the central claim of Christianity? And what do we make of Jesus' life and death, the revelation of the wondrously incarnate God? Clearly, these cannot be ignored or pushed to the side. Or if they are, then what of Christianity remains? However inconvenient, discomfiting, or mind-boggling, we Christians must grapple with the fact that our God opted for Incarnation rather than empire, power with and for rather than power over. Moreover, as the Incarnate One, God in Jesus chose to live and die according to the principle of mercy instead of the myth of mastery. On these points, the biblical witness is abundantly clear.

Where the waters get muddy, it seems, is with the question of how those of us who identify ourselves as Christians will respond to this witness, to this irrefutable endorsement of an ethic of incarnation and ingenuity. What would it mean to embrace this ethic for *our* time and context? If we were to take seriously the notion of "following Jesus," of allowing the cruciform shape of his life to (in)form our own everyday attitudes and practices, what difference would it make? What would it mean for a person or group to attempt to engage the world in a mode of "christic imagination"—facing the forces of dehumanization and mastery with creative cunning, daring to express a heterodox ethic in the midst of a powerful moral majority, and carving out a space for self-expression and self-direction despite extreme exploitation and agential delimitation?

In chapters 2 and 3, I consider two possible answers to this question. Specifically, I explore two moments when the victims of history seem to have responded to the horrors of their own systematic dehumanization with surprising spunk and gritty resourcefulness, and whose courageous creativity appears to have been rooted in significant ways in experiences of Christian faith. I begin with a small but significant pocket of medieval Christian women and the specific practices with which they resisted their dehumanization. I then focus on the moral agency of African-American Christians, both during and after slavery. I suggest that these two instances of complex and ingenious resistance to evil may be fruitfully understood as examples of a Christian ethic of ingenuity. They demonstrate that against what look like insurmountable odds, those at the margins can deploy a powerful alternate mindset to resist the forces of destruction and eke out some semblance of dignity and autonomy in the midst of extreme exploitation. What lesson the majority of us might learn from these marginalized ones remains to be seen.

True, the efforts of the moral actors I consider in what follows did not result in "victory" over the oppressor or total transformation of the status quo; most, in fact, probably had little or no sense of making real progress in the struggle toward freedom and full humanity or of participating in the in-breaking of the reign of God. It is more likely that with a few exceptions, their lives were shot through with frustration, weariness, and doubt. Glimpses of self-actualization and liberation were probably few and far between. Nevertheless, given the enormity of the forces aligned against them, the fact that these women and men were able to express moral agency *at all*, much less to engage in incisive critiques of the reigning powers, is extraordinary and worthy of note. From this vantage point, their "everyday resistances" arguably constitute what James C. Scott calls an "infrapolitics of the powerless" that, despite its modest effect, laid the groundwork for later, more remarkable transformations.[69]

The lives we encounter in the next two chapters are enormously complex, the choices made shaped by myriad motivations and influences. Consequently, no single idea or hypothesis will explain everything, or even most everything. But a good idea might shed light on *some* of what went on by opening our minds to new interpretations of old phenomena. I submit christic imagination and the ethic of ingenuity that it inspires as such an idea. It is the hypothesis that emerges from my encounter with the historical and narrative accounts of the lives of medieval Christian women and African-American men and women. Thus, we can think of an ethic of ingenuity as a modest proposal for making sense of certain behavioral trends or for interpreting complex or confounding narratives within Christian history. In addition to shedding light on the past, this exploration is intended to identify and authorize for contemporary Christians a moral posture which, although quite old, has the potential to breathe new life into our own efforts to love God and neighbor. My sense is that we are in dire need of such novelty.

2. INGENIOUS INCARNATIONS

Medieval Christian Women's Body-Centered Religiosity

Imagination is needed and new forms of disobedience

are required for the struggles to come.

—Dorothee Sölle[1]

n this chapter, I use an ethic of ingenuity as a heuristic tool for exploring the paradoxical spiritual practices of certain medieval Christian women. To do so is admittedly to engage those complex practices and their multiple potential meanings with an interpreter's imagination. It is also to recognize at the outset that the data set in question is notoriously fraught with interpretive difficulties. Nevertheless, I hope to demonstrate in this chapter that these practices constitute a rich repository of insights into how Christian individuals and communities might live in modes of christic or incarnation-shaped imagination. This chapter and the next offer extended case studies of an ethic of ingenuity. They explore the possibilities for authentic moral agency in contexts of severe constraint and moral ambiguity.

Ultimately, this chapter's case study does not reveal a simple formula for right belief or good living. Its subjects cannot claim moral purity or even clarity. This is not, then, a tale of heroism or triumph. It is not a search for moral foundations, absolutes, or even exemplars. It is, however, a story about creativity, spunk, and courage—about their surprising irruption from the margins—and it is a story I find both intriguing and inspiring. Immersing myself in the complex context, texts, and struggles of medieval Christian women has opened my eyes to a time and sensitivity very different from my own—one that I can see only through a glass darkly and yet one that has become for me a transformative prism, shedding new light and unexpected color on my own twenty-first century world and its distinctive challenges. My author's hope is that this chapter's encounter with the body-centered religiosity of medieval Christian women might evoke in my reader a new awareness of the complexities of moral agency, particularly for those who must contend with a relative lack of economic, political, and social power, as well as a fresh appreciation for the role imagination can play in the ongoing challenge to build lives, communities, and institutions of integrity and compassion.

CHALLENGES OF INTERPRETATION

The contemporary interpreter of medieval phenomena attempts to understand a time gone by—a cultural context that is at times utterly foreign and at others surprisingly familiar. (But might the "familiarity" be a product rather than a precondition of the interpretation?) In addition, the interpreter reads texts that have been translated and may well in the process have lost crucial nuances and allusions or produced others that did not exist in the original. To complicate matters even further, when one's subject matter is medieval *women*, the interpreter faces the additional challenge of getting reliable access to those whom history has largely forgotten, excluded, or aggressively contained. When, moreover, one's subject matter includes *mystical* texts—texts witnessing to extraordinary experiences, intimate transformations, and ecstatic visions—then questions about access, integrity, and understanding are pervasive. Finally, there is the all-important question of meaning: Did behavior "x" mean the same thing, or at least something similar, in the year 1200 as it means now? What intention was behind behavior "y" or comment "z"? How can we possibly find answers to these questions given the enormous gap in time and culture between interpreter and text or subject? Without such answers, what hope is there for understanding?[2]

We inevitably see the past through the lens of our own time and experience. Given this, it is crucial that we become self-aware about the lens through which we gaze, continually cross-examining our interpretations and attending as thoroughly as possible to the historical and cultural contexts that produced the texts we wish to understand. In other words, we try *not* to create a past in our own image even as we admit that our imprint will be indelibly present.

Most of what we think we know about medieval women comes from texts written not by women themselves but by the relatively privileged men who took an interest in them—confessors, scribes, and hagiographers.[3] What motivated this interest is a matter of considerable debate. In a fascinating study of contemporary appropriations of medieval women mystics by leading secular intellectuals, Amy Hollywood argues that in their depictions of women mystics, both medieval male hagiographers *and* contemporary interpreters often unintentionally project "their own and the larger culture's fears about bodily limitation, suffering, and mortality" onto their female subjects, thus contorting the evidence and creating a spectacle of women's bodies. These interpreters, says Hollywood, "ventriloquize" cultural crises such as the medieval church's opposition to the heresy of Catharism, or the modern inability to deal with the loss and limitation of mortality, through the mystic's body.[4]

Given these kinds of interpretative intrusions and overlays, some scholars argue that only female-authored texts can be trusted to offer accurate renderings of medieval women's lives and self-understanding. Hollywood's own reading of thirteenth-century Beatrice of Nazareth's "Seven Manners" demonstrates the fruitfulness of this advice. However, the exclusion of male-authored and male-transmitted texts would leave us with precious little evidence of medieval women's lives. We have few, if any, medieval women's texts that bear no extra-authorial imprint, which means we must deal as best we can with the "compromised" texts we have.

A HERMENEUTICS OF RETRIEVAL

Without a doubt, the real historical women we seek to know are not fully present in textual tradition. They are casualties not only of time and distance but also of a patriarchal culture in which writing was, as Sheila Fisher and Janet Halley remark, "a fundamentally male 'homotextual' activity: one in which male writings referred to, responded to, manipulated, and projected desire upon other men and other men's writings as much, if not more, than they claimed to represent the extraliterary world and the women in it."[5] This fact notwithstanding, I am convinced that even the formidable scope and force of this male-centered referential system did not completely obliterate medieval women's self-determination and expression. Their dogged presence and desire can be glimpsed here and there between the lines and in the silences of male-authorized texts, and peeking out from the kitchens of the domestic sphere, the halls of the convent, and the windows of the anchorhold. In recent years, careful scholarly work on medieval women's texts has produced impressive results—not in denial of the kinds of limitations Hollywood and others articulate but in thoughtful recognition of them. Strategies for wading skillfully through the quagmire of transhistorical, cross-cultural, gender-biased interpretation are gradually emerging to guide those who seek to understand, at least in part, the complex lives and moral reasoning of medieval Christian women.[6]

In full recognition of the numerous ways in which contemporary reading strategies can distort the texts and lives of medieval Christian women mystics, we can nevertheless appreciate Elizabeth Dreyer's admonition "to 'honor' these women, to grant them the right to have lived in their specific time and place, and to have their own thoughts—thoughts that are likely to be dramatically different from ours." The first step, she urges, is to engage in careful historical work, respecting the sources enough to try to understand the conditions of their production, their own interpretive categories, and their spiritual, cultural, and political aims. In sum, Dreyer says, we need to "embrace the scholarly virtues of humility and tentativeness," which means accepting "a certain amount of indeterminacy" as we allow "the past to be itself" before it is used to shed light on contemporary situations.[7]

With this admonition in mind, I present in the first part of this chapter a sketch of the medieval context in which these women mystics lived, moved, and had their being. As we will see, it was a context of powerful ideological and physical constraint—an environment that systematically curtailed women's freedom and impugned their intelligence and morality. Hemmed in on every side by the assumptions and power mechanisms of a male-centered culture and worldview, it comes as no surprise that the vast majority of medieval Christian women seem to have lived and died in miserable obscurity, apparently unable to muster the personal and social resources to resist their own dehumanization.

Astonishing is the fact, explored in the second part of this chapter, that a few *did* resist. The opposition of the few is easy to miss because it is altogether surprising in shape and consequence. History tells of no women's insurrection in medieval Europe, and why should it? The pervasive gynophobic curtailments of the time would not permit widespread organizing, plotting, or even consciousness-raising among women. Of necessity (and perhaps also by choice?), medieval women's rebellion was not noteworthy. It involved no conventional weapons or major offensives, no declarations of war or even war crime tribunals. It was, rather, a stealth campaign from beginning to end; a strategy of subversive subtleties, resistant reiterations of the unremarkable and mundane; and a leaning into the familiar with such passion and intensity as to force its bounds to give way, if only a little.

This modest but still mind-boggling expansion or stretching of the Possible was rooted in imagination, robust and courageous. As the specifics of the case study demonstrate, something akin to what I am calling an ethic of ingenuity was surely at work in the lives of these women.

After presenting the context in and against which their imagination was marshaled, I analyze the various ways these women attempted to redefine Christian tradition from within the confines of their context. Specifically, I focus on four sets of religious practices embraced by many medieval Christian women. In each case, I explore the complex, often paradoxical nature of these practices. Acknowledging that each one can be interpreted as evidence of these women's extreme victimization and perhaps unwitting self-destructiveness, I argue nevertheless for a different reading. Ultimately, I suggest that their ingenious retracing of the Christian narrative bears a compelling resemblance to the ethic of ingenuity revealed in the Incarnation.

THE MEDIEVAL CONTEXT: THE GREAT CHAIN OF BEING

To talk about the pre-modern or medieval West is to reference an entire millennium of history, politics, economics, literature, art, philosophy, and religion.[8] It is to talk about a collection of events, ideas, and people too voluminous and diverse to make for easy generalization. Nevertheless, scholars of the period find it possible to identify defining characteristics and common themes—assumptions and aims that comprise the common sense experience of the time, the taken for granted "way things are."[9] In order to make sense of medieval women's spiritual practices, we need to understand them within their proper historical context.

Without a doubt, medieval culture was hierarchically structured, with inequality an assumed norm. The metaphor of the "great chain of being," originally articulated by Augustine in 426, was an organizing idea of immense power and persuasion. It told the individual how he or she was related to other people; explained and legitimated class distinctions; and provided a compelling conceptual framework that encompassed the realities of both this world and the transcendent realm. According to this worldview, God and other spiritual beings such as angels and saints are at the top of the hierarchy; humans, who are part material and part spiritual, populate the middle tier; and nonhuman beings and nature comprise the bottom layer. Within each tier, hierarchy is again the ordering principle: God is above the angels, men are above women, and sentient beings are above non-sentient beings. In every case, that which is thought to be more spiritual ranks above and is seen as superior to that which is less spiritual. The refrain of Platonic dualism, which as we saw in chapter 1 made an indelible imprint on the thought of the early

Christian fathers, gathered strength in the medieval period. The result was the systematic devaluation of those people, things, and classes associated with materiality.

Despite its pervasiveness and persuasiveness, this thoroughly hierarchical view of the world had to be continually reiterated to sustain its normative power. The message about superior-inferior and the great chain of being—the norms of the dominant discourse—had to be continually "performed" and socially reinscribed so the masses would "buy" it. The vast majority of pre-modern people, after all, trafficked primarily in the material realm—working the land, cooking and cleaning, laboring with hands and body. Only the elite could afford to distance themselves from physical labor and concerns about material survival. To protect their privilege, these elites invested much time and energy in preserving the perception that reality is, naturally and by design, thoroughly hierarchical, with the spiritual-material dualism providing the logic of differentiation and valuation.

For evidence of the power and function of this ideology, we can turn to John of Salisbury, a twelfth-century political philosopher whom historians widely recognize as a typical medieval thinker. In his *Statesman's Handbook*, John uses the metaphor of the human body to describe the properly ordered society. Those engaged in the "higher order," the intellectual and spiritual work of political and ecclesial rule, comprise the "head" of society, while those "who discharge the humbler offices"—that is, the offices involving physical labor and "the manifold forms of getting a livelihood and sustaining life"—are identified as the "feet." John unapologetically notes that most people are, in fact, feet: "All these different occupations are so numerous that the commonwealth in the number of its feet exceeds not only the eight-footed crab but even the centipede, and because of their very multitude they cannot be enumerated."[10]

In addition to describing the social hierarchy of his age, John works to justify it. He notes, for instance, the importance of the work of the masses to the proper functioning of the whole of society, admitting that while such work does not "pertain to the authority of the governing power," it is "yet in the highest degree useful and profitable to the corporate whole of the commonwealth." Finally, John of Salisbury, typical medieval thinker, reinforces the norm with this sanguine exhortation to the masses: "It applies generally to each and all of them that in their exercise [of their duties] they should not transgress the limits of the law, and should in all things observe constant reference to the public utility. Inferiors owe it to their superiors to provide them with service, just as the superiors in their turn owe it to their inferiors to provide them with all things needful for their protection and succour."[11] From John's perspective as a member of the educated elite, the system of hierarchy with its spiritual-material dichotomy was a good and natural thing. Indeed, without it anarchy and chaos would surely ensue. For the good of the whole, he and his peers reasoned, a few must have power and authority over the masses.

THE MEDIEVAL CONTEXT: GENDER

Those few were almost always men. As a general rule, medieval men were thought to be more intellectual, more spiritual, and more capable of intellectual and spiritual pursuit than women. By contrast, women were associated with the physical, material realm. Their bodies seemed always to be undergoing change and to be drawing attention to the body's own porousness and alteration. In other words, the female body was a constant reminder of human finitude and the transitory. It was a permanent indication of how far short of the divine and the eternal humanity falls. In addition to the marked mutability of women's bodies was the fact that medieval women spent much of their lives caring for the bodies of others—feeding, bathing, nursing, clothing, and caring for young, sick, and aged bodies. Theirs was a life that revolved in many ways around bodies, a life that was necessarily immersed in and defined by the material realm. And as we know, the material world, including bodies, physicality, and nonhuman nature, as well as the classes of people whose lives were most closely tied to that world, were considered by the dominant medieval discourse to be necessary evils.[12]

Whether we look to Aristotle's description of women as "misbegotten" males in need of male rule; to Philo of Alexandria's first-century designation of woman's carnal nature as the origin of sin; or to church father Tertullian's denunciation of woman at the turn of the third century as "the Devil's gateway," evidence of the misogynist nature of the classical and medieval West is not difficult to find.[13] Not only philosophers and theologians but scientists as well articulated a robust and often creative misogyny. Consider, for example, Galen's influential fourth-century description of women as "mutilated" males with deformed sexual organs who are, nevertheless, to be tolerated because of their procreative role:

> Now, just as mankind is the most perfect of all animals, so within mankind the man is more perfect than the woman, and the reason for his perfection is his excess of heat, for heat is nature's primary instrument

. . . the woman is less perfect than the man in respect to the generative parts. For the parts were formed within her when she was still a
fetus, but could not because of the defect in the heat emerge and project
on the outside, and this, though making the animal itself that was being
formed less perfect than one that is complete in all respects, provided no
small advantage for the race; for there must needs be a female. Indeed,
you ought not to think that our Creator would purposely make half the
whole race imperfect, and, as it were, mutilated, unless there was to be
some great advantage in such a mutilation.[14]

Nine hundred years later and despite a more positive valuation of women
than many earlier Western thinkers, Thomas Aquinas came to a similar conclusion, confirming the basic medieval rationale for women's subordination by
emphasizing their essentially carnal or fleshly nature as opposed to men's "intellectual" bent, as well as their "passive power" in relation to men's "active power."
Because it is in men that "the discretion of reason predominates," Aquinas concludes that women are naturally "governed by others wiser than themselves."[15]
Just as the body's natural tendency toward lust must be continually monitored
and disciplined, medieval thinkers reasoned, so must women's natural propensity toward irrationality and disorder be reigned in by male surveillance and
authority. Man is the head and woman, the body, and while proper functioning
requires mutual responsibility, there can be no doubt about who is the superior
and who the subordinate. In the great chain of being, that powerful metaphor
of medieval existence, women were inescapably chained to and by their bodies. Together, women and their bodies appeared to pose a constant threat to the
purity and order of the social and theological universe.

By the thirteenth century and for the next few centuries, the persecution
of "witches" was fueled by a misogynist, body-loathing rhetoric of startling
ferocity and fatal consequence. Reflecting on the question of why women are
so much more likely to become witches than men, the authors of the influential
fifteenth-century inquisitor's handbook, the *Malleus Maleficarum* (the "hammer
against witches"), proffer this now-familiar line of reasoning:

Since women are feebler both in mind and body, it is not surprising that
they should come under the spell of witchcraft. For as regards intellect,
or the understanding of spiritual things, they seem to be of a different
nature from men; a fact which is vouched for by the logic of the authorities, backed by various examples from the Scriptures. . . . But the natural

reason is that she is more carnal than a man, as is clear from her many carnal abominations.[16]

At the end of the pre-modern period as at its beginning, women's devaluation was rooted in the widespread assumption of their heightened physicality. Women were inextricably linked in the minds of most medievals to the physical, material, earthly, bodily realm—the realm of change, disease, death, and decay.[17]

THE MEDIEVAL CONTEXT: STRATEGIES OF CONTROL AND CONTAINMENT

Because of the singular mutability and permeability of women's bodies, as well as their heightened signification of human finitude, mortality, sexuality, and sinfulness, it was widely believed that they required special surveillance and oversight. Such containment of women's dangerous physicality happened in diverse ways and to varying degrees. At the most basic level, girls and women were placed under the authority of their parents, notably their father, as well as of other males in family and society, such as brothers, uncles, priests, and husbands. Girls and women were expected to obey male authority and were generally confined to the household as their sphere of familiarity, freedom, and influence. Even here, the hierarchies of patriarchy meant that male power trumped female power at almost every turn.

Above all else, the medieval female was to be sexually pure—virginal outside of marriage and chaste within it. Only through constant vigilance, proper surveillance, and the fear of punishment could the forces of female lust be curtailed. And curtailed they must be lest men of all stations and pursuits be ruined by giving in to the deceptive Siren call of female flesh. Medieval scholar Claire Marshall reminds us of the emphasis in pre-modern science and theology on the unruliness of the female body.[18] Characterized in terms of "gaps, orifices and symbolic filth," the female body had an openness and porousness that unnerved and threatened those whose status depended in part on their mastery of that very body. According to Marshall, this "body was seen as pervious and excessive and her character both corruptible and corrupting. Consequently, the need to repair the natural accessibility of the female body became a moral and spiritual imperative in the medieval church's approach to women." Such correction came through "moral and physical enclosure"—specifically, practices of virginity, anchoritism, and monasticism.[19]

BODIES, BOUNDARIES, AND SOCIAL ORDER

As we conclude our examination of the context within which medieval Christian women devised their own distinctive religiosity, anthropologist Mary Douglas's work on the construction of social order is instructive. According to Douglas, human meaning depends absolutely on the drawing of lines, the erecting of boundaries. Without borders and demarcations—physical, social, and mental—there would be no order and hence no possibility of meaning. We define and differentiate order and disorder through an endless process of literal and mental fence-making.

In the pre-modern world, says Douglas, religion was the force that patrolled the boundaries, enforcing the demarcations between sovereign and subject, male and female, pure and impure. In this work, it was the body that was religion's constant reference point, the central symbol of boundary fortification and transgression. The body, as the border of the self, is the boundary humans are most familiar with. As such, it illustrates in compelling fashion the vulnerability of borders. The body's orifices are invested with intense power and danger and so must be carefully monitored and guarded. They are vulnerable to attack and disease and can be unruly and unpredictable. The body signals, simply by its being what it is, the extreme importance of well-policed boundaries for staving off danger and preserving identity.

Given the body's ambivalent import as the symbol of boundaries and their chaos-bearing transgressability, it is not surprising that the body itself, as well as those most closely associated with the body in the social imagination, are treated with a mix of fear and loathing and are deemed in need of special oversight and scrutiny. In the medieval West, it is well known that religion functioned as a powerful definer and enforcer of social boundaries. In that capacity, medieval Christianity focused with special energy on the need to police bodies, particularly female bodies with their heightened mutability and vulnerability and their tendency to be at the same time alluring and unruly. Martha Reineke effectively captures the logic behind this powerful coupling of Christian culture and the female body:

> The female body, site of processes men have perceived historically as mysterious and potentially dangerous, offers a most graphic symbolism of issues of ultimate concern. Women carry potential for order and meaning and for disorder and chaos in their very bodies. Menstruation, reproduction, and aging all testify to the triumphs and tragedies of existence. Moreover, because religions choose symbols not only to

distinguish order from disorder, but also to effect order and control disorder, the female body often has been religions' symbol of choice.[20]

Tragically for medieval Christian women, their symbolic usefulness has
not protected them from literal denigration. Quite the opposite, as Reineke
notes, "Because the female body is associated most closely with life and death
processes, authority asserted over a female body is power asserted over the
very forces of creation."[21]

Perhaps, then, it was a quintessentially human need for order and orientation in a complex and often inscrutable universe that motivated the medieval misogyny and strategies of female containment that were typical of the
medieval Christian West. Such an explanation does not, of course, expunge the
damage done. Nor does it exonerate a profoundly dehumanizing system or that
system's enforcers. Even those caught up in systems beyond their causation or
control have the freedom to respond to their situation. From passive compliance to active enforcement, the options for response are myriad. In the rest of
this chapter, we ask the question of how medieval women responded to their
own victimization, and we explore an answer that is interestingly complex. It
is also, I propose, an approach to entrenched evil that is powerfully suggestive
for our own time.

INGENIOUS INCARNATIONS

Why did medieval women tend to comply with their own dehumanization?
Why didn't they rebel, stage a walkout, or start a revolution? This question
admittedly reflects a post-Enlightenment mindset that views human history,
institutions, and norms as social constructions and human nature as fundamentally agential. However, not to ask the question of medieval women's complicity
in their own exploitation is to assume they were mere social automatons, either
helplessly or willingly allowing their bodies to be inscribed by a misogynist,
somatophobic symbol system that resulted in the systematic and very real subjugation of their bodies and opportunities at almost every turn. It may be that
medieval women *were* helpless, passive, or voluntary victims of an immutably or
intentionally misogynist system; but unless we ask the question of their relation
to that system, we limit their possibilities as surely and mercilessly as it did.

INTERNALIZED MISOGYNY?

Certainly one theory is that they internalized the misogynist assumptions about
their character and physicality that dominate the textual and artistic records

of the period. Until relatively recently, this "false consciousness" theory was embraced by most medieval scholars. If association with the body was a key cause of women's subjugation, then, it was reasoned, any woman who voluntarily affirmed or even deepened her connection to the body was obviously unmoored from reason. It is one thing to be victimized by the misogynist assumptions of a powerfully patriarchal culture and theology but quite another to participate willingly in one's own victimization. Because these medieval women affirmed and even celebrated their association with the physical—indeed, named it as their pathway to God—it was until recently assumed that they were doubly victimized, that they had internalized the misogyny of the larger culture and turned it against themselves in dramatic actions of self-loathing and self-destruction.[22]

As we saw above, pre-modern textual evidence abounds with articulations of women's physical, intellectual, moral, and spiritual inferiority. Medieval art and iconography reiterate that message. Given the widespread and generally unquestioned presentation throughout medieval culture of women's defective nature, it would come as no surprise to learn that many women internalized this portrait.

Like their male counterparts, medieval women would have yearned to live in a world of order and meaning rather than disorder and chaos, and the patriarchal worldview certainly offered a clear and comprehensive system for ordering the cosmos. Or perhaps it was simply the only system available to them—the orienting symbolics they were steeped in from birth and, as such, the only ones they could imagine. Similarly, it may have been the only worldview they were *permitted* to consider. The sophisticated containment strategies and potent norming powers of family, education, and religion may have rendered medieval girls and women powerless to do anything other than conform to the patriarchal status quo. Still another possibility is that the force and scope of these containment strategies and institutional powers may have frightened them into quiescence.

These are all possible answers to the question of medieval women's apparent complicity in their own victimization. Yet, each one reiterates the very victimization it seeks to explain. These explanations assume that medieval women were either too unstable, unimaginative, helpless, or cowardly to resist their own exploitation.

What if, by contrast, we do not assume the very worst about medieval women's mental health, moral agency, and imagination? What if, instead, we entertain the possibility that the powerfully negative forces of patriarchy, while surely taking their toll in various ways on women's psyches, behaviors, and options, did not altogether undo them? It is *this* possibility that intrigues me, particularly as I consider one of the most puzzling of all aspects of medieval Christian women's lives: their body-centered religiosity. Given the widespread assumption that women's intellectual, moral, and spiritual inferiority were rooted in their presumed "special" connection to bodies, the question of how best to make sense of the fact that a significant minority of them embraced a religious identity and spiritual practices that were peculiarly *bodily* calls out for explanation. It is in relation to their odd religiosity that the issue of imagination, and the possibility of *christic* imagination, comes to the fore.

Certainly, not all Christian women in the pre-modern period embraced the body-centered religious practices I discuss below; yet a significant number of them did. Most for whom we have useful records lived in Europe between the twelfth and sixteenth centuries. Many belonged to religious orders; others were part of a women's lay movement known as the Beguines; still others appear not to have belonged to a religious community outside of their local parish. Most of the women I consider were recognized by at least some of their contemporaries as religious leaders or exemplars, indicating that even if the majority did not embody their specific spiritual practices, those practices were nevertheless viewed in a positive light.

EXTREME RELIGION

For many medieval women, the heart of their Christian identity could be found in a range of body-focused practices including fasting, illness, and virginity-chastity.[23] Medieval historian Caroline Walker Bynum, among others, argues convincingly that these practices are to be properly understood as features of religious devotion—attempts to draw closer to the Divine. Rather than run away from the physical realm to which they were oppressively tethered by the larger culture, these women dove more deeply into it. They developed a spirituality that was radically physical. Why?

The crucial question is whether their extreme religiosity was motivated primarily by self-destructive or self-actualizing aims—whether it signaled the death of the imagination or its cultivation. To respond to this question, I consider four specific practices that characterized these women's religiosity: food asceticism, voluntary illness and suffering, sexual purity, and somatomorphic visions. Each of these practices has typically been interpreted as evidence of pathology. While this logic is not entirely unfounded, I argue that it ignores important liberative impulses and outcomes that lend themselves to an entirely different interpretation. In the final analysis, I believe there is good reason to believe that many of the women who embraced these body-centered practices may have been engaging in religiously motivated acts of imagination aimed not at their own effacement or destruction but rather at individual and societal transformation. While their notion of transformation may strike some twenty-first century readers as disappointingly weak, within the tightly-policed constraints of their own context these women appear to embody unprecedented moral courage and agency.

I. Food Asceticism in Female Religiosity

One of the hallmarks of medieval Christian women's religiosity was the practice of food asceticism. While fasting has been an important Christian practice through the ages, it was taken to unprecedented heights by medieval women. Whether their extreme embrace of the practice was an indication of internalized victimization or of resistance to victimization is our question.

In pre-modern Europe it was widely assumed that the virtues of the soul depended in part on the discipline of the body. Such discipline ordinarily included regimes of bodily renunciation such as poverty, food abstinence, and sexual chastity. It also included contemplative disciplines such as prayer, study, and meditation. Fasting was a hallmark of medieval Christian culture. It was a visible sign of one's faith and the most accessible of the four behaviors required of all Christians.[24] Food was at the center of the definitive religious ritual, the Eucharist, in which Christians "ate" their God. Among medieval ascetics, food deprivation was a favorite practice, embraced by devout women and men alike.

While standard Greco-Roman decorum encouraged moderation in eating and drinking, popular Christian views of food and diet tilted toward asceticism by lifting up God and angels, with their "light and airy" bodily constitution, as the ideal, and eschewing, by contrast, hot, lustful bodies. If the aim of Christian life was to approximate heavenly beings, then a comprehensive set of dietary rules was implied. In general, it was thought that one should avoid heavy, hot, moist foods in favor of vegetables and herbs. Even these were to be consumed in careful moderation to avoid the heat produced by belches and other gaseous emissions. Such food practices, suggested Clement of Alexandria in the late second century, would produce souls that are "pure and dry and luminous," souls poised to attain lofty heights of knowledge and contemplation.[25] With the same goal in mind, St. Jerome proposed at the turn of the fourth century that a perpetually hungry belly is ideal because it contains no undigested food to heat up the body.[26] In sum, fasting was embraced by Christian piety as a practical means of avoiding lust and sexual temptation and, at the same time, drawing closer to God.

The ideal medieval body, says historian of religion Teresa Shaw, is "cool and dry, pale and thin from fasting."[27] Such a body is well disciplined and hence able to withstand passions from both within and without. Another spiritual benefit of fasting identified by medieval Christians is its diminishing of the sex drive, a correlation confirmed by modern research. Because sex was believed to weaken one physically and morally, the religious practitioner deprived him- or herself of food in order to repress sexual desire. In addition, fasting was believed to mitigate self-love and pride by disfiguring one's appearance. Ultimately, concludes Shaw, it was believed that fasting connects the devotee to the original purity and immortality lost in the Garden of Eden via a shameful act of eating. The ascetic life becomes a way of reversing the sin of Adam and Eve and returning, at least proleptically, to "the time before bodies were sexualized and before food and bodily desire had become the downfall of humanity."[28]

Dangerous Devotion

While food deprivation was characteristic of both male and female religious devotion, it was at the very center of medieval women's religiosity.[29] Where men's ascetical options included renouncing sex, money, property, and social status in addition to food, most women were not free to determine their sexual, social, and financial lives. If something worldly was to be renounced, food was the thing over which pre-modern women enjoyed the most control, and hence it became the obvious fulcrum of their asceticism. As Bynum demonstrates in *Holy Feast and Holy Fast,* medieval women took food asceticism to extraordinary, perhaps even heavenly, heights.

Based on a study of the *vitae* of holy women who lived during these centuries in the Low Country (the lowland region near the North Sea, corresponding today to Belgium, Luxembourg, and the Netherlands), Bynum notes that "extreme fasting is a theme in every [one]."[30] For women such as Mary of Oignes, Juliana of Cornillon, Ida of Louvain, Ida of Léau, Elizabeth of Spalbeck, Margaret of Ypres, and many, many more, fasting was not a second-order devotional trapping. Instead, it was the fulcrum of their spiritual practice. This fasting, we must note, was anything but decorous. By all reports, it was at times taken to disfiguring, even life-threatening extremes. So devoted to the discipline were these holy women that, says Bynum, they "reached a point where they were unable to eat normally, where the smell and sight of food caused nausea and pain."[31] Bynum cites example after example of medieval women whose self-imposed discipline of food deprivation was carried to death-defying extremes. Two such examples are Mary of Oignes and Elizabeth of Spalbeek:

> Mary of Oignes . . . mutilated her flesh out of guilt over eating, then embarked on a program of extended fast. She ate only once a day (at Vespers or at night); she took no wine and no meat; often she ate only coarse black bread that tore her throat and made it bleed. Once, after thirty-five days of total abstinence and silence, she "came back to herself" and tried to consume earthly food. But she could not bear its odor and could sip only wine from the ablutions cup.
>
> Philip of Clairvaux reports that Elizabeth of Spalbeek ate almost nothing. She condescended, with obvious reluctance, to lap up a little milk, but she abhorred food. When relatives or companions put fruit, meat, or fish to her lips, she sucked a little juice but took in nothing of "the grosser matter." A dove consumed more in a single swallow, says Philip, than Elizabeth was willing to drink of the wine she was offered, and he remarks: "She ate and drank more to satisfy the will of others than because of her own will or even because of necessity."[32]

Clearly, these medieval women pushed their fasting to the limit, and then some. Even in relation to a cultural context tilted toward food asceticism by the assumptions discussed above, their practices of food deprivation were excessive. Medieval men fasted, too, but it was the rare exception who took food asceticism to the extraordinary lengths that were standard for holy women. Why this difference? Why were medieval Christian women so much more likely to starve themselves than men? Why, in a culture that denigrated women for their physicality, did some women focus so intensely in their spiritual practices on things physical? *Why a body-centered religiosity for those whose lives were diminished precisely by their association with the body?*

Holy Food for Holy People

Undoubtedly, medieval women's food asceticism was sometimes pathological. Like girls and women in our own day who develop eating disorders in unwitting response to perverse cultural assumptions about female health and beauty, or because they cannot live up to the inflated standards and expectations of self or others, some medieval women likely adopted a regimen of food deprivation for negative or destructive reasons. Indeed, given the force and scope of the body-fearing, woman-loathing discourse that pervaded the period, it would seem impossible *not* to soak up some of that thoroughgoing negativity. The spiritual practice of fasting at the very heart of many women's religiosity was no doubt motivated in part by these women's own deep suspicion toward the female body. Assumed for centuries to be the site *par excellence* of human frailty and sinfulness, this body would appear to be naturally in need of special oversight and discipline. If the life of the spirit were to be cultivated, then its enemy the flesh must be subdued. Female flesh, in particular, thanks to its essentially mutable and lustful constitution, must be castigated with special fervor. No wonder food deprivation became the favorite religious practice of pre-modern women: It weakened and neutralized the troublesome body, making it incapable of full functioning and forcing its subordination to the intellect and spirit.

At the same time as women's food asceticism played easily into the hands of this dominant (and dominating) logic, it also in interesting ways defied it. These women took the very thing that oppressed them and voluntarily deepened that association until, instead of causing their subjugation, it was the means to their exaltation. Viewed from this angle, the practice of depriving themselves of food was not so much a tool of self-destruction as a gesture toward self-actualization. True, these women chose to abstain from ordinary food, but they often did so in order to feast on heavenly food. They rejected normal food and drink in preparation for the spiritual nourishment provided by the holy food and drink of the Eucharist. For them, the Eucharist became a crucial avenue to self-acceptance, for in the act of consuming God, they became one with the Divine, loosening the shackles of inferiority and impurity as they were raised into holy communion with the Lover of the universe.

Of course, one might wonder whether the spiritual exaltation experienced through the embrace of eucharistic piety may have signaled not the critique or unsettling of patriarchy but rather its ultimate triumph. After all, these women were denying the everyday needs of their bodies in order to transcend the limits and miseries of earthly existence for spiritual bliss. Could we ask for a clearer reenactment of the spirit-matter dualism at the heart of medieval misogyny? Three crucial realities argue against such an interpretation. All three point to a paradoxical embrace of earthly, material existence despite the apparent rejection of it.

Service to Suffering Bodies

First, at the same time as these women were rejecting earthly food for heavenly sustenance, many of them were deeply involved in earthly ministries aimed at caring for sick and hungry bodies. They tended the wounds and dis-ease-ravaged bodies of their fellow men and women. They fed the hungry. In other words, they put their religious experience of divine mercy into concrete action in their local communities, working to transform the material existence of their neighbors.

Had these women hated the world or the multitude, of bodies that inhabit it, they would not have committed themselves to its care and transformation. Their ministries of feeding and healing reflect a theology of incarnation rather than dualism, a religiosity that requires the faithful to lean ever more coura-geously *into* the bodily and the earthly rather than to abandon them for purely spiritual realities. I imagine it was their own heightened experience of the Incarnate One, powerfully evoked by a eucharistic piety of holy fast and holy feast, that gave these remarkable women the conviction and courage to use their own culturally troubled bodies to serve the needs of the bodies around them.

To embrace physicality as they did, both in their spiritual and earthly practice, and to embrace it with such passion, despite its powerfully oppres-sive connotations and consequences, would seem to be an act of either deep psychological dysfunction or profound moral courage. In fact, it is probable that these women were motivated by both dispositions. Most likely, they found themselves by accident of birth embracing a religious tradition fraught with patriarchy and hence seemingly opposed to their own full humanity and flour-ishing. In the midst of this ambiguous embrace, they nevertheless developed a distinctive interpretation and practice of that tradition that nurtured their own moral agency, theological sensibilities and growth, and compassion for suffering others. Like those at the margins in every age, these women would not have had the luxury of escaping or defeating the reigning powers. Their lives and choices would have been necessarily bounded by powerful constraints and external authorities. Outright rebellion or escape, besides being conceptu-ally unimaginable, would have been practically imprudent—a choice for sure annihilation in one form or another. The chief aim under such conditions would have been survival with dignity, plain and simple. But such survival would actu-ally have been anything but simple given the forces of dehumanization amassed against them. Asserting one's dignity as a human being and a woman in that context would have required gritty resourcefulness, stubborn persistence, and deep pools of courage. It would have demanded ingenuity, imagination, and a source of confirmation and hope beyond the ordinary.

Evidence from every direction confirms that these women were enlivened and empowered by extraordinary experiences of divine love and intimacy and that they prepared for and responded to such experiences with the practice of food asceticism. In this context, we can appreciate the complexity of the practice at the heart of their religiosity. Admittedly, their extreme food asceticism would have reiterated normative fears of physicality, change, sexuality, and female flesh. At the same time, however, they were putting that asceticism in the service of an incarnational theology in which the Divine pulled the fleshly into intimate embrace and ultimate transformation through holy eating. As a result, that flesh was empowered for an active ministry of mercy on behalf of the least, the lost, and the last. Understood in this way, these women's food asceticism can be seen as a practice of christic imagination—a bold and creative embodiment of an ethic of incarnation and ingenuity.

An Incarnational Theology

In addition to the ministry of service to others that was inspired by the practice of food asceticism, a second factor that mitigated the practice's destructive impact was the theology it funded. In general, this was a theology not of escape from the world but of ever-deeper immersion in and service to it; a theology not of disembodied spirituality but of thoroughgoing incarnation; a theology that increasingly mirrored the paradox of vulnerability and power that characterized the lives of its female apologists. By the late Middle Ages, partly as a result of women's increased religious visibility and distinctive influence, a vernacular theology emerged that was unprecedented in its inclusiveness and fleshiness. No longer was divinity construed chiefly in terms of immutability, transcendence, and kingly power. Rather, God was often understood as the divine co-sufferer who freely chose the "indignities" and vulnerability of fleshly existence in order to heal its wounds.

Jesus was not only the resurrected and triumphant one but also, and more often, the crucified and broken one, the one who suffered in order to put an end to suffering. Depicted in startlingly feminine terms, God in Jesus was the nurturing Creator, the life-giving Mother. Religious art such as *The Savior* by fifteenth-century artist Quirizio da Murano shows a self-emptying Jesus whose blood feeds the church as a lactating mother's milk nourishes the hungry child.[33] The wound in Jesus' side from which the life-giving blood emerges is positioned by Quirizio and other artists at chest level in a clear gesture toward divine lactation. A lactating God. . . . What could be further removed from the flesh-fleeing, woman-fearing convictions of previous times? Clearly, something interesting and unexpected, something transgressive of the patriarchal norm, was going on.

Influential Women

Not only did medieval women's extreme food asceticism help inspire and sustain ministries of social transformation and a relatively holistic and inclusive theology, it also became an avenue for women's empowerment as saints, teachers, counselors, and administrators. As we know, fasting had long been an important part of Christian practice. As a result, when late medieval women took the practice to new heights, they could do so with the assumption that their behavior would be accepted as genuine religious practice, or at least that its veracity could be defended on the basis of its continuity with tradition. As it turned out, medieval women's extraordinarily intense embrace of food asceticism did evoke at least grudging recognition from the powers that be and often the respect of their peers. As a result, these women became revered as saints; they became role models for ordinary Christians; they were even tapped to lead religious houses and to advise heads of state. While there was eventually an institutional backlash against women's dramatic embrace of fasting, that reaction may be seen as an effort to monitor and contain the growing religious and social influence these women accrued, thanks to their devoted religious practice.

Taking into account the positive effects of their fasting—the active ministry it fostered, the innovative theology it helped shape, and the social and ecclesial influence it enabled—leads me to conclude that medieval women's extreme food asceticism may be best understood not in terms of false consciousness or internalized misogyny, although these factors were likely in play as well, but in terms of Irigaray's liberative mimesis or Butler's subversive performativity.[34] Medieval European society gave women a clear role to play—a role focused on their heightened and troublesome physicality. Given the ideological and institutional power of medieval culture's playwrights and directors, outright rejection of their assigned role was not a genuine option for women. Their choice, therefore, was either to assume that role submissively and enact it as scripted, or else to perform it disloyally, going through the motions of compliance while keeping an eye out for opportunities to express an alternate reality. In their practice of the religious norm of food asceticism, I see compelling evidence of medieval women's disloyalty to patriarchy.

At first glance, they appear to have enacted their assigned role dutifully, even passionately. Depriving themselves of food, they subjected their troublesome female flesh to the socially acceptable method of discipline, thereby acquiescing to the reigning dualisms of the day: heavenly food over earthly food, spirit over matter, male over female, clergy over laity. Upon closer scrutiny,

however, one notices the excesses and subversions enacted by their performance: the over-the-top character of their fasting that signals a willingness
to take risks and exceed boundaries; the propensity for soaring past ordinary
limits into ecstatic union with the Divine; the transmutation of extraordinary
passion for the Infinite into ordinary care for the finite and vulnerable; the ven-
turing forth into the world as teacher, theologian, author, and sage; the questioning of age-old social roles and theological assumptions. What we can see
encoded in medieval women's religious practice is a series of quite remarkable
innovations on the age-old theme of food asceticism—innovations that appear
to have been inspired by profound experiences of the God who, against all odds
and norms, became flesh. Perhaps emboldened by God's own momentous act
of incarnational boundary-crossing, I imagine these women developed a script
for subtle but liberative performativity, refusing to abdicate their moral agency
but smart enough to camouflage them.

II. Illness and Self-Inflicted Suffering

In addition to food asceticism, medieval women's religious practices included
voluntary illness and self-inflicted suffering. Rather than avoiding or dreading
the pain and inconvenience of illness, many Christian women welcomed it.
Some even prayed for it. Ailments ranging from occasional headaches to the
ravages of fatal disease were embraced and celebrated as important features
of devout living. In a study of 864 saints from the years 1000 to 1700, Donald
Weinstein and Rudolph Bell report that while only about 18 percent of all officially recognized medieval saints were women, a full 53 percent of those saints
whose piety included debilitating illness were women. In other words, illness
played a marked role in women's religiosity compared to men's.[35]

Bynum's study offers a brief litany of the phenomenon:

Mary of Oignies and Villana de' Botti refused prayers for relief of sickness; Gertrude of Helfta embraced headaches as a source of grace; Beatrice of Nazareth, who desired the torments of illness, was healed almost
against her wishes; Margaret of Ypres so desired to join with Christ's suffering that she prayed for her illness to last beyond the grave. Dauphine of
Puimichel even suggested that if people knew how useful diseases were
for self-discipline, they would purchase them in the marketplace.[36]

Perhaps the best-known example of the centrality of voluntary illness
to medieval women's religiosity is Julian of Norwich, who desired from God

"three graces," one of which was "bodily sickness." It was during such sickness that Julian received her sixteen showings or revelations. Here, she recounts her remarkable illness:

> And when I was thirty and a half years old, God sent me a bodily sick-
> ness in which I lay for three days and three nights; and on the fourth day
> I received all the rites of Holy Church. . . . But . . . I suffered on for two
> days and two nights . . . and on the third night . . . my reason and my
> sufferings told me that I should die; . . . so I lasted until day, and by then
> my body was dead from the middle downwards. . . . After this my sight
> began to fail, and it was dark all around me in the room, dark as night
> . . . . After that I felt as if the upper part of my body were beginning to
> die. My hands fell down on either side, and I was so weak that my head
> lolled to one side. The greatest pain that I felt was my shortness of breath
> and the ebbing of my life.[37]

In addition to illness, welcomed and even celebrated, some medieval Christian women engaged intentionally in self-destructive behaviors such as hitting, cutting, or otherwise hurting themselves. While it is true that the narration of such practices often occurred in the service of larger rhetorical aims and may well be exaggerated as a result, the general proposition that self-inflicted suffering was a genuine feature of medieval women's spiritual practice is rarely disputed. Food deprivation, which occasionally turned into fatal self-starvation, was the main form of such willed suffering, but there are also reports of women mutilating their flesh through cutting and self-flagellation. Catherine of Siena, for instance, who lived in fifteenth-century Italy and was eventually canonized as a saint, was reported to have engaged in "hours of flagellation daily."[38]

Like the practice of food asceticism, medieval women's voluntary illness and suffering puts the body front and center, indicating a deliberate intertwining of spirit and matter. Once again, we are left to wonder why those whom church and society subordinated thanks to their perceived connection to the material realm of bodies, change, suffering, and disease would intentionally emphasize and enhance that very connection. Should these women's embrace of illness and suffering be viewed as spiritual heroics, excessive self-indulgence, extreme self-hatred, or what?

Imitatio Christi

On the surface, we appear to have another example of internalized misogyny: women praying for illness and celebrating its arrival, even when it is excruciatingly painful or potentially fatal; women interpreting sickness as a blessing from God; and women flagellating and even occasionally cutting themselves. There can be little doubt that at least some of this behavior was brought on by low self-esteem, genuine self-hatred, or misguided attempts at spiritual escape from the miseries of earthly existence. Thus, we can certainly see in medieval women's practice of voluntary illness and suffering the underscoring of the very assumptions and patterns that led to and sustained their devaluation within the church and wider culture. But here again, we find an important subtext to acknowledge—a subtext predicated not on women's helplessness, passivity, or pathology but on their fundamental desire as human beings to flourish, to resist their own dehumanization, and to shape their own world in however limited a fashion.

For these women, illness and suffering were often avenues to spiritual awakening, revelation, or empowerment.[39] At other times, they were tests of one's faith and resulted, when endured, in a strengthening of one's spiritual character and resolve. As in the case of Macrina, the heroic endurance of illness was often interpreted as a kind of divine validation of a woman's saintliness. Sometimes, as for Margery Kempe and Christine de Pizan, it was viewed as a summons to a different kind of life. Occasionally, illness was linked to mystical death, with the holy girl or woman passing through a kind of death and then returning to life with a religious vision to share or with a renewed sense of purpose and authority. Christina Mirabilis and Catherine of Siena, among others, fit this model. For women who eventually became writers, such as Hildegard of Bingen, Margery Kempe, and Gertrude the Great, the experience of illness or suffering seems to have had an authorizing effect, impelling them toward new forms of self-expression and personal courage. In this excerpt from a letter of Marguerite d'Oignt, we see an example of the authorizing relationship between women's illness and their writing:

I don't know if what is written in the book is in Holy Scripture, but I know that she who put these things into writing was so ravished in our Lord one night that it seemed to her that she saw all these things. And when she returned to herself, he had them all written in her heart in such a way that she could not think about anything else, but her heart was so full that she could not eat, nor drink, nor sleep, to the degree that

she fell into such a great weakness that the doctors believed her close to
death.

She thought that if she were to put these things in writing, as our
Lord had sent them to her in her heart, her heart would be more relieved
for it. She began to write everything. . . . And as soon as she had written
everything, she was completely cured. I firmly believe that if she had not
put it in writing she would have died or become crazy. . . . And this is
why I believe that this was written by the will of Our Lord.[40]

Similarly, Hildegard comments in her *Scivias* that a prolonged illness,
interpreted by her as divinely sent, was what finally prompted her to record
and publicize her extraordinary visions.

More than anything, medieval women's illness and voluntary suffering
drew them closer to their savior and their neighbor. Within the context of
an incarnational theology in which God's audacious enfleshment to the point
of suffering and death was believed to affect the salvation of all flesh, holy
women's experience of bodily suffering became a means to identify with and
participate in God's redemptive suffering. Their torment became an intimate
window onto Jesus' hardship, and their ridicule by others, a special link to the
pain of his fateful rejection. Sinking willingly into the frailty of their own flesh,
they plunged deep into the fragility and risk of the Incarnation. There they
met their wounded but triumphant God in the depths, and there they found
a salvific vision and will with which they surfaced and ventured forth into the
world in modes of service.

Framed by an incarnational theology, these women's illness and suffering
appears ultimately to have awakened them to the infinite reach and dazzling
intensity of God's love, particularly for those who suffered at the hands of
a hard-hearted world. Moreover, it motivated them to use what health and
strength they had to participate in God's redemption of that world, channel-
ing their suffering in constructive and life-giving directions. These remarkable women understood their suffering, says Bynum, not as the consequence
or means of self-loathing but as part of a life of *imitatio christi*, imitation of
Christ.[41] Like Jesus, their suffering was meaningful not because it enacted
or reinforced social constructions of contempt or domination but because
it deepened their connection and commitment to God and to neighbor and
hence implicitly called those constructions into question. Reflecting on the
relationship between suffering and service, Hadewijch of Brabant in the early
thirteenth century counseled a young Beguine:

> We must always know that for us life must be a loving service and a
> longing exile, for so Jesus Christ lived as a man upon this earth. . . . He
> never granted Himself any respite, but lived in greater toil from day to
> day, from His first day until His last. It was His gracious will to live as we
> must live, to be what we should be, and He says to those who live now
> as He did then that where there is love there is great labour and much
> suffering. But to such men, their sufferings are sweet.[42]

In light of theological convictions such as this, we may conclude that the
willingness to suffer illness and other bodily pain is less reflective of internalized misogyny or false consciousness than of a profound identification with the
suffering One who heals the world. Instead of seeking to escape the burdens
of the flesh, Hadewijch and others found in them opportunities for drawing
ever nearer to the incarnate God and to God's suffering creatures in modes of
empathy and action. To live a life of "honourable service" to God's creatures and
"longing exile" in anticipation of perfect union with God was "to hang upon the
cross with Christ. . . . To die with Him and with Him to rise again."[43] Leaning
passionately *into* the flesh, both theirs and God's, these women may well have
experienced the surprising power of weakness, the deep joy of serving others,
the paradox at the very heart of Christian faith.

III. Virginity and Chastity

A third defining characteristic of medieval Christian women's piety was the
practice of sexual purity. Like food asceticism and voluntary illness and suffering, this was a spiritual practice at whose center was the female body. This time,
however, it was not the body as food or as sufferer that was in the spotlight but,
rather, the body as site of both unbounded energy and earthly delimitation, of
both autonomy and possession.

As medievalist Ruth Evans remarks, "Virginity is a category that the Middle Ages found indispensable to think with: unsettling and yet enormously
productive."[44] Virginity was "unsettling" because it was impossible to guaran-
tee or ascertain. How could one know for certain that another was a virgin?
There was no irrefutable empirical proof of the condition. Thus, virginity
underscores the limits of human knowledge and power. At the same time,
however, virginity functioned in the pre-modern Christian world as the ultimate symbol of fidelity, discipline, and devotion. More than any other human
act or disposition, it signaled purity of intention and action. Rooted in this
world, its implications soared heavenward. Bespeaking both the hope and the

folly of human aspirations, the symbol and practice of virginity articulated in compelling ways the complexity and paradox of medieval culture's self-understanding. It comes as no surprise, then, that "the memory of virgins was everywhere . . . in biblical drama, in popular story-collections, in lyrics and poems, in sermons, in rules and treatises for enclosed women, in manuscript illuminations, in manuals of pastoral instruction to the laity, in court poetry, interspersed with romances in household miscellanies."[45]

Although sexual purity was a cultural ideal, it was largely associated in the medieval mind with girls and women. A wide range of medieval texts, including the *Ancrene Wisse*, countless hagiographies, orthodox sermon collections, romances, medical texts, and Chaucer's *Canterbury Tales* effectively demonstrate the widespread preoccupation with female virginity.[46] Medieval girls were regularly named after the virgin-martyr saints, the tales of their heroic purity shaping the child's interpretation of her body, relationships, and possibilities for the future. The feast days of these cultural exemplars were highlighted in the calendars of medieval primers, the tales of their courageous struggle to preserve their purity recycled in different genres through the ages and their images projected onto the stained glass and tapestries of churches and sanctuaries across the land. These textual, visual, and material narratives represent variations of familiar story lines. According to one, the beautiful virgin courageously rebuffs the attempts of the opponent to ruin her sexual purity, virtuously choosing to sacrifice her life rather than her virginity. A different but related trope involves "a beautiful, virtuous Christian virgin" who "has her faith tested by pagan adversaries: tortured, imprisoned, her flesh stripped, her body dismembered, her breasts torn off, boiling oil poured over her, the virgin remains miraculously alive, her narrative of survival the very revelation of her true (Christian) self: unchangeable, indestructible, incorruptible. Her pagan opponents are converted or destroyed."[47]

The Cultural Valuation of Virginity

Women who embraced the practice of sexual purity seem to have had positive motivations such as the desire to approximate the purity enjoyed by humanity before the fall into sin.[48] Those who could not heed the superior call to virginity were encouraged to embrace chastity in marriage or widowhood as a way of cultivating virtue by overcoming the temptations of the flesh. After bearing fourteen children, Margery Kempe of fifteenth-century England became a "wilful virgin," eventually striking a deal with her husband so that she could live out the rest of her life as a chaste woman.[49]

Medieval women's sexual purity was also inspired in powerful ways by negative factors, especially fear. In addition to fears of the dangerous, unpredictable, and defiling character of female sexuality, also at play were economic insecurities, concerns about male authority and lineage, and anti-Semitism.

Economic anxieties contributed to the cultural adulation of virginity. In a system in which wealth was based on inheritance and land tenure and in which, moreover, a woman's body was considered male property, it was the wife's virginity that guaranteed the purity of the family line.[50] In such a system, men's fortunes depended absolutely on the containment of women's sexuality. Given the stakes, fathers, husbands, and sons exerted maximum control over the female bodies under their authority. A key weapon in their arsenal was the ideal of virginity, whose spectrum included chastity in marriage and widowhood.

It is likely that anti-Semitism, too, fueled the medieval Christian obsession with virginity. Popular culture embraced not only narratives of the virgin martyrs but also lurid tales about the desecration of the communion host by murderous Jews. At the heart of the central ritual of Christian practice, the Eucharist, was the belief that when the devotee consumed the host, he or she was consuming the Divine—not a piece or fragment or symbol of the Divine but God in God's perfect wholeness, thereby becoming one with that perfection in a moment of redemptive transformation. As part of a growing anti-Jewish sentiment among Christians of the later Middle Ages, tales began circulating of hostile and blood-thirsty Jews who would enter Christian churches and try to tear, puncture, or otherwise destroy the unity of the host, the most sacred object of Christian ritual practice. Stories of virgin-martyr saints whose sexual inviolability was heroically preserved despite violent opposition were used to reiterate Christian claims to the inviolability of the host in the face of Jewish attack. Conversely, Christian idealizations of virginity were reinvigorated by anti-Jewish narratives of host desecration.[51] Both discourses were useful in shoring up Christian identity and esteem during complex times in which internal threats such as the heresy of Catharism, as well as external threats such as the growth of Islam, made Christian unity seem more important than ever.

Clearly, female sexual purity was vital to the worldview, self-understanding, and everyday practices of medieval Christian culture. Whether the medieval embrace of female virginity and chastity was intended to underscore a Neoplatonic worldview, rationalize and enhance male authority, instruct girls and women in proper decorum, ensure family lineage and inheritance claims, or shore up Christian identity and unity in the face of perceived threats, the discourse of female virginity was at the heart of medieval culture. It was also a defining feature of Christian women's religiosity. It was embraced with great enthusiasm not merely by the powerful cultural elites who stood to gain from its various effects, but also by ordinary, devout women. What might these women have gained from this embrace? Or were they mere pawns in a game over which they had no control? Did they perhaps willingly participate in their own delimitation?

Virgins for Christ

From one angle, the adulation of virginity and chastity appears to reiterate the very assumptions that caused and sustained medieval women's widespread devaluation. In particular, it seems to underline the notion that sexuality is dangerous and inimical to spiritual seriousness. It implies that because of their heightened carnality, women are especially potent sources of sexual corruption and hence in need of vigilant male oversight. By choosing to embrace the ideal of sexual purity as part of their religious practice, medieval women would seem to reinforce their own subordination and containment, to sacrifice their own freedom, femininity, and fulfillment on the altar of patriarchal paranoia and power. Viewed from another angle, however, the practice becomes an imaginative way to circumvent the very delimitations that it is intended to impose.

The young girl who declared supreme devotion for God and expressed that devotion by embracing virginity and joining a religious order would have found herself living in a female-centered world free from sexual obligation to men, from the dangers of repeated pregnancies, and from a life lived in explicit subordination to husband, father, brother, and son. True, her religious order would have been overseen by men, and not always benevolently, but she would still be spared many of the daily indignities of living as a woman in a thoroughly patriarchal society. In some cases, virginity as a choice for liberation from patriarchal norms is made explicit, as in the twelfth-century *Life of Christina of Markyate*. Here, we witness Christina's protracted struggle with her parents over her desire to devote herself fully to Christ and his mother rather than consummate her marriage to Burthred, whom she was forced to wed. Ultimately, Christina runs away and lives for years in hiding, enduring great physical discomfort but also wonderful contentment at the chance to be a virgin for Christ.[52]

Again, it could be argued that declaring, as many medieval women did, that they were holy brides dedicated in body, mind, and soul to their divine bridegroom was, in fact, the height of medieval women's folly. Weren't they, after all, merely replacing finite male authorities with an infinite one—the one widely believed to have ordained the patriarchal order itself? That is a legitimate concern, to be sure, and yet the bridegroom to whom these women betrothed themselves was no tyrant but a caring and reciprocating lover who desired their fulfillment. Nothing could be further from coercion or domination than Hadewijch's description of her bridegroom: "Then he gave Himself to me in the shape of the Sacrament, in its outward form, as the custom is; and then he gave me to drink from the chalice, in form and taste, as the custom is. After that he came himself to me, took me entirely in his arms, and pressed me to him; and all my members felt his in full felicity, in accordance with the desire of my heart and my humanity. So I was outwardly satisfied and fully transported. . . . Then it was to me as if we were one without difference."[53]

In her study of Hadewijch and two other thirteenth-century bridal mystics, Ulrike Wiethaus grapples with the fact that some medieval holy women expressed explicitly negative appraisals of the body.[54] While the visionary language of Hadewijch, Mechthild of Magdeburg, and Beatrice of Nazareth is highly sensual and even erotic, Wiethaus points out that it nevertheless articulates a clear desire to leave the body behind. In her description of the highest stage of mystical experience, for example, Beatrice offers this thoroughly dualistic declaration: "And now this earth is for the soul a cruel exile and a dire prison and a heavy torment . . . and it is for the soul a great punishment that it must live in this estrangement and appear so alien. It cannot forget that it is in exile."[55]

Interestingly, rather than interpret this body-soul antithesis as a case of internalized misogyny or reinscribed Neoplatonic dualism, Wiethaus suggests that it was employed by Beatrice and others as a rhetorical strategy for criticizing the patriarchal domination to which as women they were continually subjected. Like the soul, women were exiles in a strange land. Through their hopeful words of release from the bodily sphere, they expressed their fervent desire for "emancipation from limiting feminine role expectations." Thanks to their experiences of bridal mysticism in which Jesus came to them in distinctly non-patriarchal modes and empowered their own pleasure and even divinization, these women discovered "that limits as limits can be destroyed, that femininity can be constructed as a symbol of power, authority, boldness, mental and spiritual well-being and freedom."[56] I imagine that Beatrice, Mechthild, Hadewijch, and others took what was at hand—the powerful body-spirit dichotomy that pervaded medieval culture—and used it against its own intentions to decry the alienating effects of patriarchal gender roles and to cultivate hope for a different reality. Their bold and inventive christic imagination would have been enabled and energized by experiences of divinity-as-mutuality instead of domination, of God as Lover of the unlovable.

While the practice of virginity-chastity freed some women *from* the gendered strictures of their world and *for* heightened devotion to God and betrothal to Christ, it awakened others to the reality and extent of their own exile from full personhood and energized them for the crucial task of critique. For many women, the practice of virginity-chastity also offered access to people and opportunities they would not otherwise have had. For St. Leoba in the eighth century, it was her decision to live a virginal life that allowed her to study under the tutelage of Mother Tetta and eventually be chosen to join St. Boniface on his mission to Germany. Hildegard of Bingen's commitment to virginity was thought to be a key to her own learning as well and allowed her to enter into dialogue with God without the usual assumptions of female inferiority.[57]

While it may be that the choice for virginity-chastity constituted for some women a rejection of their femaleness, it seems likely that for most women, what was sought was freedom from gender—the cultural interpretation of maleness and femaleness that was to medieval women's distinct disadvantage. Hildegard, for instance, is clear in her conviction that women cannot be ordained into the priesthood because their bodies are "defective," by which she means not self-sufficient because they need men's help in order to reproduce.[58] Because a woman cannot inseminate herself, "just as the earth cannot plow itself," Hildegard concludes that she cannot by herself "do the work of consecrating the body and blood" of Christ in the Eucharist.[59] Of course, had women not been culturally identified with the task of biological reproduction, this analogy would have broken down or else applied just as easily to men, who are even further than women from self-sufficiency in reproduction. Still, even from within her sexist context, Hildegard continually names Mary as the model for priestly activity: just as Mary creates the body of Christ in her virgin womb thanks to her faithful response to God, so the priest, if he has a similar faith, can confect the body of Christ in the Eucharist. Ultimately, Hildegard proposes that women's faithful embrace of virginity gives them access to the priesthood: "A virgin betrothed to my Son will receive Him as Bridegroom, for she has shut her body away from a physical husband; and in her Bridegroom she has the priesthood and all the ministry of My altar, and with Him possesses all its riches."[60] Hildegard thus begins with a reiteration of the culturally assumed inferiority of women based on their physicality but then moves, ingeniously, to a bold affirmation of their spiritual capacity.

Given the above, it would be difficult to conclude that medieval women's embrace of the practice of sexual purity was solely or even primarily an instance of self-negation or hatred of the fleshly or earthly. There is simply too much compelling evidence to the contrary. While it is highly likely that some women chose virginity in order to submit to parental or ecclesial expectation, flee the impurities and sinfulness of female sexuality, or reject their femininity altogether, we cannot ignore the myriad ways in which the practice of sexual purity was a relatively liberative one. In their paradoxical embrace of sexual purity, a practice intended to respond to and reinforce cultural assumptions of their heightened physicality and concomitant spiritual inferiority, medieval women appear to have enacted a disloyal repetition of misogynist norms. Thanks to their strategic ingenuity, the practice of virginity-chastity sometimes became an avenue toward self-understanding and -expression, autonomy and freedom, social critique, religious and secular authority, and profound spiritual transformation.

IV. Somatomorphic Visions

We turn now to a fourth and final body-focused characteristic of medieval women's religious practice—their somatomorphic visions. During the Middle Ages, direct experience of God via mystical vision was considered to be a vital part of religious life for the religiously serious man or woman. The most popular genre of vision was the tour of heaven and hell, eventually perfected in Dante's *Divine Comedy*. This genre began to be eclipsed in the twelfth century, says historian of religion Bernard McGinn, as a new form of vision became increasingly popular. This new genre, rather than featuring "once-in-a-lifetime extended trips to heaven and hell," involved "repeatable encounters with a wide range of heavenly figures." It also often involved "a personal, deeply emotional, and even erotic encounter with Jesus, the Divine Lover."[61] This new kind of vision, which bore witness to "manifestations of the supernatural realm within the world of common experience," was part of a larger cultural shift toward what McGinn calls increased democratization and secularization.[62] Where the earlier religious ideal was largely elitist, involving a select few who withdrew from the world in order to contemplate heavenly matters undisturbed, the early thirteenth century saw an emphasis on God's availability not merely in the cloister or to the cleric but everywhere and to everyone.[63] Traditionally rigid boundaries between sacred and secular, spiritual and material, scripture and experience began to soften.

This shift or softening was motivated, says McGinn, by the emergence of the mendicant orders of Franciscans and Dominicans, as well as the Beguine movement for women, all of which moved theology out into the world in unprecedented ways. Bernard of Clairvaux's influential recognition that in addition to scripture, personal experience was a legitimate source of spiritual authority contributed to the shift as well by lending credibility to everyday insights and experiences and implying that revelation was not purely a heavenly, esoteric matter. Taken together, these developments constituted a general democratizing and secularizing trend that allowed for a new genre of mystical vision that was itself more affective, earthy, and inclusive. This genre was one aspect of a new "vernacular theology" that articulated "an understanding of faith that was not bound to the professional school or the cloister" but was more expansive, diffuse, and accessible to society's non-elites.[64]

In contrast to the mainly cerebral, non-sensual, Latin-focused theology of the universities, this vernacular theology supported an affective piety in which believers were encouraged to meditate on biblical stories such as the nativity and passion of Christ and to imagine themselves present at these events, identifying with Jesus in his joys and struggles and determining to exemplify him in their own everyday life.[65] As McGinn is quick to note, this shift took place over the course of several centuries and was often highly contested, so we are wise not to oversimplify or romanticize it. Still, it helps explain the marked profusion during the later Middle Ages of visionary texts and experiences, and the notable increase in women's visibility and influence as visionaries.

Disputed Visions

For medieval women during the later Middle Ages, visions became a key feature of spiritual experience. By the later Middle Ages, they were a commonplace of devout women's religious practice. Indeed, as Nicholas Watson notes, "in the beguinages and convents of northern Europe, visionary experience seems to have been not only common but expected."[66] Despite this fact, women's visions were often treated with suspicion and even outright condemnation by religious authorities and scholars of the day. In influential medieval texts such as the *Ancrene Wisse*, Richard Rolle's *Form of Living*, and Walter Hilton's *Scale of Perfection*, readers were warned that visions should be treated with skepticism because they may well be demonically generated.[67] Again and again, medieval women were admonished that while their visions may feel authentic, and the rare one may even *be* authentic, they should all nevertheless be presumed deceptive because it is impossible to be certain of their origin and intention.

Suspicion towards women's mystical visions increased as the Middle Ages unfolded, perhaps due to the steady growth in the number of female visionaries and to the potentially subversive content of their visions.[68] Jean Gerson's powerful opposition to women's visionary experience reflects just how deep clerical suspicion of female mystical claims ran. In his fifteenth-century *De probatione spirituum*, a treatise on spiritual discretion, Gerson suggests that women's visions are caused by degenerative brain disease or mental illness: "Since the judgment of the intellect is affected by an injured brain, if anyone who has been thus injured is subject to strange fancies, we do not have to inquire further to discover from what spirit those neurotic and illusory visions come, as is evident in cases of insanity and in various other illnesses."[69]

Suspicion and condemnation notwithstanding, large numbers of medieval women claimed to have experienced powerful and transformative visions of divine realities, and their visions were occasionally acknowledged as genuine by the male elite. A few were published and widely disseminated, embodying the new vernacular theology in important ways.

A Hierarchy of Visions

Physicality was at the heart of most women's visions. In fact, it was the body-saturated or somatomorphic nature of these women's visions that set them apart from their male counterparts. Rosalynn Voaden reminds us that thanks to Augustine's early analysis and categorization of religious visions, it was a medieval commonplace to privilege "intellectual" experiences of incomprehensible and inexpressible union with God (*unio mystica*) over more "sensual" visions of divine realities, no matter how imagistically vivid, personally powerful, or theologically astute these visions may have been.[70] In the fourteenth-century *Scale of Perfection* by Walter Hilton, the secondary status of visions is made abundantly clear:

> By what I have said you will to some extent understand that visions or revelations of any kind of spirit, appearing in the body or in the imagination, asleep or awake, or any other feeling in the bodily senses made in spiritual fashion—either in sound by the ear, or tasting in the mouth, or smelling to the nose, or else any heat that can be felt like fire glowing and warming the breast or any other part of the body, or anything that can be felt by bodily sense, however comforting and pleasing it may be—these are not truly contemplation.[71]

We know that the only transcendental experience medieval women were believed to have access to was the inferior, sensual form of vision. Nevertheless, medieval women's religiosity tended to embrace visions that were highly sensual and materially concrete—visions in which they saw, touched, breathed, and tasted the Divine. Despite the fact that most of these visions were discounted as "a flawed and suspect expression of a flawed and suspect spirituality," devout women insisted on their veracity and transformative effect. Many of them became renowned for their extravagantly sensual visions.[72] Once again, the fact of medieval women's body-centered religious practice begs the question: Why? Why did they choose to deepen their association with the body when it was precisely that association that was a primary source of their devaluation and subjugation? Were they too dumb to understand what they were doing, too weak or unimaginative to resist society's norms, or simply bent on self-destruction?

Visions and Visionaries

Here again, the story is more complicated than one would expect at first glance. It is highly likely that medieval women embraced somatomorphic visions because they were the socially acceptable form of vision for women to have. In this sense, these women would have been complying with patriarchal norms and, inevitably, reinscribing women's presumed inferiority. But to stop there with our analysis is to sell these women terribly short. As with food asceticism, voluntary illness, and sexual purity, their embrace of somatomorphic visions appears to have had liberative intent and effect. As such, it witnesses to the transformative power and ingenuity of the incarnate God, as well as to the moral courage and imagination of the marginalized.

Medieval women's often extravagantly sensual visions allowed them to experience spiritual fulfillment and authority that they could not otherwise have claimed. In the face of the widespread and passionately held belief that they did not have the moral or biological constitution to be spiritual beings or to exercise religious authority, women claimed firsthand experience and knowledge of the Divine. They experienced visions in which God granted them access to profound religious truths and admonished them to share those truths with others. Far more than the other religious practices they embraced, women's visionary experiences were difficult for patriarchy's enforcers to police. As a result, they offered their female practitioners unparalleled opportunities for spiritual exploration, fulfillment, and leadership.

Discretio Spirituum *and Its Circumvention*

Because these women were testifying to direct mystical encounters with God, Jesus, and the saints, and because they were claiming authority on the basis of these encounters, their experiences and claims to authority were practically impossible to discount altogether. Who, after all, could say for certain that God had not revealed divine realities to these female claimants? In response to this reality, the church developed an elaborate system of checks and balances to monitor, interpret, and, when necessary, discredit or disallow women's visions. At the heart of this system was the ecclesiastical doctrine of *discretio spirituum*, the discerning of spirits, that was developed by church authorities as a means for defining visionary experience and evaluating the relative legitimacy of the purported visionary and her vision.[73] The doctrine was basically a "code of conduct" that delineated the acceptable way for the purported visionary to present her or his revelation; the demeanor appropriate to a genuine visionary; the mandate that the visionary have a spiritual director; and the character of the relationship with that spiritual director.[74]

A true visionary, specified the *discretio spirituum*, is meek in temperament, exemplifying a humble and contrite heart. She does not seek attention or notoriety but subordinates her own interests and personality to God's. She is reluctant to share or publicize her experience and must often be motivated by supernatural persuasion or divinely wrought illness to publish her vision. Indeed, she is her own vision's harshest critic, predisposed to denounce it as the work of the devil unless and until it is verified by another. Becoming perfectly transparent to the divine will, she is as an empty vessel waiting patiently to be filled by the wisdom of another. She is, of course, submissive to her spiritual director at all times, trusting his judgment about the relative veracity of her visionary experience and how best, if at all, to share the experience with others.

Interestingly, given the constraining intentions of the doctrine of *discretion spirituum*, those female visionaries who became skilled at complying with the doctrine were able to develop their own religious and secular voices and agendas with relative freedom and even with support from the reigning religious establishment.[75] Bridget of Sweden, for example, complied with enough of the doctrine's conventions to receive the enthusiastic support of her male spiritual director and hence to produce and widely disseminate a textual account of her visionary experience, *Revelaciones*. Recognized as a model visionary according to the strictures of *discretio spirituum*, Bridget was able to achieve exceptional social and political influence, offering counsel to kings, popes, and emperors, establishing her own religious order, and eventually being canonized as a saint. Catherine of Siena, Julian of Norwich, and Hildegard of Bingen, too, enjoyed extraordinary autonomy and influence, thanks in large part to their compliance with the conventions set forth for visionaries. Each of these women had the advantage of being educated and hence well versed in the demands and effects of proper decorum, but each also made a decision to abide by those demands.

In full awareness of cultural assumptions of their intellectual inferiority and the demand of *discretio spirituum* that the visionary's individual will be extinguished, these women peppered their sometimes subversive visionary accounts with humility formulas and portrayed themselves as passive mouthpieces for God. Their accounts often include explicit mandates from God, Jesus, or Mary that the visionary and her vision be recognized as authentic and given a proper hearing. In some cases, these accounts narrate the woman's great reluctance to record her visionary experience and, in response, a divine directive to record and disseminate it on pain of divine disapproval or reprimand. In a context in which visions were easily and frequently denounced as demonically inspired, and women were presumed to be constitutively sinful, the female visionary's very survival might depend on adoption of the *discretio spirituum* norms. Beyond survival, if she wanted to express her religious experience and vision and have any chance of influencing others with them, the appearance of compliance was a must.

Envisioning Critique

It is impossible to know for certain whether these women's adoption of visionary convention was genuine or strategic. Given the fact that the content of their visions was at times highly unconventional, it seems likely that their compliance was largely strategic rather than ideological. Examples of women's visionary non-conformity to patriarchal norms abound. Many visions contained critiques of political corruption and social immorality. A favorite focus of critique was priestly power and pride. Some women's visions went so far as to bypass priestly authority altogether, depicting Mary or even the visionary herself fulfilling priestly duties, including presiding over the holy sacraments. Such narratives of women's blessedness and empowerment functioned also as tools of social commentary and critique.

Another popular visionary trope featured an intensely intimate, sometimes highly erotic relationship between the visionary and Christ. In these visions, the woman's own pleasure and worth are emphasized as important to her divine beloved. When the visionary's individuality is itself eclipsed in these visions, it is in experiences of ecstatic transcendence of all limitations on the way to beatific union with the Lover of the universe. Medieval women's visions often prominently featured food and feeding, the central preoccupation of women's everyday life. In them, Jesus is depicted as feeding a spiritually hungry world with his own flesh and blood. He is a nurturing, healing, self-giving God who shares and hence sacralizes the sensibilities and experiences of women.

Again and again in their visionary experiences, women found their individual worth confirmed and their spiritual potential underscored—in stark contrast to their systematic devaluation in the mundane world. Also, in contrast to the larger culture's strong body-spirit dualism, women's visions tended to be highly sensual and materially concrete, filled with bodies that ate, drank, loved, and suffered as God's body did.

Far from being escapist fantasies that diverted the visionary's attention away from the everyday world, these women's visions appear most often to have inspired deep self-reflection, social critique, and spiritual transformation. In the face of powerful forces of dehumanization and devaluation, medieval women's embrace of sensual, "inferior" visions empowered them for active engagement in the world. Elizabeth Petroff says, "A vision in such circumstances thus becomes a way of strengthening, of firming the self; the vision provides the experience of an inner 'I' against the crippling and maiming that the external world seems bent on inflicting."[76] In addition to enabling a re-centering of the self, the vision also helps the visionary redefine the outside world and her role within it. Inspired by visionary experiences of their own lovableness and moral agency, as well as of God's desire to comfort and heal a suffering world, these women ventured forth into the world to teach, write, found hospitals and schools, build convents, and serve needful others in myriad ways.

As we conclude our discussion of women's visions, it is important to recall that the claim here is not one of women's unbridled liberation or uncensored self-expression. Rather, the claim is that given the limitations of the day, including the confinements of the doctrine of *discretio spirituum*, there were medieval women who were remarkably effective at transgressing the bounds of those limitations. And typically, their transgressions involved an ingenious and disloyal embrace of the very conventions and assumptions designed to subordinate them. Shrewdly, it seems, they used the appearance of submission to male authority and conventional norms as a front for their not-so-submissive experiences and insights. Rooted as their spiritual practice was in an incarnational theology in which God's shocking enfleshment is the means to the salvation of the world, one can detect a compelling resonance between these women's moral courage and liberative imagination and the redemptive ingenuity of the God they adored. It is not a stretch, then, to appreciate their innovative spirit and activity as an instance of a Christian ethic of ingenuity and to aspire in our own lives and for our own unique historical context to emulate their divinely inspired creativity and courage.

CREATIVITY AND COURAGE FOR TODAY'S CONTEXT

In the face of long-standing patterns of inequality and injustice, powerful and pervasive cultural norms and assumptions that feed these patterns, and the realization of one's own entrenchment and inevitable complicity in such patterns, it is easy to become disillusioned or paralyzed. Nothing I do or say could make any real difference anyway, so why bother? Even if I determine to take action, to try to be part of a solution, I have no idea where to begin. The problems are so complex and widespread, and the other side is so well organized and funded. Besides, how can I be critical of a system that benefits me in so many ways? Maybe the world we have is the best we can expect. . . .

Who among us has not been through a similar train of thought? Being a human being, a moral agent or actor, in today's world means living constantly in the tension between responsibility and despair. On the one hand, we know in our bones that we are meant to shape our own lives and the world around us— that we are response-able beings rather than mere automatons. Those of us who are Christian understand ourselves to be responsible for loving God and loving our neighbor. On the other hand, it seems that more and more, we don't know *how* to respond. What does loving our neighbor mean when increasing numbers of us live in or aspire to live in gated communities or homogeneous suburbs where we intentionally close ourselves off from all but our look-alike neighbors? Sometimes it seems that in our global village we are more "connected" yet more isolated than ever before: We are increasingly alienated from the most basic processes of life—birth and death (hardly anyone with a choice opts anymore for real connection with the physical realities of life's beginning and ending, preferring anesthetized unknowing instead); the production of food (Who knows where it was grown or with what chemicals and labor practices?); sustained relationship to people and land (only the helpless, hopeless, or unmotivated stay in one place long enough to put down real roots).

What does it mean, in our time, to love God and to love our neighbor? Despite the predictions of the pundits, religion is still alive and well, and many of us appear to be at least working on the loving God piece of the Christian mandate. But what of our responsibility to love the neighbor? Who *is* my neighbor, anyway? Is she still, after all this time, the one robbed, beaten, and left for dead? The one on the side of the road whom no one wants to acknowledge or assist? The ones left behind when the hurricane hits and the storm surge devastates? If so, what would it mean in our contemporary context of global trade and communication networks to see and attend to the legion ones on the sides of today's superhighways, byways, and floodways? How might we, as individuals and communities of faith, begin *to see* those robbed, beaten, and left for dead by international trade agreements, corporate mergers, and big box economics? How could we become response-able for nursing them back to life? How might we, moreover, change the conditions that caused their suffering in the first place? Rather than conceive of Christian responsibility primarily in terms of crisis response—rallying our hearts and troops only when a dire need is on our doorstep—what if we were to think and organize for the long term, aiming to prevent the crises too often caused by individual malaise, institutional greed, and national hubris?

If there is one thing we cannot do without on this journey into Christian responsibility, it is imagination, robust and patient. The situation is too complex, the problems too entrenched, the suffering too acute to rely on convention. Creativity and the courage to employ it are essential. However, the truth is that as Christians, most of us have heard far too little about imagination and far too much about doctrine, commandment, and authority. Theological ethics has too often been the terrain and tool of the dominant classes, the espousing of universal norms and categorical imperatives, and the privileging of cool rationality and impartial reasoning. In the face of all this, the ones on the side of the road cry out, and their suffering demands new ideas and fresh energy.

It is time for the imagination to come front and center in Christian ethics. It is time to reclaim the theological tradition of a God who confronts evil not with mastery or violence but with an ethic of incarnation and ingenuity, a God who deftly turns convention against itself, sinking deep into the paradoxical and, in so doing, surprising the reigning powers with a non-normative morality that confounds and discredits their own power politics. We find witnesses to this ingeniously Divine One at the margins of Christian history—in the christic imagination of medieval women who performed an illogical but transformative body-centered religiosity and, as we will see in the next chapter, in the hidden transcripts and everyday insurrections of African-American men and women.

3. MAKING A WAY OUT OF NO WAY

Christic Imagination
in African-American Tradition

Under the appropriate conditions, the accumulation of petty acts can,

rather like snowflakes on a steep mountainside, set off an avalanche.

—James C. Scott[1]

Got one mind for white folks to see,

'Nother for what I know is me;

He don't know, he don't know my mind.

—African-American folk song[2]

F rom slavery's "invisible institution" to the lunch-counter protests of the Civil Rights movement and the sophisticated innovations of jazz, African-American cultural, religious, and political life has been profoundly shaped by imagination. No matter how brutal the oppression or thoroughgoing the discrimination, how far from loved ones, or how close to tragedy, a life-affirming, freedom-loving spirit of gritty resourcefulness and subversive creativity has characterized the moral reasoning and lives of African-American men and women. In this chapter, I consider four moments in African-American history when this ethic of ingenuity was manifest in remarkable fashion: slavery's "invisible institution" and related cultural practices, the development of the independent black church movement in the nineteenth century, the strategy of nonviolent direct action as embraced by Dr. Martin

Luther King Jr. and the Civil Rights movement of the twentieth century, and twenty-first-century womanist theology and practice. In each instance, religious experience of a God who above all else loves and liberates, often in inventive and surprisingly subversive ways, is at the heart of the human exercise of imagination. Each case, I propose, constitutes a clear and compelling incarnation of the gestalt of religiously-inspired ethical ingenuity and, hence, is evidence of the centrality of this gestalt in African-American history, culture, and daily life.[3]

SLAVERY: DEEP POOLS OF RESILIENCE AND RESISTANCE

To foreground in a discussion of American slavery the moral agency of slaves was for a long time unheard of. It was simply taken for granted by many early historians and interpreters of slavery that slaves lacked the personal and communal power to critically assess and meaningfully influence their situation.[4] Thanks to several decades of careful historical work largely conducted by African-American scholars, the theory that black people were impotent in the face of the horrors of slavery has been decisively debunked.[5] The evidence is clear: Slaves resisted their own dehumanization consistently, courageously, and creatively. Far from being completely stripped of all cultural and moral resources for preserving their identity and dignity, slaves brought the traditions and wisdom of their African heritage to bear on the challenges of "the peculiar institution" of slavery. They worked the old into the new by weaving African strands together with American strands to create a distinctive fabric, a novel worldview and culture. This truth was historically overlooked, suggests Dwight Hopkins, because scholars focused attention almost exclusively on the period from "sunup to sundown"—that is, on the times and spaces most dominated by the master class. In doing so, they failed to appreciate "sundown to sunup" time, or the alternative mindset, spaces, and activities that were generally "hidden from the plantation owners," even though they were often "displayed before their unseeing eyes."[6] It was in this interstitial space, says Hopkins, that slaves were able to "operate on their own turf and rhythm," developing a wide range of survival, resistance, and transformation tactics in order to "engineer a new self" in the face of all those who sought to diminish, enslave, and destroy that very self.[7]

Attention to this alternative "sundown to sunup" sphere reveals that slaves constructed their own "hybrid" cosmos or world of meaning, thus demonstrating that they were far from helpless or destroyed. The world the slaves made placed a premium on imagination and shrewd inventiveness. In truth, the extreme brutality and systematically dehumanizing effects of slavery meant that survival itself was a notable achievement requiring great inner and communal resources and ingenuity. Beyond that, the fact that large numbers of slaves devised strategies for actively resisting their own victimization, usually in the face of dire consequences such as separation from family, physical beatings, or even death, implies a strong moral foundation, vision, and community. In numerous ways, including the trickster traditions of oral culture, the innovative revising of the slaveholder's religion, and a wide range of everyday practices, African-American slaves employed a spiritually inspired imagination to make a way out of no way. Without a doubt, a dominant trope of their religiously funded moral agency was ingenuity.

I. Trickster Traditions and the Cultural Valuation of Inventiveness

The Africa-informed oral tradition developed by slaves reveals a fondness for trickster tales. Whether in human or animal form, the trickster functioned in slave culture both to reflect and reiterate the importance of ingenuity, even as it also invited critical reflection upon the ethical limits of trickery and deception.[8] The best-known trickster figure is surely Brer Rabbit, who playfully outwits his adversaries by exploiting their pretensions to power.[9] The scrawny hare does not have the physical prowess of Brer Bear, the social status of Brer Lion, nor the presumed intelligence of Brer Fox. Indeed, the rabbit is the natural prey of these bigger, stronger predators. Without the trappings of power, Brer Rabbit must rely on his wit, imagination, and scrappy resourcefulness if he is to survive in the jungle. And in tale after tale, he does just that—cunningly upending the expectations and ego of the powerful with feisty creativity and surprising shrewdness. When caught by the mighty and voracious Wolf, for example, Brer Rabbit escapes sure destruction by exploiting Wolf's desire for mastery. Knowing that Wolf will do precisely what will most terrify his victim, Brer Rabbit desperately entreats him to do anything except throw Rabbit into the briar patch. Wolf obliges, of course, attempting to terrorize his pleading victim by plunging him into his most feared scenario, only to find, to his utter dismay and fury, that this is precisely what Rabbit had planned. Scampering toward freedom, Brer Rabbit triumphantly reminds Wolf that the briar patch is "de place me mammy fetch me up."[10]

A Complex Moral Sensibility

Given the clear parallels between the relative powerlessness and limited resources of Brer Rabbit and the slaves who fashioned myriad tales about him, it is interesting to note that even while Rabbit's inventiveness and *joie de vivre* are positively valued in the trickster narratives and do indicate a kind of endorsement of such dispositions in slave culture, he is nevertheless not depicted as enjoying moral purity. That is, although rabbit usually wins out over his adversary, thanks to his inventiveness and quick wit, he is also periodically lampooned in these tales as arrogant and overly aggressive. He is certainly never portrayed as an entirely innocent victim of the jungle hierarchy.

Such a full-bodied characterization of the trickster implies a recognition on the part of slaves of the complex and often messy character of moral existence. When one lives at the margins of social, economic, and political power, one must of necessity see and experience the carnage created by life's "winners." In the process, one becomes acutely aware of the universality of human weakness and the illusion of moral purity. For their part, slaves did not hesitate to denounce the immorality of slavery and its supporting assumptions, institutions, and cast of characters. There was certainly no ambiguity in their minds about the evil of chattel slavery. At the same time, however, they exhibited a certain humility about their own moral system—a recognition of its limitations and weaknesses.[11] Perhaps they saw Rabbit's (and their own) embrace of cunning and guile as a provisional moral strategy. It was necessary and even morally legitimate, given the context of inequality and injustice within which slaves were forced to carve out their moral agency, and yet its legitimacy was always in question and constantly in danger of being undermined when aimed toward self-aggrandizement or violence.[12]

Trickster tales invited African-American hearers to consider not only the positive valences of ingenuity—the possibilities for deploying limited resources to confront and sometimes even undermine the unjust status quo—but also the (im)moral framework of the slaveholding culture that created the need for an ethic of ingenuity in the first place. As Lawrence Levine suggests, when slaves told stories of a morally compromised trickster, they may have been commenting on the "irrational and immoral side of [their own] universe":

> The life of every slave could be altered by the most arbitrary and amoral acts. They could be whipped, sexually assaulted, ripped out of societies in which they had deep roots, and bartered away for pecuniary profit by men and women who were also capable of treating them with kindness and consideration and who professed belief in a moral code which they held up for emulation not only by their children but often by their slaves as well. It would not be surprising if these dualities which marked the

slaves' world were not reflected in both the forms and the content of their folk culture.[13]

While the trickster's inventiveness usually aimed toward the positive good of cultivating among the oppressed a genuine moral agency, a taste for freedom from oppression, and a critical awareness of the morally bankrupt ways of the mighty, it also sometimes tended toward the glorification of power, the desire to avenge and destroy the oppressor, or a survival-at-any-cost mentality:

> Trapped by Mr. Man and hung from a sweet gum tree until he can be cooked, Rabbit is buffeted to and fro by the wind and left to contemplate his bleak future until Brer Squirrel happens along. "This yer my cool swing," Rabbit informs him. "I take a fine swing this morning." Squirrel begs a turn and finds his friend surprisingly gracious: "Certainly, Brer Squirrel, you do me proud. Come up here, Brer Squirrel, and give me a hand with this knot." Tying the grateful squirrel securely in the tree, Rabbit leaves him to his pleasure—and his fate. When Mr. Man returns, "he take Brer Squirrel home and cook him for dinner."[14]

Thus, trickster tales sometimes functioned to reiterate the very brutalities that created and sustained the system of slavery itself. Even in stories of the trickster's violence, however, the initial aggressor is usually not the trickster but a member of the powerful elite, and the spirit of the tale is "one not of moral judgment but of vicarious triumph."[15]

Sacred Texts

If understood as at least partly autobiographical or self-referential, the massively popular trickster tales give witness to the vital importance and positive social function of an ethic of ingenuity in slave culture. By presenting positive portrayals of the underdog's agency, along with pointed critiques of the oppressor's abuse of power in narratives that could at least claim ideological neutrality (They were only stories, right?), trickster tales were important sites of moral education for slaves. They entertained and encouraged the downtrodden, gave them confidence in their own ability to resist dehumanization with creativity and humor, and schooled them in the dangers and excesses of worldly power and the unharnessed ego. It seems clear that stories of Brer Rabbit, High John the Conqueror, and other tricksters were, for many slaves, sacred texts. They were enduring communal narratives of identity formation, struggle, and transformation that helped men, women, and children orient themselves in relation to the forces and choices around them. They were complex and multivalent texts, rich with interpretive possibilities and welcoming of new and returning interlocutors. As Riggins Earl Jr. notes, the telling of trickster tales was a central ritual of slave existence, a key means for educating the younger generations and preparing them for the complexities of adulthood in a morally tainted universe. It was especially the older slave men, so often assumed by the master class to have reached a point of docility and harmlessness, who told and retold trickster tales in order to keep the fires of ingenuity and resistance stoked.[16]

These sacred tales signaled a mature awareness of the complex nature of human morality and, in particular, of the ways in which ethical principles and strategies are often dependent upon both context and intention. Employing guile or deception as a strategy of resistance to exploitation and dehumanization, as well as with an aim toward freedom and mutual flourishing, is something altogether different than deceiving in order to humiliate, punish, or dominate another, even one's oppressor. The trickster traditions of slave times highlight both the freedom-loving inventiveness and the complex moral sensitivities of African-American women and men. They also lead naturally into a discussion of slave religion, where both emphases find crucial articulation.

II. Slave Religion

The moral system that helped rationalize and support slavery was funded by what many now recognize as "slaveholding Christianity." This was the dominant version of Christianity in the United States from the time the Pilgrims arrived until the slaves themselves created a rival version of the religion. It featured a provident and all-powerful God who was believed to sanction the system of chattel slavery and to punish those who opposed it.[17] Ex-slave Peter Randolph offers insight into the content and methods of slaveholding Christianity:

> The prominent preaching to the slaves was, "Servants, obey your masters. Do not steal or lie, for this is very wrong. Such conduct is sinning against the Holy Ghost, and is base ingratitude to your kind masters, who feed, clothe and protect you." Furthermore, the preacher often continued, "It is the devil . . . who tells you to try and be free." And again he bid them be patient at work, warning them that it would be his duty to whip them, if they appeared dissatisfied—all which would be pleasing to God![18]

Notice here that proper moral behavior is defined as obedience to the slavemaster and his property.

Deceiving the master by taking from him, lying to him, or escaping his authority was in the view of slaveholding religion a chief sin. In addition to being an affront to God, such behavior demonstrated contempt for the "benevolent" institution of slavery and was viewed as a threat to the entire social fabric.[19] As defined by slaveholding Christianity, then, moral agency for slaves involved obedience to and gratitude toward both God and master, whose intention and authority were practically identical. Such views were incorporated into the official teachings of the church, as is evidenced by this catechism used with slaves in South Carolina:

> Who gave you a master and a mistress? —*God gave them to me.*
> Who says that you must obey them? —*God says that I must.*
> What book tells you these things? —*The Bible.*
> . . . What makes you so lazy? —*My own wicked heart.*
> How do you know your heart is wicked? —*I feel it every day.*
> What teaches you so many wicked things? —*The Devil.*
> Must you let the Devil teach you? —*No, I must not.*[20]

A different catechism communicated a similar message:

> Q. What did God make you for?
> A. To make a crop.
> Q. What is the meaning of "Thou shalt not commit adultery"?
> A. To serve our heavenly Father, and our earthly master, obey our overseer, and not steal anything.[21]

Despite the best efforts of the proponents of slaveholding Christianity, as well as threats of divine wrath and eternal punishment, slaves were by and large not persuaded to embrace the religious worldview espoused by the master class. In most cases, it appears, slaves' own religious experiences and convictions led them to denounce this view as an atrocious perversion.[22]

The Invisible Institution

Slaves developed their own form of church or religion, dubbed the "invisible institution" by scholars.[23] It was, says Albert Raboteau, "an extensive hidden religious life."[24] The slave church might be located anywhere, from a cabin to a cotton field to a clearing in a swamp. Because independent slave gatherings were against the law and could incur stiff penalties, they were necessarily "invisible" to the master class and its surveillance teams, often shifting from one location to another to avoid detection.[25] Various strategies were used to conceal religious gatherings, some of them quite ingenious. The most frequently mentioned one is the "turned over pot," a strategy explained by ex-slave Minnie Folkes: "So to keep de soun' from goin' out, slaves would put a gra' big iron pot at de do'." Ex-slave Katie Blackwess Johnson concurs: "I would see them turn down the pots to keep the folks at the big-house from hearin' them singin' and prayin'."[26] Another technique, described by ex-slave Arthur Greene, was the creation of a temporary bush arbor, or "hush harbor," in which slaves would gather to worship and enjoy momentary respite from the slaveholder's world: "Well-er talkin' 'bout de church in dem days, we po' colored people ain' had none lak you have now. We jes made er bush arbor by cuttin' bushes dat was full of green leaves an' puttin' em on top of four poles reachin' pole to pole. Den sometimes we'd have dem bushes put roun' to kiver de sides an' back from der bottom to der top. All us get together in dis arbor fer de meetin'."[27] Another strategy of concealment was to hang wet quilts on trees or shrubs to dampen the sounds of the meeting.[28] As Raboteau notes, "The external hush harbor symbolized an internal resistance, a private place at the core of the slaves' religious life" that was ingeniously shielded from the destructive intrusions of white power.[29]

In order to undermine the efforts of the white patrollers who scoured the plantations and countryside for illegal gatherings of blacks, slaves created their own scouting operations, decoys, and even booby traps, as ex-slave West Turner recounts: "Well, dey made me de lookout boy, an' when de paddyrollers (the patrollers) come down de lane past de church . . . well, sir, dey tell me to step out f'm de woods an' let 'em see me." Heading into the woods after the fleeing Turner, "Dem ole paddyrollers done rid plumb into a great line of grape vines dat de slaves had stretched 'cross de path. An' dese vines tripped up de horses an' throwed de ole paddyrollers off in de bushes."[30] Whether through active "guerilla warfare" tactics or more subtle evasions, many slaves were motivated by an exploitative, dehumanizing system to embrace deception as a positive moral good.

Where slaveholding Christianity focused intently on the biblical passages and past precedents that appeared to support power inequities and slavery, the slaves fashioned quite a different Christianity. They based their alternative on the Exodus tradition of God liberating the Israelite slaves from bondage in

Egypt; the Hebrew prophets' denunciations of the greed and cruel indifference of the ruling classes; and the words and actions of Jesus, which expressed care especially for the widows, orphans, strangers, and the poor—in other words, for those without status, connections, or socioeconomic power. Jesus was also often viewed as a second Moses who would lead his people to freedom.

Imaginative Alternatives

While slaveholding Christianity functioned in both form and content to support and strengthen the authority of the master class and its undergirding assumptions of race-based superiority and entitlement, the religion of the slaves focused in both form and content on resisting those very assumptions and that very authority. Slave religion was itself a work of the imagination. It took what was at hand—the religion of the master class—and turned it into a new hybrid reality that actively opposed that class's intentions.[31] Traditional African beliefs in one supreme creator God, the sacredness and interconnection of all things, and the individual's embeddedness within and responsibility toward the community were creatively woven together with biblically based commitments to a creator-liberator God, the dignity and worth of all creatures, and a savior who both suffers with the despised and redeems them from that suffering. The end product was an Africa-informed, freedom-centered version of Christianity that was a key source of comfort, guidance, and courage for slaves and their descendants.[32] Born as it was in the womb of the imagination and in response to experiences of a liberating God who became incarnate in the savior Jesus, it is no wonder slave Christianity embodied a robust ethic of incarnation and ingenuity.

At the very heart of this ethic were profound encounters with divine creativity. According to Dwight Hopkins, slaves and their descendants understood and experienced God as the Way Maker, "a being so infinite in abilities that anything is possible."[33] From the shards of human tragedy and suffering, the twisted remains of shattered dreams and forcibly broken relationships, the scraps of resistance and rebellion, God makes a way for God's people. God restores dignity, renews relationships, and announces a new day for those who suffer. God is understood not so much as the one who creates out of nothing— the triumphant master who tames the dark chaos—as the one who can make do with what is on hand. As Hopkins suggests, "The Way Maker can take a crooked stick—the problems of life, the oppressed conditions of the poor, the humanly impossible—and hit a straight lick, a correction of all the ailments and infirmities suffered by society's victims. The Way Maker takes the frailties of the human condition and out of that which is ill-formed changes human relations into a dreamed-of newness."[34] As the Way Maker become fully human, Jesus is the trailblazer, the one who clears the path. Like a second Moses, Jesus leads the way. Jesus is also a compassionate co-traveler whose own experience facing suffering and humiliation with courage and creativity offers comfort and inspiration to others on the journey.[35] Created in God's image and befriended by Jesus, slaves and their descendants embraced a life-affirming ethic of ingenuity as they sought to en-flesh and incarnate divine creativity and christic imagination.

Sacred Song and Sweat

The confluence of religious experience and everyday imagination is especially noticeable in the slave songs or spirituals, which were sung not only in religious meetings but throughout the day. These songs seem to have been constantly in the air, providing a kind of background music of consolation and courage to slaves as they endured the hardships and humiliations of enforced, unpaid labor as well as a personal and communal universe that was over-defined by the authority and assumptions of the master class. According to Lawrence Levine, the spirituals functioned alongside other spoken arts such as folktales, jokes, proverbs, and secular music to allow slaves "to voice criticism as well as to uphold traditional values and group cohesion."[36] In the spirituals, slaves articulated a worldview or cosmology that could oppose the chaos and cruelty of everyday reality. They were, according to John Lovell, "a positive thing, a folk group's answer to life."[37] Says Levine, "The spirituals are the record of a people who found the status, the harmony, the values, the order they needed to survive by internally creating an expanded universe, by literally willing themselves reborn."[38] In these songs, they narrated, celebrated, and reiterated their connection to the sacred, the One who created, sustains, loves, and dignifies them, the God who "makes a way out of no way."

Slaves also used those very songs to make their *own* way out of no way. The call and response pattern used in singing the songs forged bonds of connection among slaves by placing the individual singer "in continual dialogue with his community."[39] Thus, while the chattel system seemed intent on destroying the bonds of family and affection, slaves used their music to establish and reinforce humanizing connections with each other. As for the content of the songs, Levine tells us that "the most persistent single image . . . is that of the chosen people. The vast majority of the spirituals identify the singers as 'de people dat is born of God.'"[40] In their sacred music, at the site where the master class intended

"Slaves, obey your master" to be the sole refrain, came instead mischievous melodies and strains of subversion. Deftly employing the double entendre, slaves
communicated not only genuine religious experiences and keen theological
insights but practical information about upcoming slave gatherings, friends in
need, and planned escapes or revolts.[41] Using a language of "stealth and ambiguity" in both song and everyday spoken communications, slaves created what
Dwight Hopkins calls "a deceptive linguistic culture of survival" whose aim was
"to subvert white theological discovery of genuine slave thought."[42]

A key liturgical feature of slave religion was the "shout," and here again
we see clear evidence of slaves' religion-centered ingenuity. Anthony Pinn
describes the shout as a ritual in which black bodies whose very blackness
inspired a racist aesthetic and an extensive "economy of discipline" nevertheless
became sites of sacred connection between slaves and the divine. In defiance of
a social and economic order rooted in assumptions of black bodies as inherently
unruly, grotesque, and impure—the literal embodiment of sin—slaves enacted
a religiosity in which black bodies were bodies of worth, beauty, and complex
subjectivity. The rhythm and sweat of the shout effected a transvaluation in
which "the Black body as ugly and impoverished . . . was transformed into a ritual device through which the glory of God and the beauty of human movement
were celebrated. Through ecstatic modes of Black worship," says Pinn, "the
body was rescued because it became a vessel holding cosmic energy."[43] More
often than not, slaves' sweat was a marker of their enforced subordination,
their coerced labor used to enrich their oppressors; but in stolen moments of
sacred time, their sweat became a sacrament, concrete evidence of the vitality
of the Holy Spirit enfleshed in beautiful black bodies.

Through their worship, music, biblical interpretation, and theological
worldview, slaves created a freedom-loving, flesh-affirming version of Christianity that served as an effective antidote to the powerful poison of the white
slaveholders' religion and worldview. As James Cone suggests, "The essence of
ante-bellum black religion was the emphasis on the *somebodiness* of black slaves.
. . . Because religion defined the *somebodiness* of their being, black slaves could
retain a sense of the dignity of their person even though they were treated
as things."[44] At the heart of the slaves' spiritual universe was God the Way
Maker, whose own inventiveness in the face of evil empowered slaves to defy
the morality of obeisance, quietude, and self-loathing encouraged by the white
master class and to forge their own moral system.[45] Within this system ingenuity, parody, irony, shrewdness, humor, and cunning were valued as primary
individual and social goods.

III. Everyday Insurrections

Thanks to a resilient spirit, a cultural heritage that nurtured the imagination, and a religious worldview and set of practices that emphasized divine and human creativity, most African-American slaves managed not only to survive the terrors of the chattel system but intentionally to resist its dehumanizing intentions.[46] Whether in their parenting, communicating, economic transactions, or any number of other everyday practices, ingenuity was a defining trope. In contrast to earlier trends in scholarship that assumed that only outright rebellion or revolt constituted resistance to slavery, it is now widely acknowledged that a far wider range of slave activities and dispositions count as genuine resistance.[47] The fact that these less dramatic forms of protest were ignored or discounted for so long is a testimony both to the subtlety and inventiveness of slaves, whose own survival depended on the avoidance of detection, *and* to the assumption among scholars and interpreters of slavery that slaves were incapable of such subtle ingenuity. In this final section of our discussion of slaves' moral universe, we consider several forms of everyday resistance— the content of what some might call slaves' "secular" existence but which was clearly continuous with and undergirded by their religiously saturated worldview.[48] These forms of protest fell short of armed rebellion, but they nonetheless constituted a significant "atmospheric disturbance" that arguably prepared the way for the future in-breaking of a new day of freedom.[49]

Parenting as Protest

One of the worst terrors of slavery was its destructive effects on slave families. Not only were husbands and wives often forcibly separated through sale, but slave parents' ability to *be* parents to their children was undermined at every turn.[50] This state of affairs threatened both the emotional health of parents and children and the prospects of transmitting the slaves' culture of resistance to future generations. Far too often, mothers and fathers found themselves helpless to protect their own children from the predacious behaviors of slaveholders and overseers. As Caroline Hunter of Virginia relates, "Many a day my ole mama has stood by an' watched massa beat her chillun 'til dey bled an' she couldn' open her mouf'." Hunter lamented that "During slavery it seemed lak yo' chillun b'long to ev'ybody but you."[51] Indeed, slave children did not "belong" to their parents but to their "owners."

Nevertheless, slave parents smartly manipulated plantation realities so they could exert their parental prerogative. Slaveholders needed fathers and mothers to be productive workers, and slaves were quick to use that need to their own advantage. Slave owners knew that a forlorn mother or resentful father was likely to work more slowly, be more distracted or destructive, and rebel more easily than a more parentally contented one. In addition, parents who felt meaningfully connected to and responsible for children were presumably less likely to risk life and limb by attempting escape or plotting insurrection. Furthermore, it was to the slaveowner's economic advantage to increase his holdings by ensuring that slave children survived childhood and were well enough cared for to become productive laborers themselves. Especially after the United States Congress put an end in 1808 to the international slave trade, slaveholders were compelled by economic necessity to "grow" their own slaves. Knowing all of this gave slave parents some leverage against the slaveholder. If he desired productive workers for the plantation as well as a continual replenishing of the labor force, then that very desire could be used against him. And, indeed, it was. Thus, while law determined that slave children did not belong to their parents, many parents nevertheless found ways of wresting parental authority away from the master class.[52]

Not only was the experience of parenting a source of individual and familial esteem, dignity, and agency for slaves; it was also a vital key to the cultivation of a culture of resistance. By actively resisting slaveholders' legal right to parental authority, slaves offered their children vital emotional, cultural, and spiritual resources for maintaining their own dignity and developing a counter-hegemonic worldview that could oppose the dominant ideology and morality. "Through families," says Marie Jenkins Schwartz, "children learned to judge bondage, and the men and women who enslaved them, in terms other than those employed to justify the institution."[53] Parental resistance took several forms, one of which was the attempt to preserve family unity. When family separation could not be avoided, energy was focused on postponing it long enough to allow children to gather the emotional and material resources necessary for survival in a parentless world. Slave fathers, in particular, would use the power of their labor to keep their families intact, running away and then sending word that they would return to work only once their children were removed from the auction list.[54]

Much emphasis was placed on teaching young children how to be self-sufficient and respectful of adults so that, should they be removed from their parents, they could nevertheless survive and, with a little good fortune, be cared for by surrogate slave parents. Through storytelling, songs, and their own example, slave parents and other adults intentionally schooled young children in plantation survival strategies such as how to display signs of proper

deference to whites, how to keep certain matters (for example, the clandestine slave economy or escape plans) "in their sleeves"—that is, within the slave
community—and how to pace their official work in order to save energy for
unofficial work such as gardening, weaving, and hunting.[55] Such work, in addition to supplementing a meager subsistence diet, developed in children a taste
for independence and self-reliance.

A key point of leverage for slaves was the widespread claim made by the
master class that slavery in the United States was uniquely humane compared
to other slave societies. In contrast to slavery in Latin America and the Carib-
bean, where slave deaths outpaced births, slaves in the United States had much
better life expectancies, creating a largely native-born slave population.[56] This
meant slavery could continue to be a vital economic and social reality long
after the international slave trade had waned. Indeed, "by 1860, the United
States had achieved the dubious distinction of becoming the largest slaveholding nation in the world, with more than four million slaves."[57] The naturally re-
populating dynamic of North American slavery meant that before long, most
African-American slaves had never known any reality other than slavery. Black
bondage within a white system was simply the way things had always been.
Given this, the fact that so many slaves actively resisted their enslavement testifies to the robust and compelling nature of the counter-hegemonic religious
and cultural traditions they developed and passed down to future generations
via parenting.

American slaveholders and their allies used the record-setting survival
rates and life expectancies of slavery in the United States to argue that slavery
was actually a benevolent institution. They argued that the opportunities that
slaves in the United States enjoyed for vocational training (read: forced labor),
cultural enlightenment (read: learning white ways of seeing, being, and thinking), religious truth (read: conversion to slaveholding Christianity), and daily
luxuries (read: subsistence-level food, clothing, and shelter) made them positively privileged by the world's standards for black people. It was precisely this
assumption of slavery's benevolence that slaves used to their own advantage
in a variety of arenas.[58] If slaveowners refused to allow slave children to be
parented by their biological parents, then they had to contend with a different
kind of resistance from parents and their slave allies, who used tactics such as
work slow-downs and feigned illness to pressure masters and mistresses into
allowing slave parents to *be* parents.

Slaveholders sought to undermine parental authority not only to gain
short-term benefits from the labor of slave children but also, and more

importantly, in order to ensure the long-term viability of the plantation system and the slaveholding way of life, particularly as abolitionist sentiments
became more widespread. Toward that end, slaveowners tried to cultivate slave
children's loyalty both to individual slaveowners and their families *and* to the
overall social order and worldview of plantation slavery.[59] Slaveowners, says
Schwartz, wanted "to ensure that boys and girls learned how to work as well as
how to play subservient parts in the paternalistic drama that passed for southern race relations."[60]

In the face of these kinds of deep and systemic intentions, and in spite
of their own apparent powerlessness, slave parents made ingenious use of the
meager resources they had. They used their labor power, the master class's
prideful assumption of benevolence, the privacy of the slave quarters, and the
time from sundown to sunup to resist one of the most dehumanizing intentions of the slave system. Schwartz concludes that parental strategies, which
were supported by the larger slave community, created "a buffer between the
slaveholder and the young slave" that helped "assuage the child's physical and
emotional sufferings under the slave system."[61] Thus, parenting functioned as
a key site of protest against slavery and a crucial means for the cultivation of
moral agency among those whom the dominant culture assumed were neither
moral nor agents.

Working the Work

Slaves were, first and foremost, workers. As such, they were the wheels
that turned the Southern economy. They were both completely at the mercy
of the white master class and, ironically, absolutely necessary to that class's
dominance. And they were wonderfully adept at working that tension in an
attempt to protest their own exploitation, undermine the authority and economic well-being of slaveholders, and cultivate their own autonomy, community, and moral agency.

A favorite strategy of resistance was the work slow-down or stoppage.
To protest a particularly egregious misuse of slaveholder power, comment on
a recent decision or event, challenge an overseer's authority, or express any
number of other concerns, slaves would simply slow down the pace of their
work, take unscheduled breaks, or feign illness. Such behavior, which was hard
to detect and hence punish, might seem harmless enough, but it created very
real economic consequences for the plantation owner. Work lost was money
lost. A related form of protest was work performed sloppily, which could
result in damaged machinery, wasted materials, and shoddy outcomes.

Another preferred method of resisting slavery was pilfering or stealing from the master's storeroom, field, chicken coop, or barn. As Gilbert Osofsky explains, "Inventiveness was necessary if one was to avoid detection. Aunt Peggy, for example, was an artist at stealing little pigs. One day, the 'Philistines were upon her' as she was boiling her catch in a large kettle. Peggy put a door on the kettle, seated her daughter on the door, covered the young girl with a heavy quilt, and told the inquisitive overseer the child had a heavy cold and was taking a steam bath."[62] Interestingly, such behavior was not considered unethical by slaves. They reasoned that they were merely helping themselves to wealth that they themselves had produced. They were, in other words, "taking" what was already theirs. Indeed, slaves generally reserved the term "stealing," as well as the moral condemnation it implied, for thefts against other slaves or non-slaveholding whites. Slaves reasoned that since they were considered by the plantation economy to be property, just as the pigs and corn were property, it did not make sense to accuse them of stealing. After all, when the master's horse ate the master's hay, the horse was not stealing from the master; rather, the master's property was simply being moved around.[63] Ingenious thinking, to be sure.

Still another way of rethinking slaves' thievery involved putting such behavior in its proper context, as this runaway slave did in a letter to his mistress: ". . . you say I am a thief, because I took the old mare along with me. Have you got to learn that I had a better right to the old mare, as you call her, than Mannasseth Logue had to me? Is it a greater sin for me to steal his horse, than it was for him to rob my mother's cradle, and steal me?"[64] Here, the slave's "immorality"— the stealing of the master's horse—is dwarfed by the master's immorality. Even so, the reigning moral paradigm of the day indicted the slave and absolved the master. By contrast, from the standpoint of the slaves' moral system, theft was justifiable when undertaken in the service of freedom because it demonstrated obedience to a higher good than mere earthly authority—that is, the God who liberated Israel from bondage in Egypt and who intends freedom for all God's creatures. One slavemistress confided to her son: "The conduct of the negroes in robbing our house, store room, meat house, etc. and refusing to restore anything shows you they think it right to steal from us, to spoil us, as the Israelites did the Egyptians."[65] Furthermore, theft undertaken as a protest against injustice or as a means to survival might also claim moral authority insofar as it aimed toward the full personhood and dignity of "the least of these."[66]

A similar logic was used in relation to another common form of slave resistance: running away, which has been described as "the hardest blow an individual could strike against the regime."[67] While a successful permanent escape to a free state in the North was relatively rare, far more common were permanent and temporary escapes within slaveholding states.[68] The main tool employed by runaways of all types was ingenuity, both as they planned and implemented their escapes and as they learned to survive on the other side of slavery. As Gilbert Osofsky reports, escapees had to be "wise in the ways of nature, [as well as] knowledgeable in animal lore and in techniques for foraging and living off the land." Elaborate ruses were sometimes devised: "Some [escapees] had themselves packed in crates or barrels and shipped north. One man tied himself to the underside of a night passenger train. Those pursued by bloodhounds sometimes put red pepper on their limbs or dug into graves and used the dust on their bodies to throw off their human scent."[69]

Those who escaped usually joined the "clandestine slave economy" that involved a variety of guileful conventions. John Hope Franklin and Loren Schweninger recount that covert contacts with slave friends and families would supply the runaway with food and supplies "taken" from the master's storehouses. Often, such goods were bought, sold, and bartered on the "black" market or in towns and cities where the escapee would pose as legitimately free or as on an errand for a hypothetical master. In addition, runaway slaves would band together with other escapees, free blacks, and even white merchants to create occasionally extensive trade networks. In some instances, note Franklin and Schweninger, "the items pillaged [for escapees] wound up back on the same plantations."[70]

Temporary escapes from plantations were not at all uncommon. Typically, a slave would exit for a day or two to run an important errand, visit a loved one, blow off steam, take a rest, or lodge a protest against his or her master. Occasionally, a runaway slave would negotiate the conditions of his or her return, bargaining with the slaveholder about the punishment to be imposed or the negative conditions that motivated the leave-taking in the first place. Almost always, runaways endured punishment, often quite brutal, upon their return. Yet, the work of historians like Franklin and Schweninger suggests that significant numbers of slaves ran away at least once during their lives.

Running away was a key weapon in the arsenal of resistance, and as with many other dimensions of slave life, it relied on an ethic of ingenuity that was supported by an imagination-focused religion. One window of opportunity exploited by slaves was provided by the death of a master. "Taking advantage of a breakdown in discipline, failure of communication, or conflicts among whites at the time of the owner's death," the crafty slave would slip away and often "be absent for days before it was known."[71] Once again, we have a compelling example of a slave ethic of ingenuity.

The Moral Minority

A telling commentary on the very different moral epistemologies of slaves and masters is the fact that while slaves felt morally compelled to resist the injustices and indignities of slavery by, for instance, running away, pilfering, or working sloppily, slavemasters felt morally wronged by such behaviors. Masters certainly objected on economic grounds, but they also used religious and moral arguments to denounce slave resistance. We have already seen how white sermons and catechisms demonized slave disobedience and deception as sins against God and the divinely sanctioned social order. Another common tactic used by the master class was to insist that slaves had a moral obligation to treat their owners with respect and gratitude. As Franklin and Schweninger note: "Again and again, slave owners used the same word to describe runaways: ungrateful. They had been treated well and humanely; they had been given proper food and clothing; they had been well housed and provided with other necessities . . . .Yet, at the first opportunity they had set out on their own.They had neither honor nor gratitude; as a race, they were deceptive and deceitful."[72]

What it is possible to recognize in hindsight—a recognition that is essential to an adequate understanding of the moral lives of slaves as well as other marginalized groups in Christian history—is that the slaves' deceit was, in fact, a *moral* response to their situation.[73] It may have violated the precepts of the dominant moral system and from that vantage point appeared as an egregious character flaw and indicator of group pathology, but the dominant system's dominance was won precisely through the intentional, systematic, and extreme *domination* of an entire race of human beings. It was, in other words, a profoundly immoral system. Slaves were quick to realize this and to develop a complex set of resistances that, because opposed to that system, were inevitably repudiated as themselves immoral.Yet, as we have seen, slaves could turn to powerful cultural and religious warrants, including their trickster traditions and a Way-Maker God, to support their moral reasoning, non-normative though it was.[74]

THE BLACK CHURCH TRADITION

African-American slaves' responses to the system of terror known as slavery were wide-ranging and complex—far too numerous and diverse to acknowledge, let alone address adequately, in a single chapter.Yet, we have seen that one conclusion to be drawn is that a significant feature of many of these responses was an ethic of ingenuity fueled by a freedom-seeking theological tradition and imagination. Despite its significance, frequency, and range, however, slave resistance seems to have been largely imperceptible to the ruling classes.[75] During slavery, African Americans' ethic of ingenuity was both a constant, vital, and indeed life-saving reality *and*, at the same time, a relatively unremarkable one to observers of the period.

A second major "moment" in the life of this ethic, and one with a much more overt character, is the independent black church movement. This movement was born out of the womb of slavery and matured into what scholars have variously termed "a nation within a nation," "the first black freedom movement" in America, and "the cultural womb of the black community."[76] From its origin to its content and method, the black church tradition has reverberated with christic imagination, moving with the Way-Maker God and the co-suffering Savior into the gaps caused by white racism and incarnating there a non-normative morality of justice, mercy, and shared creaturehood that would eventually transform a nation.

I. A New Creation

During slavery's twilight years and into the period of Reconstruction, what had been for centuries an "invisible" institution came into full view and claimed its own public identity and space. While there had always been black-led churches, formal recognition of and associations among these scattered congregations had been disallowed, if not by law then by extra-legal pressures. Pushed out of mainstream (white) Christianity by the insult and indignity of segregated worship spaces, racist biblical interpretation, and a host of other provocations, pioneers of the late eighteenth and early nineteenth centuries like Richard Allen, Absalom Jones, and Thomas Paul formed their own congregations and, eventually, denominations.[77] Risking failure among the black community and recrimination from whites, these church planters were emboldened not only by the negative energies of white bigotry but also, and more importantly, by a positive, full-bodied vision of human dignity and equal civic, economic, and religious opportunity for all. No longer invisible, black independent churches, nevertheless, had much in common with the slave church, effectively functioning as the moral, social, and political center of African-American life and relying on the Way-Maker God for inspiration and example.

Independent black churches played an especially crucial role during what has been called the "nadir" of race relations—the avalanche of discriminatory laws and practices adopted during the final years of the nineteenth century.[78] The relative freedom of the Reconstruction years, during which African Americans were able to embrace various political and economic rights and privileges, was tragically short-lived. As Jim Crow laws were affirmed by a parade of southern states during the closing decades of the nineteenth century, the nation's highest court betrayed black Americans first by declaring the federal Civil Rights Act of 1875 to be unconstitutional and then by announcing the powerful "separate but equal" doctrine. With racism once again the official law of the land, black Americans found themselves systematically discriminated against in nearly every aspect of life and death: "employment, housing, places of amusement, public transportation, schools, hospitals, and cemeteries."[79]

No longer able to vote or hold office, and unable to protect themselves or their families from humiliating curtailments of basic human rights, black men and women turned to the church for solace, support, and opportunity. The black church, Evelyn Brooks Higginbotham reminds us, was uniquely positioned to respond: "As the 'invisible institution' of the slaves, the church had long promoted a sense of individual and collective worth and perpetuated a belief in human dignity that countered the racist preachings of the master class. In the decades following Reconstruction, the church's autonomy and financial strength made it the most logical institution for the pursuit of racial self-help."[80] As in slave times, so once again after Reconstruction, a distinctively African-American variation of Christianity became the glue that held most black lives together. Despite the fact that religious energies were now able to move less surreptitiously than in slavery, they nevertheless continued to generate and rely upon a robust moral imagination and an ethic of ingenuity.

II. A Way-Making Church

Simply to keep hope alive during the extreme turmoil and disillusionment of the late 1800s required stubborn imagination. The sources of despair were legion. In one seven-year period, for instance, more than 2,500 lynchings of African Americans were recorded.[81] Black people were systematically disenfranchised and depoliticized, stripped of basic civil and human rights, denied economic and educational opportunity, subjected to myriad daily humiliations, and asked in countless ways to accept and internalize their own inferiority. In the midst of this all-out assault on their humanity, African-American men and women found the will, somehow, to keep hope alive, to love each other into survival, and to imagine each other into resistance. The black church tradition was the crucible within which this will, hope, love, and imagination were effectively fired and fueled. As we have seen, the church was itself rooted in the audacious creativity of slaves and ex-slaves whose disloyal repetition of the master's religion yielded a new, freedom-loving Christianity. And it was once again a feat of imagination and courage to extricate that distinctive religiosity from both strategic invisibility and exploitative white-washing by forming churches and denominations devoted to proclaiming God's love for *all*—even, and perhaps especially, those whom "the world" despises. Finally, then, it should come as no surprise to learn that the independent black church movement yielded a novel kind of church that was not only indebted to the christic imagination of its forebears and founders but also wonderfully generative of new creative energies and forms.

In response to white Christianity's tenacious assumptions of black inferiority and spiritual incapacity, black Christians drew on pivotal texts such as the Exodus narrative and the suffering servant tradition of Isaiah to develop in rich and compelling ways the analogy between themselves and the Israelites of old, who so often suffered at the hands of powerful oppressors. In the New Testament, black preachers like Daniel Coker in 1810 found solace and inspiration in texts such as 1 Pet. 2:9: "But ye are a chosen generation, a royal priesthood, and a holy nation, a peculiar people." As one scholar of the nineteenth century notes, texts and traditions such as these "provided a hermeneutic lens" with which black people could "account for their condition," "articulate a faith that God was active in history," and celebrate "the uniqueness of black people and their relation to God."[82] While the dominant culture maligned them as subhuman, the black church tradition offered powerful affirmations of black humanity and blessedness. This happened not only in the church's theological tradition but in its concrete practice as well. Benjamin Mays and Joseph Nicholson offer this now-classic description of the transformative effect of black ecclesial existence:

> A truck driver of average or more than ordinary qualities becomes the chairman of the Deacon Board. A hotel man of some ability is the superintendent of the Sunday church school of a rather important church. A woman who would hardly be noticed, socially or otherwise, becomes a leading woman in the missionary society. A girl of little training and less opportunity for training gets the chance to become the leading soprano in the choir of a great church. These people receive little or no recognition on their daily job. There is nothing to make them feel that they are "somebody." Frequently their souls are crushed and their personalities

disregarded. . . . But in the church on X Street, *she* is Mrs. Johnson, the Church Clerk; and *he* is Mr. Jones, the chairman of the Deacon Board.[83]

In a culture predicated on the deliberate dehumanization of black people, experiences such as these were not merely personally edifying; they were world-preserving. By pulling black men and women out of the fragmentation and nihilism caused by exploitation and contempt and into a reliable, coherent cosmos, these snatches of stability, dignity, and recognition were vital cultivators of the vision, conviction, and imagination necessary for genuine moral agency and personal and communal courage in the face of enormous obstacles.

At the heart of the black church tradition, says Peter Paris, stand two fundamental principles: the parenthood of God and the kinship of all people.[84] These two principles, so robustly evident in scripture and yet so clearly denied by the dominant church, distinguished the black church from the white church. They also, Paris notes, created a certain ambivalence within the black church tradition insofar as they aimed it toward reconciliation with its white oppressor even while serving to differentiate the two traditions. While God as Parent may have been the dominant metaphor of African-American Christianity during the difficult post-Reconstruction period and beyond, the notion of God as Way Maker remained a potent reality as well. The continued vitality of an ethic of way-making or ingenuity was manifest in numerous ways, not least of which was the creative bringing together of religious sensibilities, commitments, and forms with social, political, economic, and cultural needs and realities.

III. Making Connections

Predating the formation of independent black churches in places like Philadelphia, Boston, and New Haven was the establishment of voluntary associations among African Americans—associations aimed at mutual support and assistance. Bearing names such as the Free African Society and the African Union Society, these benevolent associations aimed, in the words of one society's preamble, to include black people "without regard to religious tenets, provided the persons live an orderly and sober life, in order to support one another in sickness, and for the benefit of their widows and fatherless children."[85] In a hostile world, black people created their own social safety nets, vowing to take care of one another in life and in death. Despite the secular ring of these mutual aid societies, they were, in fact, motivated by deep religious convictions, founded by black preachers and laypeople, developed in close partnership with newly forming black churches, and often eventually folded into those churches. So, for instance, the Free African Society of Philadelphia, founded by Richard Allen and Absalom Jones in 1787, gave birth in 1794 to Mother Bethel A. M. E. Church, also founded by Allen and Jones.

Just as in Africa, where sacred and secular realms were closely interconnected, so in America, the religious and socio-political spheres were viewed by black people as properly integral to each other. Where white America saw the two areas as in a continually tensive and sometimes conflictual relationship, black Americans affirmed a creative and fruitful partnership. Not surprising, then, is the fact that the church was the cultural "womb" of black America, giving birth to, housing, and nurturing a wide range of institutions and practices and constituting what E. Franklin Frazier famously described as "a nation within a nation."[86] The very raising of the funds and overseeing of the building of countless black churches was itself a feat of imagination, hard work, and follow-through—one that W. E. B. Du Bois called the "first form of economic cooperation" among black people.[87] Because they were usually the first, and often the only, black-owned and black-controlled institutions in communities both small and large, black churches opened their doors to members and non-members alike and became community centers, theaters, music halls, schools, political training academies, publishing houses, and lending institutions. In 1926, the Mayor's Interracial Committee of Detroit characterized the role of the black church this way:

> The Negro has been humiliated in so many public and privately owned institutions and amusement places that he has resorted to church as a place in which he can be sure of spending his leisure time peacefully. To a large extent it takes the place of the theatre, the dance hall, and similar amusement places, and fills the vacancy created by the failure of public and commercial places of recreation and amusement to give him a cordial welcome. Consequently, the average Negro church in Detroit keeps its doors open constantly for the use of the community. Numerous suppers, lectures, recitals, debates, plays, and the like are given by clubs and individuals from without and within the congregation.[88]

The seamless weaving together of what in the dominant white culture were often disparate and even competing worlds—religion and politics, religion and economics, religion and the arts—into a new public space or commons constituted a bold and imaginative response to widespread attempts by the dominant culture to curtail and contain the energy, hopes, creative spirit, and moral agency of black people.

Ultimately, the independent black church during the nineteenth century constituted a new public space. Its sanctuaries, halls, classrooms, and yards played host to a diversity of community groups and programs, both secular and religious, in a time when "blacks were denied access to public space, such as parks, libraries, restaurants, meeting halls, and other public accommodations."[89] It also, and perhaps more significantly, became what Evelyn Brooks Higginbotham describes as "a discursive, critical arena—a public sphere in which values and issues were aired, debated, and disseminated throughout the larger black community."[90] As such, says Eddie S. Glaude Jr., "black churches . . . were the sites for a public discourse critical of white supremacy and the American nation-state as well as the spaces for identity construction. Here, African Americans engaged in public deliberation free of humiliation (at least by whites). They also spoke in a self-determining voice, defining a cultural identity through a particular idiom and style."[91] On the issue of the black church's expansive identity and function, Peter Paris offers this insight: "The black church independence movement provided for blacks what the Declaration of Independence provided for the nation, namely, the condition for freedom and self-actualization."[92] In sum, the black church functioned in the post-slavery context as a forum, training ground, and medium for moral, civic, political, and economic engagement and leadership. Rejecting majority assumptions of the separation of the sacred and the profane, the black church tradition artfully wove disparate realms together to create a new whole, a novel union.

IV. Heavenly Promise

A variation on this capacity to hold disparate things together in imaginative and effective ways is found in the black church tradition's handling of eschatology, or beliefs about the end times (heaven, hell, last judgment, and so on). Many scholars over the years have noticed the proliferation in African-American religious texts of language about heaven and have concluded that black religion embraces a largely otherworldly mentality. Given the hardships and brutalities of this racist world, it is natural to assume that black people would yearn for escape. Yet, to interpret the fondness for eschatological imagery as an indication of an escapist mindset—one that focuses on a timeless place far removed from the everyday world—is to miss the black church's important interweaving of present and future, the now and the soon to be, the actual and the possible.

Heaven was not so much an unattainable fantasy world as a *promised* land—a reality that was vitally in the making, on the horizon, soon to be embraced. And its very plenitude of justice, dignity, and mutual flourishing functioned for African Americans both as an energizing summons and as grounds for righteous critique of the status quo.[93] Whereas white people's language about heaven might have had little implication for the here and now, essentially underwriting the unjust status quo, black people's eschatology "arose in the sanctuary as the ecstasy of a vision of paradise at one moment, and in the next it drove believers into the streets to give that vision material actuality in the structures of society."[94] As such, black religion's eschatology constituted what Gayraud Wilmore recognizes as a kind of "psychological guerilla warfare"—another tool of "underground resistance," a "kind of attack on the flanks and from the rear of the enemy."[95] Like the formation of the black church itself, as well as that church's distinctive bringing together of religion with politics, economics, and culture, this unique interpretation and use of eschatological realities testifies to the powerful presence in African-American history of a religiously based ethic of ingenuity.

V. Accommodation or Resistance?

The black church tradition's embrace of this ethic has not been seamless or unambiguous. Like all human efforts, the movement has at various times faltered and lost its focus. Even for those whose devotion to the Way-Maker God is sure, the way itself is fraught with complexity. And, of course, ingenuity itself offers no moral guidance.[96] Hence, the Incarnation of God made known in concrete modes of human relationship and daily activity is important. An ethic of ingenuity, it seems, is good news for Christians only when it is guided by the norms and aims of the Incarnation: the principle of mercy, the mandate for social justice, and the aim toward mutual flourishing for all God's creatures.

Scholars have long wrestled with the question of how to evaluate the moral wisdom and practice of the black church tradition in its many-splendored diversity. Some worry that it has been too accommodating of the dominant culture's means and aims, effectively abdicating its distinctive identity and vision in favor of a morally compromised status quo. Others fret that the tradition has pushed too hard in the other direction, making resistance at all costs its mantra and ignoring the call of the Prince of Peace.[97] No doubt, it has erred in both directions. But excesses and blind spots notwithstanding, the fact remains that the independent black church movement of the nineteenth century and beyond stands as a crucial moment in the history of African-American religiosity and ethics, and for the purposes of my discussion in this book, it constitutes an important instantiation of a moral posture long devalued by Christian tradition despite its deep roots in that very tradition.

VI. A Larger Moral Landscape

An ethic of ingenuity guided by incarnational norms and aims was by no means the only moral posture or trajectory that characterized the independent black church movement, but it was a vital and easily overlooked one. Certainly, black preachers, leaders, and parents encouraged the goals of hard work, honesty, thrift, and sobriety, and they did so in good faith. However, even as these norms and goals were embraced and endorsed with conviction, they were also recognized as to some degree tainted by their complicity in a system of political, social, economic, *and* moral domination.[98] And so these values were generally contextualized within a larger moral landscape. That is, they were placed within an overall framework defined by the primary moral goods of black dignity, freedom, and self-determination and by the primary theological affirmations of the parenthood of God and the kinship of all people. Once *these* values were viewed as definitive, then forms of agency such as wit, cunning, humor, and subterfuge could be recognized as potentially moral in character, depending on their intent and context.

African Americans did not reject the dominant (white Christian) morality whole cloth or merely because it was embraced by the master class. Rather, they rejected the underlying intent and outcome of this morality—its legitimation and perpetuation of white superiority. This complex valuation of the dominant morality meant blacks were free to endorse various of its features while still resisting its underlying logic. It also meant that African Americans could endorse behaviors and strategies deemed morally deviant by the dominant moral paradigm insofar as those behaviors contributed to the overarching aims of black dignity, freedom, and self-determination and did not violate the norms of the parenthood of God and the kinship of all people.

NONVIOLENT RESISTANCE TO EVIL

When civil rights activists embraced in the 1950s and 60s the strategy of nonviolent direct action to combat racial and economic discrimination, black Americans' long-standing ethic of ingenuity became manifest in a dramatic and highly visible way. Far from being a "hidden" transcript, this was a self-consciously and necessarily *public* discourse. Indeed, nonviolent resistance was successful only insofar as it was able to create a *new* public, an awareness among histori-cally separated peoples of their shared humanity and destiny. Despite its public character and aims, however, this was a thoroughly ingenious moral posture. It was deeply subversive of the status quo; it was in many ways counterintui-tive despite its compelling logic, requiring people to rethink things as basic as human nature and instinct; and, like the ancient narrative of God outwitting the devil, it functioned by luring the powers of evil into excess, thereby creat-ing a new moral clarity and consensus.

Given our historical proximity to the American Civil Rights movement, it is easy to forget how truly revolutionary were its aims and tactics. The heyday of Reconstruction with its new freedoms for African Americans had by the early years of the twentieth century become a fleeting dream, a cruel tease. Full and equal participation with whites in electoral politics, education, health care, housing, employment, and social life seemed nothing but a pipedream. Perhaps most tragically, many black churches and ministers appeared to have lost their resolve—sinking into despair, embracing an other worldly, pie-in-the-sky religiosity, or expending scarce emotional and financial resources on internal power struggles that kept them from developing effective networks of solidarity and action.[99] Yet, as Martin Luther King Jr. was himself to identify, a gradual coalescence of factors began to set the stage for a new movement, a new day.[100]

With the Montgomery bus boycott of 1955–56, a fresh incarnation of African Americans' religiously rooted ethic of ingenuity was born. Modeled after Mahatma Gandhi's crusade against British colonial rule of India and claiming as a key theological warrant Jesus' own way of being in the world, the American Civil Rights movement embraced nonviolent direct action as a strategy for effecting social change.[101] For King, nonviolence was not only a temporary tactic but a philosophy for living, a spiritual discipline, a faithful response to the summons of the Prince of Peace and the Way-Maker God. Its ultimate aim was what King called "the beloved community"—humanity gath-ered in modes of peace, justice, and mutual flourishing. This aim could never be reached, King insisted, through violence—neither the structural violence of master-class politics and economics, nor the reactionary violence of the underclasses. The means and the end must not conflict. King was resolute and unwavering on this point. If justice and peace are the aim, then they must be peacefully sought, else their attainment will be illusory and short-lived: "In the long run of history, immoral destructive means cannot bring about moral and constructive ends."[102]

At the same time, King was equally resolved that peaceful means need not be impotent. Resistance to injustice can be both nonviolent *and* fierce, both peaceful *and* world-changing. In a 1957 article in the journal *Christian Century*, King avers:

> This is not a method for cowards; it *does* resist. The nonviolent resister is just as strongly opposed to the evil against which he protests as is the person who uses violence. His method is passive or nonaggressive in the sense that he is not physically aggressive toward his opponent. But his mind and emotions are always active, constantly seeking to persuade the opponent that he is mistaken. This method is passive physically but strongly active spiritually; it is nonaggressive physically but dynamically aggressive spiritually.[103]

Large-scale economic boycotts, for example, may be nonviolent, but they are far from passive. Boycotts actively direct resources away from targeted areas, creating an unreliable and often unsustainable financial situation for those being targeted and compelling them to attend to the claims of the resisters. In addition, boycotts often direct resources in new directions, thereby rewarding or rejuvenating non-offending vendors or motivating the creation of new vendors. Finally, and perhaps most importantly, boycotts and other forms of nonviolent direct action mobilize and energize the disenfranchised, giving them opportunity to respond actively, constructively, and corporately to their victimization. In so doing, boycotts cultivate esteem, agency, creativity, and solidarity. As King reflected in 1960, "the nonviolent approach does not immediately change the heart of the oppressor. It first does something to the hearts and souls of those committed to it. It gives them new self-respect; it calls up resources of strength and courage that they did not know they had."[104]

I. Rehumanization

In addition to being profoundly active, nonviolent resistance as practiced by civil rights activists was also deeply humane and visionary. As King often noted, "nonviolent resistance does not seek to defeat or humiliate the opponent, but to win his friendship and understanding."[105] Where violence destroys and dehumanizes, essentially rejecting the opponent's claims to full humanity, nonviolent direct action explicitly assumes the opponent's humanity and challenges him or her to lean more genuinely *into* that reality by responding humanely to those whose humanity is under assault by unjust systems, laws, and mores.

Nonviolent resistance seeks not to dehumanize but to *re*humanize—to sum-
mon the perpetrators of injustice into new being, new connection, and new
possibility. Protest and nonconformity are tools intended precisely to jolt the
master class into awareness, to awaken in them a kind of species-consciousness,
a recognition that the resisters and protesters are, like them, human beings
with a right to humane treatment. Ultimately, said King, the aim of nonviolent
resistance is not revenge or overthrow but "redemption and reconciliation. The
aftermath of nonviolence is the creation of the beloved community, while the
aftermath of violence is tragic bitterness."[106]

Just as the protestors call the unjust toward rehumanization, so the resisters themselves must be grasped in their hearts by an ethic of love rather than of
vengeance or mastery. A key to nonviolence, taught King, is its internalization
by those who would practice it: "In struggling for human dignity the oppressed
people of the world must not allow themselves to become bitter or indulge
in hate campaigns. To retaliate with hate and bitterness would do nothing but
intensify the hate in the world." Real change requires that we give up on violence, as counterintuitive and countercultural as that may be: "Along the way of
life, someone must have sense enough and morality enough to cut off the chain
of hate."[107] Because the powerful benefit from the violence their systems per-
petrate, it is highly unlikely that they will turn away from violence of their own
accord. Indeed, they can hardly recognize their violence *as* violence; it appears
to them simply as the proper order of things, the way things are, have been, and
always should be. Thus, the task of opening the eyes of the powerful to their self-
induced and self-aggrandizing state of moral blindness falls so often to their victims. It is they, paradoxically, who hold the power to awaken, to transform. But
this power, warned King, must be guided and limited by "the ethics of love" if it
is to effect lasting change. It must be a new kind of power—communal and life-
affirming rather than self-interested and death-dealing. And in many instances,
this power will be achieved paradoxically, through the abdication of power.

Motivated and framed by a love deeper than hate, nonviolent direct action
takes the world's un-love and inhumanity by surprise, prompting unprecedented questions and moral reckonings: How can it be that this person whom
my own politics and daily practice dismiss as subhuman is sitting before me in
a mode of full humanity? From whence come this dignity, resiliency, and self-
actualization that refuse to cower or retaliate under the force of my blow? What
quality of character, what depth of resolve it must take to put one's body, one's
pride, one's *life* on the line in the face of staggering odds and certain defeat.
What astounding il-logic! What mind-blowing conviction!

The sheer surprise wrought by the nonviolent direct action of civil rights protestors, even among those who had heard of its method but had not been faced with its actualization, cannot be underestimated. To witness the enactment of full humanity by those presumed to be subhuman is to have one's assumptions rattled. To encounter the gaze of equality from one presumed to be inferior, the righteousness of one discounted as morally incapable, is to feel the unhinging of one's categories of understanding, the destabilizing of self and world. Even if only for a moment, this unexpected undermining of assumptions and certainties raises a specter of doubt and extends an invitation to be transformed.[108]

II. A Moral Crossroad

To reject this invitation is to compound one's culpability, to harden one's heart. As so often happened during the Civil Rights movement, it is precisely in this moment of steely resolve that one is likely to strike out foolishly and to expose one's hard heart to the world, unintentionally creating in the observer an instinctive recoiling from that moral callousness. At this moment of excess, of the overflow of hate, fear, or self-protection, a crucial moral bifurcation occurs. The observer distances her- or himself from the hateful act and actor, seeing for perhaps the first time their moral untenability.

It is precisely in order to evoke this experience of moral clarity in the oppressor or uncommitted bystander that nonviolent resistance is necessarily public, corporate, and sustained through time. A key to direct action is that it happens in public, where the opponent's reaction to it will be observed and scrutinized. The coverage of civil rights demonstrations on television, radio, and in newspapers drew increasing numbers of Americans, both black and white, into the moral debate. It forced white people to acknowledge and attempt to defend racist practices and systems, exposing them as self-interested, narrow-minded, and cowardly. When it did not soften the oppressor's heart, nonviolent resistance exposed the hardening for all to see, taunting it into self-defeating excess. In other words, nonviolent direct action lured whites into discrediting themselves in the eyes of the public. When policemen, enforcers of the white-defined status quo, aimed powerful fire hoses at women and the elderly; when they set dogs loose on children and beat peaceful, unarmed men; when white merchants and customers shouted insults and poured milk or coffee on the heads of passive would-be consumers at lunch counters, the ugliness and inhumanity of "the rule of law" and its associated economic and moral systems were laid bare for all to see. In essence, a moral bifurcation was performed, and its audience—first-hand observers, television watchers, radio listeners, newspaper readers—had to choose a side.

The sustained, repetitive character of nonviolent protests was also a significant piece of the strategy. The seemingly never-ending train of protestors and the persistent character of protests such as boycotts and sit-ins sent the message that the resistance would not end until its aims were realized. Ignoring today's protestors would do no good because they or their allies, with their confounding tactic of nonviolent resistance, would be back tomorrow, and the next day, and the next day. As King intoned, "All history teaches us that like a turbulent ocean beating great cliffs into fragments of rock, the determined movement of people incessantly demanding their rights always disintegrates the old order."[109] The protestors' persistence was fueled by regular meetings, rousing music, and a powerful theology that centered on the conviction that, as King said, "God is on the side of truth and justice," offering the protestors "cosmic companionship" in the struggle. True to the creative eschatology of slave and black church traditions, King's theology brought heaven and earth, the now and the yet to be, together to motivate, sustain, and nurture black resistance and hope. He offered this reflection in the midst of the Montgomery bus boycott:

> This belief that God is on the side of truth and justice comes down to us from the long tradition of our Christian faith. There is something at the very center of our faith which reminds us that Good Friday may reign for a day, but ultimately it must give way to the triumphant beat of Easter drums. Evil may so shape events that Caesar will occupy a palace and Christ a cross, but one day that same Christ will rise up and split history into A.D. and B.C., so that even the life of Caesar must be dated by his name. So in Montgomery we can walk and never get weary, because we know that there will be a great camp meeting in the promised land of freedom and justice.[110]

At other times, King chided his fellow black Christians for embracing an impotent, otherworldly theology:

> It's alright to talk about "long white robes over yonder," in all its symbolism. But ultimately people want some suits and dresses and shoes to wear down here. It's alright to talk about "streets flowing with milk and honey," but God has commanded us to be concerned about the slums

down here, and his children who can't eat three square meals a day. It's alright to talk about the new Jerusalem, but one day, God's preacher must talk about the new New York, the new Atlanta, the new Philadelphia, the new Los Angeles, the new Memphis, Tennessee. This is what we have to do.[111]

III. The Power of Love

No matter how hard the struggle or what the personal cost, King continued to believe that "love is the most durable power in the world," the "highest good," the principal that "stands at the center of the cosmos." This conviction was rooted in powerful encounters with the compassionate and liberating God who became incarnate in Jesus of Nazareth: "As John says, 'God is love.' He who loves is a participant in the being of God. He who hates does not know God."[112] Convinced that nonviolent direct action was the only way to resist the evils of segregation, racism, economic exploitation, and war in a mode of love—that is, without succumbing to the logic and tactics of evil itself—King and his allies sought to know and participate in the Divine. Even while they embraced an "ethics of love," however, they did not shy away from criticizing the reigning religious paradigm of the day, exhorting their fellow Christians, black and white, to rethink their version of the gospel: "Any religion that professes to be concerned about the souls of men and is not concerned about the slums that damn them, the economic conditions that strangle them and the social conditions that cripple them is a spiritually moribund religion awaiting burial."[113]

Similarly, nonviolent resistance embodied a stubborn critique of unjust moral and legal systems insofar as it involved protestors in concrete acts of civil disobedience. These acts aimed to expose the immoral underpinnings of "unjust laws"—their violation of basic human rights, their defiance of "the moral law of the universe" that accords all creatures the right to dignity and self-determination.[114] Thus, King defended and even advocated the breaking of unjust laws on the basis that "noncooperation with evil is as much a moral obligation as the cooperation with good." Far from exhibiting disrespect toward law and justice, the breaking of unjust laws and the willingness to accept the consequences of such defiance expresses, said King, "the very highest respect for the law."[115]

In the face of concerns from within the black community that the strategy of nonviolent resistance merely played into the hands of the dominating powers, King insisted that "true nonviolent resistance is not unrealistic submission to evil power. It is rather a courageous confrontation of evil by the power of love."[116] King readily admitted that this strategy was unorthodox and difficult within the reigning paradigm to appreciate because it required those with the least power willingly to abdicate some of that power—specifically, the power to hate, destroy, and seek revenge. Rather than seeking such power, King argued that the victims of the powerful should accept the suffering their resistance brought on in modes of reconciliation and with an eye to the overall aim of structural transformation.

Rejecting negative power did not mean, however, a rejection of all power. Indeed, as the struggle persisted, King became increasingly convinced of the crucial importance of black participation in power and, more broadly, of poor people's participation in power. As he became increasingly aware of the structural connections between white superiority and American economic and cultural imperialism, King realized how deeply entrenched and systemically broad were the patterns of inequality and injustice that he and others hoped to change. As a result, he began to consider how the strategy of nonviolent resistance could be used to dismantle the complex network of systems and powers that eventuated in racism, poverty, war, unemployment and underemployment, nuclear weapons proliferation, and a host of other injustices. Despite a new appreciation of the extent of the challenge, King continued to believe that orchestrated and sustained campaigns of civil disobedience and nonviolent protest offered the best hope for effecting lasting structural change. As counterintuitive and unorthodox as this strategy was, King was convinced that it was the only hope for genuine transformation and real social change.

IV. Moral Jujitsu

It was likely the heterodox character of the strategy of nonviolent direct action—its inconceivability from within a violence-saturated culture, its simple but mind-bending logic, its pure intentions and moral clarity—that made it initially so successful but ultimately too threatening, too subversive, to permit. Like the early Christian notion of divine ingenuity in which the Incarnation was understood as a masterfully cunning challenge to the powers of evil—a willing abdication of power that lured the powerful into unwitting but discrediting excess—the strategy of nonviolent direct action effects what Eugene TeSelle calls a kind of "moral jujitsu": "Non-violent direct action takes control of the situation away from the ruling powers, poses a dilemma to them, puts them in a double bind: they must either consent to an act of disobedience (and thus appear weak, or give legitimacy to the dissenters) or exert their authority against it (and thus seem bullying and be morally discredited). It is a kind of moral 'jujitsu' that uses an opponent's strength to defeat him."[117] In the case of the Civil Rights movement, the opponent's "strength" was, on the one hand, the economic and social power of the white middle and upper classes. This power was turned against itself as business owners, police forces, and white community leaders responded to the pressures of nonviolent protest by exerting excessive force and hence exposing their raw will to power. Dramatized in clear public view, this excess ignited moral clarity and outrage among the American masses, both black and white.

An additional "strength" that was effectively turned against the white power structure was its stated commitment to democracy and the American Constitution. Just as slaves used the white master class's rhetoric about the relative humaneness of American slavery to argue for *more* humane treatment, so civil rights activists turned the American ideals of democracy and justice against the white American elite, insisting that they stop applying them selectively. By the time of King's death, his sights were set higher than ever, aiming not merely to apply constitutional rights to African Americans but, more radically and comprehensively, to redistribute political, social, and economic power so that all God's people might experience full participation in the human community. As ever, he stood by his conviction that only courageous and creative nonviolent resistance could ever hope to transform evil into good.

In the final analysis, the strategy of nonviolent direct action advocated and put into practice by King and his colleagues in the Civil Rights movement represented a bold attempt to be faithful to the legacy of an African-American ethic of incarnation and ingenuity—an ethic whose roots extended deep into the independent black church movement, slavery, and the early Christian church.[118] Like the body-centered spirituality of medieval women and the subversively creative religiosity of the slaves' hush harbors, the nonviolent direct action of the Civil Rights movement engaged those at the fringes of social, economic, and political power in ingenious practices of resistance and liberation. In ways both dramatic and subtle, it drew them into authentic relationship with the God who makes a way out of no way, the One who took the modest resources at hand—human flesh, genuine caring for the other, a passion for justice—and used them to recreate the world. Armed with christic imagination, King and company fashioned what has come to be regarded as "the most significant and redemptive moral revolution of the twentieth century."[119] Unconventional and unorthodox? Yes. Surprising and subversive? Absolutely. Moral? Without a doubt.

WOMANIST IMAGINATION

This chapter's discussion of an African-American ethic of ingenuity explores four incarnations of that ethic—four related but distinct moments in which religiously inspired black people have responded to evil with gritty resourcefulness, courageous creativity, and liberative imagination. In the creation of slavery's invisible institution and its related cultural practices, the formation of the independent black church movement in the nineteenth century, and the embrace of the strategy of nonviolent direct action in the twentieth century's Civil Rights movement, we see clear and compelling evidence of what I am calling an ethic of ingenuity at the very heart of African-American life and history. Moving into the twenty-first century and the contemporary context, I lift up a fourth incarnation of christic imagination: womanist theology and ethics. While other contemporary moments or movements may also fit the bill, womanist theology and its attendant moral wisdom and practices resonate profoundly with the gestalt of ingenuity. They constitute an undeniable incarnation and expansion of this key African-American moral tradition. While space will not allow a full discussion of womanist theological insights and practices, I will highlight for consideration a few of the key ways in which womanist thought and practice constitute a significant demonstration and deepening of a religiously inspired ethic of ingenuity.

If African Americans as a people have had to endure a long and brutal history of dehumanization, exploitation, and neglect at the hands of the white majority culture, then African-American women have been particularly victimized. As blacks, they have been racially villified by whites and, eventually, lighter-skinned immigrant populations. As women, they have been victimized by the patriarchal assumptions and personal and institutional practices of both white and black cultures. Caught between a rock and a hard place, black women have been forced to develop a complex set of resistances, alliances, and self-understandings in order to live with integrity, humaneness, and self-determination in a usually hostile world. As Gloria T. Hull, Patricia Bell Scott, and Barbara Smith have famously characterized the situation, "all the women are white, all the blacks are men, but some of us are brave."[120]

I. Defining Our Terms

"Womanist" thought, theology, and practices are those that are embraced by freedom-loving women of color who refuse to abdicate their race, their gender, their self-respect, or their unique experiences and hard-won wisdom in the face of the oppressive forces that surround them. While this disposition and set of commitments stretch as far back as Africa and the galleys of the Middle Passage, the term "womanist" comes from Alice Walker's use of the folk term "womanish" in her 1983 book, *In Search of Our Mothers' Gardens*.[121] Subordinated on the basis of race and gender, black women have also disproportionately poor and working class.[122] In the face of this harsh reality, the cultivation of "womanist" wisdom and audacity, of a deep and unrelenting spiritual foundation and hope, and of a feisty love of self and community, has been less a luxury than a life-saving necessity. Beyond that, it has been a font of individual and communal affirmation, resilience, and imagination. Womanist Emilie Townes proposes that "this [womanist] perspective—which flows from surviving, as women, in a society based on inequalities rather than justice—is one that yearns for glory. Such glory is found in seeking a new heaven and a new earth—a world crafted on justice *and* love that holds us all in God's creation rather than in a hierarchy of oppressions."[123] For Townes and other womanist theologians, it is the Way-Maker God who became incarnate in Jesus the Christ's real-life ministry of justice, mercy, and liberation who inspires and sustains black women's distinctive spirituality and ethics.

II. Womanist Ethics

Katie Cannon's groundbreaking work on womanist ethics reveals that at the heart of the lived moral philosophy of African-American women is a vibrant ethic of ingenuity. This ethic, which so often runs counter to the dominant ethic of the capitalist political economy and its undergirding moral economy rooted in master class Christianity, has been viewed by those discourses as "either immoral or amoral." Where the dominant ethic "makes a virtue of qualities that lead to economic success—self-reliance, frugality and industry," Cannon notes that these virtues are based on the assumption that "success is possible for anyone who tries"—an assumption proved false by black women's centuries of experience in the American workforce.[124]

In addition to defining as "moral" a set of virtues based on an economic context that excludes many black women, Cannon points out that the dominant ethic rests on the assumption that the moral actor is "free and self-determining."[125] It is commonly assumed, in other words, that the moral agent can (and should) take full responsibility for her choices and actions and, hence, that her position in the world is the result of her own free choice. Again, this assumption does not mesh with the realities of black women's existence, which has been largely defined by forced subordination and a relative lack of freedom. Moreover, the dominant moral paradigm assumes that a wide range of choices is available to the moral agent and, hence, that she is always free to choose the ideal option and make the morally "correct" decision. This assumption ignores the extreme delimitation of choices experienced by most African-American people, past and present. In sum, the dominant ethic fails to account for the kinds of powerful, systemic constraints that define the everyday reality and moral landscape of black women. Not surprisingly, black women's real-life moral wisdom and practice tend to be unrecognizable *as moral* by the dominant culture.

III. Real-Life Virtues

So what does this "real-life moral wisdom and practice" actually look like? What specific shapes does a womanist ethic of ingenuity take? The first thing to note, suggests Cannon, is that black women's moral wisdom "is not identical with the body of obligations and duties that Anglo-Protestant American society requires of its members." Rather, out of black women's unique cultural context has emerged a distinctive "analysis and appraisal of what is right and wrong and good or bad." This appraisal may or may not line up with the dominant system's interpretation of what is morally upright. Furthermore, Cannon avers, black women's moral wisdom "does not appeal to the fixed rules or absolute principles of the white-oriented, male structured society."[126] It is, rather, a complex, multiform, and continually unfolding set of sensibilities and commitments that is nimble enough to respond to changing circumstances, new experiences, and fresh insights, as well as to the need for continual self-critique and self-correction.

This essential flexibility notwithstanding, Cannon points to three moral dispositions or aims that have become constitutive of African-American women's ethic: invisible dignity, quiet grace, and unshouted courage. These ethical values, created and cultivated in the cauldron of racism, sexism, and classism and given voice within black women's literary tradition, have allowed black women "to prevail against the odds, with moral integrity, in their ongoing participation in the white-male-capitalist value system."[127] Beyond mere survival, these values have allowed African-American girls and women to push back against dehumanizing systems of power by developing a rich hidden transcript of texts, traditions, and practices that are life-affirming, community-building, and world-transforming.

African-American women have never had the luxury of innocence. Generally speaking, they have lived in a morally compromised universe with diverse causes and shapes: the loss of sexual innocence at the hands of a rapist slave

master or the dominant class's brutal stereotyping; the daily pretense of deference and compliance in relation to white people and black men; the sad task
of teaching one's children not to shine too brightly in a world intent on their
destruction. All too often in the exercise of their own moral agency, the "right"
or "good" choice has been the one that would inflict the least suffering, that
would do the least harm. Only rarely has the line between good and evil been
simple, clear-cut, or within reach.

In such a world of moral ambiguity and constraint, African-American
women have cultivated what Cannon identifies as the virtue of "invisible dignity." Facing the loss or absence of innocence not with denial or depression but
with stubborn resolve and grace-filled imagination, black women like Zora
Neale Hurston learn "to appreciate that surviving the continual struggle and
the interplay of contradictory opposites" is itself a virtue. They learn to celebrate their own survival as a positive good and to appreciate the ethical task as
"a balance of complexities" rather than the expression of a clear and static ideal.
As Cannon says, to embrace the virtue of invisible dignity is "to maintain a
feistiness about life that nobody can wipe out, no matter how hard they try."[128]
Despite its invisibility as a moral good, the art of dignified survival in a hate-
filled, morally compromised world is, indeed, an accomplishment to celebrate
and a moral good to recognize and nurture.

A second characteristic of black women's moral agency is found in their
ability to convert their "never practiced delicacy" into the virtue of "quiet
grace." Where virtue for white women has often included "elitest attributes of
passive gentleness and an enervative delicacy," black women have not had the
luxury of such dispositions. Modesty, daintiness, and pretenses of vulnerability or frailty have been practical impossibilities for African-American women,
indicating once again the lack of fit between the realities of their lives and the
expectations of the dominant moral paradigm. And yet, says Cannon, black
women have deftly turned their "never practiced delicacy" into the virtue of
"quiet grace"—a "special ethical quality" by which they "evoke, sustain, and
augment their actions in order to avert capricious and uncalculating perils."
With little time for "wound licking frailty" or other elitest conventions, and
without "reverence or protection from the dominant powers in society," black
women nevertheless cultivate a strategic quietness that allows them to "deci-
pher the various sounds in the larger world" and make wise decisions about
when and how to make themselves heard. African-American women's search
for truth may be inaudible to others, but for those who have ears to hear, it is
most certainly there. It is nurtured by the virtue of quiet grace, which allows

them "to venture on, to continue taking risks, to push against limits that deny their beingness."[129]

The third and final virtue Cannon identifies as part of black women's distinctive moral wisdom is "unshouted courage." Once again, this virtue stands in contrast to the dominant moral paradigm, which associates courage with the willful and usually heroic vanquishing of fear or opposition. For black women past and present, fear and opposition are permanent structures of reality— not to be vanquished but rather endured, managed, and strategically lessened. Courage, in this context, is not so much a heroic choice of the free will—the Herculean untethering of the self from the constraints and contexts of fear—as it is the conversion of "forced responsibility" into an opportunity for self-actualization. Unshouted courage, says Cannon, "is the quality of steadfastness, akin to fortitude, in the face of formidable oppression." Far more than a "grin and bear it" mentality, "it involves the ability to 'hold on to life' against major oppositions . . . to chip away the oppressive structures, bit by bit." It is "the often unacknowledged inner conviction that keeps one's appetite whet for freedom."[130]

Together, these three virtues—invisible dignity, quiet grace, and unshouted courage—constitute the heart of African-American women's moral wisdom. This wisdom has informed the self-understanding, spirituality, politics, and daily practices of women of color in multiform ways through the centuries. In order to get a feel for the specificity of this distinctive moral tradition, let us briefly consider three concrete instantiations of black women's ethic of ingenuity, each from a different moment in Christian history.

IV. An Alternative Work Ethic

The system of chattel slavery in the United States was devised to procure cheap labor for a complex agrarian society without a large enough indigenous labor base to create the desired productivity and profit. Within this system, black women's lives were defined primarily by their role as laborers. They were valuable insofar as they were productive workers and insofar as their reproductive labor created new generations of workers. In other words, black women slaves were bought and bred to labor. The system of enforced labor was undeniably the source of their exploitation and dehumanization. It was also, argues womanist Joan M. Martin, a site of ingenious resistance to their own victimization.[131] We saw above that slave women used cunning and imagination to wrest important parental control away from their children's legal owners in order to protect, guide, and teach slave children the ways and wisdom of black culture and community. What we learn from Martin is that even at the point of their greatest exploitation—work—slave women managed to express genuine moral agency, push back against master-class hegemony, and make strides toward self-actualization and communal flourishing. Through their work, slave women helped construct alternative social spaces, a discourse of resistance, and a work ethic that subverted the dominant white culture's notions of the value and meaning of work.

Specifically, slave women's narrative testimonies such as those of Harriet Jacobs, Lucy Delaney, and Elizabeth Kleckley demonstrate a countercultural interpretation of work. The dominant moral paradigm defined the slave work ethic solely in terms of obedience and hard work. The larger Protestant work ethic suggested that one's work was divinely ordained and was to be embraced as a vocation or calling. For their part, slave women were resolute in their view that the exploitative work of the chattel system was a human-created evil displeasing to the God of freedom. Furthermore, they insisted that work was a positive moral good, a vocation or calling, only when it "contributed to the community by affirming the interdependence of self and self-in-community in the ongoing struggle for emancipation and freedom."[132] Thus, slave women's work of "provision gardening"—their uncoerced labor aimed at supplementing their family's subsistence diet—was viewed as good and meaningful work, as was their work as mother, midwife, root worker, and keeper and transmitter of intergenerational wisdom and moral authority. Conversely, the work they performed for "the profits and power" of the unjust institution of slavery was seen as neither a moral good, an opportunity for self-improvement, nor a part of God's will. Thus, although the dominant moral paradigm saw work as a primary "defining characteristic of what it means to be human," black women developed their own interpretation of moral agency and goodness.[133]

According to this interpretation, we are truly human when we contribute to the survival and flourishing of the community and the self-in-community. Work is "good" and agency is "moral" inasmuch as they contribute to these ends and safeguard the embodied integrity and dignity of all involved. Underscoring black women's ingenuity, Martin notes that in a situation of extreme delimitation, slave women nevertheless managed to create a "self-understanding of work *unchained* from slavery's meaning, yet *arising out of those very chains*."[134] In the real-life practices of slave women as reflected in their own narratives, we find an ingenious if hard-won rethinking of the meaning of life, the value of work, and the character of the moral. This creative alternative to an exploitative system of living, working, and valuing was inspired and sustained by powerful experiences of God as "the God of life, freedom, and protection"—a creative

Divine incarnated in Jesus and in the christic imagination and humanizing work of black slave women.[135]

V. The Politics of Respectability

At the turn of the twentieth century, women within the black Baptist church tradition created an important and complex movement aimed at social justice, spiritual edification, and enhanced moral agency for African-American women. Womanist scholar Evelyn Brooks Higginbotham offers a compelling analysis of this bold and imaginative movement in her book, *Righteous Discontent: The Women's Movement in the Black Baptist Church, 1880-1920*.[136] During this period, the National Baptist Convention (NBC) was by far the largest black church *and* the largest Baptist church in America. It was, moreover, the third largest Christian denomination in the nation, black or white. The Women's Convention of the NBC, which was founded in 1900, quickly became a national force, creating effective alliances with black men and white women alike, but also maintaining a distinctive identity and set of commitments and objectives. Of the movement's many characteristics and accomplishments, it is these women's embrace of a "politics of respectability" that I want to lift up as a notable incarnation of an African-American ethic of ingenuity.[137]

In the early 1900s, white Christianity's moral system made a virtue of the white middle-class ideals of sobriety, thrift, personal decorum, and industriousness. Such virtues, it was thought, were keys to morally upright and economically successful lives. Given the decidedly non-normative character of the alternative work ethic and moral wisdom developed by black women during slavery, it is perhaps surprising to note that during the early 1900s, a generation of black women enthusiastically embraced the white bourgeois morality of respectability. Or so it appeared. In reality, as Higginbotham's study makes clear, black women imaginatively converted the dominant culture's morality of respectability into a *politics* of respectability that functioned in important ways to undermine the very moral system upon which it was predicated. At a time when black people were struggling for respectful treatment from whites and aiming toward racial self-determination in a thoroughly racist culture, black Baptist women activists embraced the prevailing morality of respectability— with an essential twist or two—as a means toward both objectives.

By emphasizing in their moral discourse the importance of clean living and hard work, black women hoped to dismantle white assumptions of black people's "natural" laziness, dirtiness, and moral licentiousness. They also sought to put an end to what they saw as negative practices among their fellow African

Americans. By encouraging reform of individual attitudes and behaviors, they aimed to improve race relations at the structural level in order to enhance freedom and opportunity for black women and men.

Racist stereotypes and pseudo-science abounded in white culture in the early 1900s. In addition to Social Darwinism, which suggested that struggling and oppressed peoples were weak members of the species and should basically be allowed to die off, a host of racist stereotypes paraded as objective. These included "the immoral black female teacher as cause for the weakness of black schools; the immoral black mother as responsible for the degeneracy of the black family; the acquiescence of the black husband to his wife's infidelity; and the widespread belief that black women were unclean."[138] In the face of such stereotypes, black Baptist women insisted on the moral uprightness of African-American women. They demonstrated through their own impeccable decorum and fastidiously organized conventions the falsity of the stereotypes that black women were inherently lazy and promiscuous. In their speeches and reports, they commended the hard work of "daily toilers" and praised the accomplishments of black professionals. In countless ways, the rhetoric and activities of African-American women leaders in the early twentieth century affirmed the morality of respectability—of hard work and clean living—that white America embraced and often used as a weapon against black Americans.

However, these influential black women's apparent affirmation of the dominant morality was in many respects a disloyal repetition of that morality. It was a subversion of the script they were given by the dominant culture, a deliberate mimicking of the public transcript. Their creative reappropriation of ethical norms was aimed, ultimately, not at the undermining of the morality of respectability itself but, more radically, at the dismantling of the unjust white power structure altogether. The virtues endorsed by the leaders of the black Baptist Women's Convention may have been hallmarks of white bourgeois culture, but they used those very virtues to prove that poor, working-class black people were worthy of respect. As Higginbotham's study reveals, "by claiming respectability through their manners and morals, poor black women boldly asserted the will and agency to define themselves outside the parameters of prevailing racist discourses."[139]

By exhibiting the virtues of respectability such as sobriety, thrift, cleanliness, and politeness, black people embodied a method for refuting, in concrete and verifiable ways, the logic behind their own subjugation. In concrete, everyday ways, they developed what Pierre Bourdieu might name a heretical discourse. Turning the dominant morality on its head, these women rejected

"the definition of the real that was imposed upon them."[140] This politics of
heterodoxy was understood to complement other strategies for dismantling
unjust power structures, as this 1915 statement by the Women's Convention
articulates: "Fight segregation through the courts as an unlawful act? Yes. But
fight it with soap and water, hoes, spades, shovels and paint, to remove any
reasonable excuse for it, is the fight that will win."[141]

It must be admitted that the embrace of the morality of respectability by
black women leaders could and sometimes did function unintentionally as an
uncritical repetition of the dominant morality—as, for instance, when their
denunciations of some black people's moral improprieties reinforced stereotypes of blacks as immoral, or when their emphasis on individual behavior
implied that blacks were responsible for their own victimization. This fact notwithstanding, Higginbotham's careful study leads her to conclude that although
black women's politics of respectability was not "radical" in its critique of white
culture and morality, nor unambiguous in its effects, it nevertheless constituted an important expression of black women's agency in a time of great
delimitation, a key "'bridge discourse' that mediated between black and white
reformers," and an impressive attempt to push against the dominant system by
using that system's assumptions and values in a heterodox or disloyal fashion.[142]
Black women's politics of respectability at the turn of the twentieth century
laid "the very groundwork for protest, voting, and other traditionally recognized forms of political activity" that would, within the succeeding decades,
"escalate the assault on race and gender discrimination."[143]

VI. Kitchen Poetry as Resistance

In our contemporary context of the twenty-first century, numerous examples
of a womanist ethic of ingenuity could be identified. The one I lift up here is
the practice of "concealed gatherings" as experienced and narrated by Lynne
Westfield in her book *Dear Sisters: A Womanist Practice of Hospitality*. According
to Westfield, a key way in which African-American women nurture resilience,
hope, and solidarity in the face of the "tridimensional phenomenon of race,
class, and gender oppression" is through simple, concrete practices of hospitality such as those embodied in what she calls concealed gatherings of diverse
black women.[144] Concealed gatherings are those that occur away from white
people and from African-American men—often around the kitchen counter
or in living rooms, simple or ornate. They are spaces of genuine hospitality
where black women "have neither to defend nor to deny their place or their
humanness."[145] These gatherings are distinguished, says Westfield, by:

. . . raucous bantering, comic tales of then and now, outrageous anec-
dotes, new/old jokes, playing of the dozens, snappy comebacks, dissing,
sarcasm, absurd and sick humor, lies, philosophizing, theologizing, recited
poetry, new poetry, tired clichés, sage wisdom, tales of how we got over,
stories of back when and back then, dreams of right living, right loving,
and new ways of being. The gatherings are high energy and fast-paced
events. . . . The rhythm of the conversation is often syncopated and double
syncopated with several women talking at one time—a varietal symphony
of verbal and bodily expression. The gatherings are verbally and linguisti-
cally treacherous—not for the dull, slow, or faint of heart.[146]

In these sensuous and full-bodied contexts, African-American women
practice and inculcate radical hospitality—learning first to welcome and
embrace their own souls and bodies and then reaching out to others. They aim
not at mere survival, insists Westfield, but at creative resilience and defiant
celebration no matter what the odds.

These "poets of the kitchen" spin tales and craft language as strategies of
self-care and resistance to evil. In their poetry and prose, their subversive humor
and serious play, they ask deep questions and consider profound possibilities:

What is it?
that keeps a Black woman's head UN-bowed
back UN-broken
spirit IN-tact?

What is it?
that keeps her
fresh alive
vibrant still?
. . .
Who is it? Or What is it?
that enables
dance without benefit of orchestra
flight with just one wing
full voluptuous laughter
deep down belly deep laughter
side splitting
show-every-tooth-in-her-head laughter?

that powers her
to charge forward
to take charge
to be in charge
to lead
doing more with less than seemingly possible
making fancy garments from plain threads
creating banquets from crumbs
building warm nests even in the midst of ice poverty?

it must be something
not of this world
something which bubbles
forth from Mystery
given at conception
reenforced at birth
refined honed along life's way
melded tested each & every day
it must be large
delicate
tunelessly changing
& eternal.[147]

When the white world is inhospitable, the black church is unwelcoming,
or the daily grind of life is almost too much to bear, concealed gatherings invite
black women to uncover their wounds and fears in the company of healers.
More constructively, these gatherings nurture the development of a positive
kind of double-consciousness that equips black women with a worldview "able
to respond to a multicultural, postmodern reality."[148] In spite of the gravity
and complexity of the challenges, humor remains an indispensable and oft-
used tactic for resisting despair and dehumanization. As Daryl Cumber Dance
proposes, "If there is any one thing that has brought African-American women
whole through the horrors of the middle passage, slavery, Jim Crow, Aunt
Jemima, the welfare system, integration, the O. J. Simpson trial, and Newt
Gingrich, it is our humor." "Laughter," she says, "is not simply funny; it's serious
medicine; it's righteous therapy."[149]

As "moral bricoleurs," contemporary African-American women formu-
late ethical decisions for complex situations and times, using the sometimes

meager tools at hand to carve out life-affirming options and to seek self-sustaining and community-sustaining ends. "The bricoleur's tools," says Westfield, "are discernment, envisioning, cunning, guts, and ingenuity for the transforming of unholy conditions."[150] Reflecting on the long legacy of black women's creative moral agency, Nikki Giovanni recalls:

> We are the folk who took rotten peaches and made cobblers; we took pieces of leftover cloth and made quilts; we took the entrails of pigs and cleaned them and rinsed them in cold water until the water ran clear then chopped up onions, shredded some red peppers, dropped a few fresh bay leafs and one large whole peeled potato in the pot to let it simmer over the open fire until we returned from the fields so that our families would have a hot meal at the end of the day. Every time something was taken away we took something else and made it work.[151]

In the twenty-first century as in days gone by, freedom-loving African-American women embrace an ethic of ingenuity. The self-care and sisterhood nurtured in concealed gatherings is often undergirded by deep connection to the God who makes a way out of no way. This God is the moral bricoleur *par excellence* who somehow crafted divinity out of humanity and salvation out of suffering. This is the God who, like Lynne Westfield's granny, "take a little/ from here & there/ & there & here/ create enough for all/ & still/ have some to spare."[152]

VII. A Way-Making Ethic

From slavery to the contemporary context, African-American women have responded to oppressive assumptions and conditions with intelligence and humor, finding ever-new ways to preserve dignity, cultivate hope, and plot resistance. Smartly, stubbornly, and with the help of a way-making theology, they have embodied a set of virtues—invisible dignity, quiet grace, unshouted courage, subversive humor, moral bricolage, and life-affirming solidarity—as positive moral goods despite the fact that these goods have usually stood in tension with the value system of the dominant culture. This tension, we have seen, is both oppositional and creative. It is oppositional insofar as these womanist virtues form an ethic that opposes the implied mastery and univocality of the dominant paradigm. It exposes the self-interested, partial, and socially constructed character of that paradigm by articulating a different, yet equally legitimate moral philosophy. At the same time as it opposes the dominant system, however, this minority tradition also stands in fruitful, creative tension with that system. As we have seen, the moral wisdom cultivated by African-American women has resulted from a communal process of imaginative and subversive riffs on the dominant paradigm. Created from within the constraints of social, political, economic, and religious marginalization, black womanist ethics takes what is at hand—master-class moral assumptions and prescriptions—and uses it to forge a distinctive set of moral norms and practices. This distinctive tradition, imaginatively shaped from the refuse of oppression, prizes ingenuity, scrappy resourcefulness, and feisty creativity. It aims toward social justice, human dignity, and mutual flourishing for all. As such, black women's moral wisdom testifies to the presence and vitality of an African-American ethic of ingenuity.

This larger African-American moral tradition—what we might call a way-making ethic—has not been the only tradition of moral wisdom embraced by black people. But because of its deeply nonconformist character and aims, the ethic of incarnation and ingenuity of African Americans has been largely unrecognized or underappreciated by the majority of American Christians and moral philosophers. Even among African-American scholars who have contributed brilliantly to the uncovering and thematizing of black ingenuity through the ages, there is sometimes a reluctance to lift this strand of tradition up for moral affirmation, a hesitation to name it as a legitimate and compelling moral posture.[153] There are good reasons for such hesitation, but they should not be allowed to obscure the vital presence throughout African-American history of an ethic of ingenuity with deep religious roots.

This ethic is fundamentally creative in nature; it is not a static set of ideals or behaviors but takes shape in response to the continually unfolding realities and challenges of real-life experience. This very dynamism makes an ethic of ingenuity difficult to define and discipline, which can create worries about moral relativism. Given the historic accusations of black immorality as well as the continual need to take firm stands for justice and against oppression, such worries cannot be ignored, but neither should they be allowed to determine the rules of moral engagement. As I discuss in the final chapter of this book, an ethic of incarnation and ingenuity is not without its own set of robust intentions and guidelines. Indeed, its aims and frames strike me as particularly well-suited for the complex moral universe in which we twenty-first-century Christians live, move, and have our being.

4. INCARNATING IMAGINATION

A Christian Ethic of Ingenuity in Contemporary Context

o live with integrity in today's world can sometimes seem impossible. In the context of globalizing practices, transnational capitalism, and biogenetic engineering, everyday practices like a trip to the grocery store can become painful moral dilemmas. If we are to complete the mundane tasks of daily living with our sanity intact, it seems necessary to detach ourselves from the complexities of global markets and nanotechnologies and to ignore our complicity in unfair labor practices and any number of other destructive patterns, policies, and institutions. We learn to keep other people at arm's length, especially those whose neediness or pain indicts our own habits of living. And yet, Christians are called into relationships of compassion and justice. We are called to be neighbors, not detached observers; and to be a neighbor is to care not merely for our own well-being but also, and even especially, for those who are hurting.[1] It means that we cannot simply pass by on the other side, but we must get involved; we must take action.

One of the biggest obstacles to taking action today is a lack of imagination. Given the entrenched complexities of our world, it is difficult to conceive how we could meaningfully respond to the hurt we see around us. We can put a dollar in a cup, send a year-end contribution, drive a hybrid, or spend a few hours in community service, but what difference will it make? While most Christians know we are called to live in modes of mercy and to be neighbors to those in need, we rarely know how to enact such commitments in anything other than narrowly personal ways. Our lack of imagination affects not only our ability to act but even our capacity to *want* to act. As theologian Paula

Cooey reflects, many of us today suffer from a diminished capacity for desire. We easily desire the good for ourselves and those within our narrow circle of primary concern, but we have a much harder time desiring the good for those who fall outside that circle. In other words, we have lost our ability genuinely to desire the *common* good, the good beyond and perhaps in tension with our own good. Even when we do want others to flourish, we often assume *we* know what is best for *them*. "In short," says Cooey, "our desire for the good is both too narrowly extended and authoritarian." Those of us who enjoy relative privilege and power simply "do not know how to desire a good that we do not control." Whether we realize it or not, we "suffer from an impoverishment of the imagination regarding what we hope for as good."[2] Evidence of our lack of embodied passion for the common good is everywhere—in emergency rooms filled with hardworking Americans who clock forty-hour work weeks but still cannot afford health insurance; in public schools without art, music, updated books, or money for paper; on death row, where the vast majority of inmates are poor men of color with substandard legal counsel whose crimes cause far less damage than the white-collar affluence and corporate greed many of us aspire to; in a fossil-fuel-centered, consumerist lifestyle and economy that depend upon the ravaging of the earth and its most vulnerable workers.

Even when at a conceptual level we "see" the problems, even when we "know" we need to act, we frequently lack the will to do so. Our will is powerless—bound by our fear of change, of losing what we already have; bound by our inertia, by the exhaustion so many of us feel, thanks to the frantic pace of our 24/7 lives;[3] and bound by a profound lack of imagination, by our inability to conceive of viable solutions to the problems we confront. A diminished imagination is only one piece of the causal nexus, but it is a vital piece. As the ancient biblical writer knew, "Without a vision, the people perish" (Prov. 29:18). Without imagination—the constructive coming together of energy, experimentation, hope, and vision—the common good cannot be enacted. Imagination is the midwife of possibility and the catalyst for action. It is also deeply pleasurable, welcoming our whole selves into creative engagement and exercising our fantasies of individual fulfillment and mutual flourishing.[4]

Have we forgotten that the Incarnation—the essence of the good news we Christians have to offer the world—was an audacious act of divine *imagination*? Do we fail to appreciate that we were created in the image of the Great Imaginer? *Imago dei*, indeed. Surely, part of what it means to be human is to be imaginers, people of vision who refuse to let each other perish, people created *imago imaginationis*. Taking our cue from God's profoundly imaginative response to our brokenness and bondage, one way of conceiving of Christian discipleship is in terms of "disciplines of ingenuity"—the cultivation of dispositions and embodied practices that do not cower, anesthetize, or despair in the face of complex, systemic problems like racism, sexism, militarism, and consumerism but that instead exercise the imagination—yours and mine, ours and theirs—on behalf of all God's creatures. The truth is that viable solutions to today's complex social, economic, and ecological problems *already exist*. They have been imagined and are even being enacted on a small scale in various places across the globe. If we are to see widespread and systemic change, we will need *more* ingenious ideas as well as the will to perform them. But we also need to *incarnate* our imagination, to enflesh it with courage, compassion, *and* a growing circle of companions. Ingenuity cannot be only about the ideas, the conceptual play, the theories of resistance, performativity, and transformation. It's got to be enacted. We've got to put flesh on those bones.

One paralyzing dynamic that seems to affect many Christians is the lack of apparent connection between today's dauntingly complex problems and biblical realities. When we look to our sacred texts for help and do not find in them specific examples of how to embody compassion in relation to the sophisticated economic and technological systems that define contemporary existence, many conclude that it cannot or should not be done. We may assume the Good News of love incarnate is personal—applicable in one-on-one encounters with discrete others but irrelevant or impotent in relation to more complex relationships or to those whose good is not directly linked to our own. Too often, we Christians assume the answers to contemporary challenges are already defined in our texts and tradition and that our sole task is to return to the past in search of *the* definitive answer.

EXCAVATIONS

Certainly, the impulse to return is at the heart of the religious sensibility. The Latin roots of the word "religion" (*re-ligio, religare*) mean "to tie or fasten" or "to retrace." Religion, then, rightfully involves its practitioners in journeys of excavation and pilgrimage. In our liturgies and study, we fasten ourselves to old stories, return to sacred times and places, and hope to encounter wisdom for our own struggles and times. Importantly, though, our retracings are not exercises in ventriloquism. We do not merely recite the past in an intention-free vacuum. Rather, our speaking of old narratives breathes into them new life, novel possibilities, unforeseen applications. Religion as a retracing, then, does not excise the imagination so much as it exercises it, summoning it into action. Much of this book has been spent on just this sort of imaginative retracing of Christian pasts.

Many contemporary Christians are discomfitted by the idea that the human imagination plays a necessary role in all encounters with sacred texts and traditions. For them, the authority of the text lies precisely in its inviolability, its absolute immunity to the whims and bias of human interpretation. For most Christians, "imagination" comes far down the list of Christian virtues, if it appears at all. For many, it is a nemesis of virtue, a source of contamination and dangerous unpredictability. This devaluing or maligning of imagination notwithstanding, I claim it as central not only to practices of biblical interpretation and theological construction but to the very story to which Christians as a people seek to tie ourselves. As a small but significant minority of the Christian faithful has realized, including a handful of church fathers, dozens of medieval women, and generations of African Americans, the Incarnation was a profoundly imaginative response to the world's brokenness. It defied expectation and confounded logic. It was no weak deception but a muscular creativity, an audacious Way-Making. Confronted by the entrenched habits and systems of a species bent on self-destruction, God responded with outrageous ingenuity, unrelenting creativity. Becoming not only flesh/vulnerability but a fleshly one committed to the weakest and most vulnerable and, more outrageously still, to a ministry of creative nonviolent resistance instead of mastery, divinity was revealed in the mode of ingenuity. Discipleship, then, requires christic imagination.

RISKY BUSINESS

Imagination, full-bodied and courageous, is exactly what today's world with its complex character and challenges requires of Christian persons and communities. For Christians, creativity is not an option but a mandate. Fastening ourselves to the Christian story means retracing with our own lives a path blazed with christic imagination. It means embodying in times both ordinary and extraordinary an ethic of incarnation-inspired and -guided ingenuity.

But this is tricky business, this embrace of ingenuity. The fact is, we live in an enormously complex world where moral reasoning is not a simple matter of selecting an action, decision, or value from the "good" or "righteous" column as opposed to the "bad" or "immoral" column. Moral wisdom is a much messier affair than that. It usually involves the careful sifting through of multiple possibilities, none of which may be ideal. More often than not, we are forced to ennoble or redeem a less than ideal option. Always, ethics involves the critical assessment of context and possible outcomes. It ultimately requires that we step out in a mode of risk, wagering that we have done the best we could to make a humane and defensible choice.

Particularly in situations of significant agential constraint—contexts in which the moral agent or community is faced with few if any options or with a choice between non-ideal options—an ethic of ingenuity can empower the moral actor or community. It inspires a search for novel possibilities, an exploration of new angles, the posing of different questions, and the consideration of unorthodox approaches to moral challenges. It can, moreover, empower one to call into question the very assumptions of "the moral" and "the good" that are imposing the constraints within which one is attempting to maneuver. As we saw in the previous chapter, African-American men and women have developed into an art precisely these kinds of novel considerations and moves as they have devised ever-new strategies for survival with dignity and, beyond that, genuine freedom and structural transformation. To discount this hard-won moral tradition, this sophisticated moral art, as a mere coping mechanism or as a minor thread within the larger moral fabric, is to overlook or downplay the intelligence and agility of generations of moral actors and communities.

True, an ethic of ingenuity is fundamentally flexible in nature, raising concerns about moral relativism. Its elastic, fluid character defies the containment strategies and totalizing intentions of solid mechanics, onto-theologies, and master discourses. And yet, we insist, it is not wholly amorphous or unruly. This ethic has clear intentions. Its liquid imagination works tirelessly to stir up waves of resistance to human evil, wear down the rough edges of violence, and re-route the channels of bigotry and oppression in new, life-affirming directions. The prophetic refrain of Amos and Martin Luther King Jr. is the imagination's constant aim: "Let justice roll down like waters, and righteousness like an ever-flowing stream" (Amos 5:24).

It is important to note that concerns about moral relativism, while legitimate, are applicable to *all* traditions and strategies. *Any* particular moral posture or tradition is viewed as "moral" *in relation to* a certain framework of understanding and valuing, a specific set of experiences and interpretations, and a particular view of authority and accountability. In this respect, an ethic of ingenuity is undeniably "relative"—or, more accurately, "relational." The question to pose, then, is not about the *fact* of relativity or relation, since it is a predicate of all moral systems. Rather, the crucial question has to do with the *quality, scope, and aim* of the relations that constitute the moral tradition: Whose experiences are recognized as worthy of consideration? Whose interpretation of texts and events is granted authority? Toward what ultimate condition or situation does the tradition aim? Who, in other words, counts as human?

For the African-American ethic of ingenuity described in chapter 3, the answer to these questions is rooted in a Way-Making theology that affirms the universal parenthood and compassionate creativity of God, the shared creaturehood of all, and the life-transforming power and praxis of Jesus the Christ. Similarly, we considered in chapter 2 that medieval Christian women's audacious conversion of the degraded into the divine grew out of their shockingly unorthodox conviction of God's radical availability and universal care for all. These two case studies prompt us to recognize that although an ethic of ingenuity may emerge from the margins, it nevertheless aims to recognize the full and shared humanity and dignity of *all* persons. This primary intention defines not only the ethic's end or aim but its means or strategies as well. Thus, despite its fluid and responsive character, an ethic of ingenuity calms fears about moral relativism or nihilism. Despite its cultivation of creativity and cunning, it is consistent in its affirmation of the dignity of human life, the worthiness of human freedom and community, and the self-defeating, other-effacing nature of pretensions to mastery and domination over other people and beings. In sum, an ethic of ingenuity embraces fluidity, flexibility, heterodoxy, and hybridity in the service of clear and consistent commitments and aims. A Christian ethic of ingenuity is inspired and guided by incarnational norms and aspirations.

Still, it must be admitted that there is risk involved in this endorsement of a Christian ethic of ingenuity. God may well be a bold and effective Way Maker, but discerning the implications of this theological affirmation for our own finite seeing and being is far from simple. Our exploration into two concrete manifestations of the ethic reveals the contested, ambiguous character of moral agency, action, and community. Rarely are there moments of absolute moral clarity or outcomes that are morally uncomplicated or unequivocally good. What is experienced far more often than clarity, certainty, or moral "success" is the risky business of choosing a way forward without knowing what the outcome will be or how it will interact with larger contexts of power. Despite this ultimate unknowing, a Christian ethic of ingenuity challenges women and men of faith to act boldly. We are to be an incarnational people, enfleshing love, embodying justice, and using all the resources of the imagination to outwit, unseat, and otherwise resist the forces of destruction and dehumanization we encounter in our world.

EDGING OUT VIOLENCE

The question of which particular efforts, movements, or strategies may be considered "christic" is less important than the conviction that included in a Christlike disposition and praxis is the virtue of ingenuity. If in our own lives and communities we are attempting to discern the next step in a christomorphic ethic, we can turn not only to the hopeful stories of our own time and of Christian communities gone by, but also to our tradition's sacred texts, which offer us not a detailed recipe for victory but a proposed vision—not unlike the picture on the jigsaw puzzle box or the clue to the crossword that we return to again and again as we work to fit the pieces together or find the perfect word. The biblical vision guides and inspires our work; the picture it portrays is so compelling, so worthy. That vision functions proleptically, summoning us towards future fullness, showing us what is possible. It also offers us a kind of frame for our work—a set of edges and corners, some boundaries and limits.

My own sense of scripture's vision is that it edges out violence and seeks to limit human acquisitiveness and mastery. With each glimpse of the sacred I catch, those corners are reiterated, that ethical framework reinforced. Yet, I am aware that some who share the same overall vision as I do spy different boundaries, boundaries that do not exclude violence as a response to evil. To be sure, advocacy of nonviolence can appear to be simply another quieting tactic of the ruling elite—a strategy for quelling resistance and outrage in order to preserve an unjust status quo. Often, those who advocate nonviolence among the disenfranchised turn a blind eye to the institutionalized violence of racism, heterosexism, and capitalism, as if to say that petty acts of physical insubordination like looting or vandalism count as "violence" while "justice" systems that result in staggering incarceration rates for people of color, or taxation systems that systematically privilege large corporations and the wealthy elite, are not "violent." I make no such assertions. Neither do I propose that petty acts of violent insurrection among the underclass are the same as institutionalized systems of marginalization. The latter are premeditated and systemic—different, therefore, in both intention and scope than spontaneous outbursts of rage or resentment.

That said, I follow Jesus, Gandhi, King, and others in recognizing that while the spontaneous outbursts may be powerfully provoked and, hence, completely understandable, they are, nevertheless, not the best choice.[5] A middle path between passive submission and violent protest is almost always possible, and that path has the best potential for transforming evil without succumbing to its death-dealing strategies. Although violence may seem justified as a response to situations of extreme exploitation, a robust, imaginative, nonviolent response has the potential to effect deeper change, and change is, in the final analysis, the desired outcome. As Walter Wink implores, "Violence simply is not radical enough, since it generally changes only the rulers but not the rules. What use is a revolution that fails to address the fundamental problem: the existence of domination in all its forms, and the myth of redemptive violence that perpetuates it?"[6]

In truth, an ethic of ingenuity is an edgy ethic. It puts us on edge because of its unrelentingly liminal character. Even when we recognize its existence, trace its presence, and argue for its strategic usefulness and moral worthiness, we do not permanently soften its edges. Acknowledging an ethic of ingenuity *as* an ethic means acknowledging also our inability, and everyone else's as well, to determine once and for all what specific behaviors count as "the good," "the moral," or "the ethical." It means relinquishing control, or better, recognizing the illusory nature of our aspirations to control. Taking an ethic of ingenuity seriously, then, means taking ourselves a little *less* seriously; seeing our own constructions of meaning *as* constructions—well intended, we hope, and occasionally productive of the common good, but also inevitably compromised, flawed, and complicit in systems of power that inflict pain. To incarnate ingenuity is not only, then, to recall that we are *imago dei* and, as such, *imago imaginationis;* it is also, and equally importantly, to remember that we are dust and to dust we shall return.

MODEST INTENTIONS

When medieval women like Catherine of Siena and Julian of Norwich chose to dive ever more deeply into the dust, into the physical as an essential ingredient of spiritual practice, they were wagering that such an approach would bear fruit, that somehow a body-hostile culture and woman-fearing church would make room for their paradoxical expression of self, community, and religiosity. Surely, they did not expect their mimetic strategy to free them from the powerful constraints of their time, to "liberate" them from "the oppressor." The aim of their moral agency does not appear to have been unilateral power or self-righteous purity but a much more modest goal: a modicum of self-actualization, a moment of spiritual plenitude.

Perhaps, their wager paid off. Certainly, it is possible to read their practices in this way. Ultimately, however, we admit that such an interpretation is *our* wager. Our contemporary retracing (*religare*) of their stories no doubt tells us as much about our own desire for religious understanding and moral courage as about theirs. Like them, we live in complicated times characterized by sophisticated discourses of power and knowledge. Where church and patriarchy dictated the terms of medieval women's lives, our own reality is defined primarily by transnational markets and global capitalism, with other master(ing) narratives such as sexism, racism, and classism playing key supporting roles. In our day as in pre-modern times, moral agency must be embodied within powerful constraints. In neither context would it make sense to claim moral purity or absolute certainty. Our intentions must be more modest, more pragmatic, or else we will find ourselves quickly disillusioned and defeated. Our imagination can and should soar; it should be unbounded in its consideration of alternative systems of thought and practice. But it must ultimately be applicable to current realities, even if it intends to deconstruct them from the ground up, and it must avoid becoming a new master(ing) narrative.

An encounter with medieval women's body-centered religiosity leaves us with a new appreciation of the ways in which individual moral agency is necessarily co-defined by larger relationships of power. It impresses upon us that ethics does not happen in a vacuum but is a process of continual negotiation in contexts of constraint and ambiguity—a process whose aim is not escape from or denial of constraint or ambiguity but the pragmatic sizing up of and moving forward with what is possible from within those contexts. The short-term goal, then, is not some kind of miraculous or triumphal assertion of moral heroism, surety, or purity but something more modest, more realizable, and perhaps more transformative: a modicum of self-actualization, a moment of spiritual plenitude, an experience of genuine healing or of justice in the making, and, so importantly, of company along the way. The accumulation of such modest moments can, over time, create tremendous change, new ways of defining and organizing power, new paradigms for thinking and living. Of vital significance for Christians in this process of effecting change is the example and Spirit of the Way-Making God whom we claim was incarnate in Jesus of Nazareth. In ways ancient and new, we experience and hope for the audacious creativity of the God who, then and now, makes a way out of no way in the pursuit of mutual flourishing for all God's creatures.

For our medieval women friends, incarnating ingenuity meant imitating Christ with their bodies, embracing the mystery and mundanity of God's body, and ministering to the bodily needs of the suffering. What might a body-focused ethic of ingenuity look like in a twenty-first-century American context? Answers to this question will be as varied as the problems we identify and the people determined to solve them. One thing seems certain, however:

The particularities of a twenty-first-century ethic of ingenuity will depend on the embodied wisdom and imagination of those on the ground, those whose everyday, material lives are most disfigured by the problems. Those at a distance, those "on the top," simply cannot know how best to solve the problems of the suffering, how best to promote the *common* good, unless and until we become true allies, real comrades, of the wounded. This means leaving the ivory tower, the board room, and the insulated suburbs and going to where the problems are most deeply felt. It means, as the medieval Beguines clearly knew, leaving the cloister and going to where the wounded are. For some, this leave-taking may mean physical relocation, moving home or business from the suburbs to the inner city, for instance. For most of us, however, it will mean something less dramatic but still significant: redirecting more of our primary work towards the common good, or relocating and reallocating our money so it serves wider goods.

Still, unless we engage our *bodies* in this work—unless this departure involves regular face-to-face, flesh-to-flesh encounters with the wounded—our efforts are likely to fall back into models of hierarchy and patronage. Our imagination must be an incarnational one. Certainly, the experiences, knowledge, skill set, connections, and material resources of the privileged are necessary to this work. But as we have seen time and again, they are simply not enough. The "haves" have got to seek out, learn from, and take direction from the "have nots." As we are learning in my Mississippi workplace, those of us behind the gates have got to "shut up and listen" to our more vulnerable neighbors. And this listening, this reaching out, cannot be a one-time or only occasional gesture; it must be our permanent way of operating. If it does not change at a fundamental level the way we do business, our self-understanding and institutional mission, and our allocations of time and resources, then it is just one more empty gesture, one more feel-good media ploy, one more betrayal of public trust. The privileged and the poor are not patrons and clients; we are *partners*. Together, we must exercise our imaginations, and together, we must put our bodies on the line in the work for justice and mutual flourishing. To enflesh genuine partnership, day in and day out, is to engage in an incarnational ethic of ingenuity.

Let me reiterate that ingenious solutions to today's toughest problems will emerge from the real-life experiences and hard-won insights of the flesh and blood people whose lives are seriously diminished by those problems: the poor, the unemployed, people of color, the handicapped—the "least of these" for whom our God Incarnate showed special concern. The rest of us must find the humility to re-imagine our roles, to move from being well-meaning overlords and patrons to being shoulder-to-shoulder co-workers in struggles for humane living for all. We must, as evangelical minister and social activist Jim Wallis contends, improve our "proximity to the poor" and marginalized.[7] And I am not thinking here of increased intellectual or electronic access to each other, although those kinds of connections do have a role to play, but of increased *bodily* encounters: face to face conversations, shared meals, common classrooms and play spaces where our children regularly engage each other. Medieval Christian women seemed to know that when *bodies* encounter each other, ethics is enlivened, goodness is summoned, and transformation is imaginable. So even when the body is the source of pain or of stigma, as it clearly was for those women and as it is for so many people today, it is at the same time a key site of resistance to suffering, a vital source of connection to the wider universe, and a conduit of pleasure, creativity, and joy.

Can we Christians, people of the Incarnation, appreciate that our ethic of ingenuity in the face of today's complex moral challenges must be a robustly embodied one, a commingling of our body with the bodies of the wounded, a taking into ourselves—into our hearts, minds, and daily concern—the material realities of those at the margins? I believe we must. Inspired by God's audacious becoming of body in the Incarnation and medieval women's incarnation-based affirmation of the paradoxes of body for their own time, we must imagine a new kind of eucharistic piety for our own context—a piety defined by embodied communion with the suffering.

A WAY-MAKING PRAXIS

If what we hold onto from our glimpse of medieval women's religiosity is an appreciation of the complex context of the ethical task, as well as a clear mandate for a body-centered ethic of ingenuity aimed at enfleshed communion and full partnership with the suffering, then perhaps it is further illumination of the content and fresh insights into the method of our ethic for which we can turn to the African-American traditions of chapter 3. Certainly, the recognition and experience of the Way-Making God is a profound and indispensable contribution to an ethic of ingenuity. Indeed, it is this African-American notion of God that most compellingly reinvigorates the early Christian experience of the Divine as the one who, as an expression of justice, creatively outsmarts and unravels the powers of evil. At the heart of a Christian ethic of ingenuity—its origin, sustaining hope, and proleptic lure—is without question the Ingenious Divine, who was and is powerfully articulated by those at the social, economic, and political margins.

What is made additionally clear in the moral wisdom and practices of African Americans from slavery through today is that this Way-Making God empowers and perhaps even requires a *Way-Making praxis* among humans as a faithful response to God's amazing grace. This practical mandate for ingenuity has been most explicitly articulated in the trickster tradition and its kin. Significantly, this tradition underscores and amplifies the enormous potential of human Way-Making to advance causes of justice-seeking and mutual flourishing while at the same time recognizing that ambiguity is a mark of all human moral efforts. Perhaps it is this simultaneous embrace of both liberation and ambiguity that makes the trickster of particular interest to some of today's most astute minds.

Within the past couple of decades there has been a profusion of interest in and theorizing about trickster figures—mythical, biblical, medieval, Shakespearean, Native American, African, Asian, and the list goes on.[8] Many of these studies explore the link between trickster narratives and the peoples and cultures that produce and reproduce them, leading one expert, William J. Hynes, to propose that these tales of mischievous shape-shifters function within society in one or more of the following six ways: (1) to entertain; (2) to vent and hence *dissipate* social frustrations; (3) to reaffirm the dominant belief system by embodying a *mythical* transgression of boundaries that results in the *practical* underlining and reinforcing of those same boundaries for hearers or readers; (4) to evoke the surfacing of repressed feelings or values, thus initiating *psychic* adventures into creativity, otherness, and ingenuity; (5) to transcend and disrupt the bounds of monoculturality and univocality by playing the role of liminality, multivocality, and pluri-positionality; and finally, as a result of (5), (6) to open up spaces of excess and plenitude out of which genuinely *new* discourses, logics, and identities might emerge.[9] I have tried in this book to push those who traffic in Christian ethics to consider the possibility that the trickster trope or gestalt with its myriad embodiments of play, ingenuity, wit, cunning, imagination, and subversion, and with its multiple psychological and social functions as outlined by Hynes, points to a real moral posture, an ethical stance that merits attention, thematization, and careful evaluation, and one that, moreover, has deep roots in Christian tradition and history.

I am not alone in appreciating the illuminating potential of this gestalt. Among contemporary scholars who find the trickster trope useful for thinking about today's ethical challenges are Ada María Isasi-Díaz, Donna Haraway, and Sharon Welch. My own appropriation of the trickster theme in terms of an ethic of ingenuity has emerged not only in conversation with African-American scholars but also in relation to these three important thinkers. For Isasi-Diaz, a Cuban *mujerista* theologian, it is the concept of *burla* or mockery that best describes the innovative moral agency of Hispanas/Latinas.[10] She argues that despite the considerable constraints imposed by economic and racial subordination, Hispanas/Latinas have learned how to "tur[n] marginalization into a creative space of struggle."[11] Relegated to the margins of society, to "in-between" spaces that are generally forgotten, unrecognizable, or explicitly devalued by the dominant classes, Hispanas/Latinas have used their imaginations to transform those spaces into "fertile in-betweens." They have converted the apparent negativity of "living on the hyphen" into opportunities for resistance and transformation by recognizing that their "interstices have not been and are not silencing spaces."[12]

No matter what exclusivist or dominating dynamics may have produced the hybrid or in-between positionality of Hispanas/Latinas, Isasi-Diaz argues that it is possible to use that subjectivity imaginatively, disloyally, in surreptitious "raiding" activities aimed at "taking hold of what I find useful in my colonizing condition for building the future." To turn the very space to which one has been "exiled" into a strategic "refuge" where hope is nurtured and new visions are cultivated is to mock the intentions and power of the colonizers. It is irreverently to convert "the confinement/spaces to which we are assigned into creative/liberative spaces"—spaces that "little by little we turn into our own."[13]

At the same time as she appreciates the need to critique dominating discourses, Isasi-Diaz emphasizes that such deconstruction must be understood as a temporary and strategic backward glance endured for the sake of moving forward, of "remembering myself and my people" in order "to make it possible to move ahead." Thus, she thinks of the work of critique and deconstruction as a "memory forward."[14] Tricking or evading the oppressor through mockery or mischievousness is, insists Isasi-Diaz, "a most healthy antidote for any sense of 'victimhood' that we [Hispanas/Latinas] might be tempted to embrace." It is also a strategic way of confronting one's oppressor, of "asserting ourselves as sujetos históricos (historical subjects) engaged in la lucha (the struggle) and refusing to value suffering in itself." To engage in strategic practices of *burla* or trickery is not to repeat the status quo but, rather, to be reminded of what should *not* be repeated, of what is "worthy of mockery." As Isasi-Diaz concludes, "This is our ultimate burla: to turn the elements of confinement in the tiniest of interstices into those needed to create una sociedad en la que quepan todos, a society in which all fit, from which no one is excluded."[15]

From the vantage point of this "raided" space, this "fertile in-between," the marginalized can create utopian projects that envision and begin to embody new spaces, new forms of moral agency. Contrary to some views of utopia, Isasi-Diaz defines this utopian project as the work of envisioning "our preferred future"—a future that, once imagined, "takes root in us as a community of struggle" and becomes "tangible in concrete projects."[16] Imagination is the key to this taking root, for the work of utopia is not merely "a condemnation of the existing order" but a bold and positive "proclamation . . . the forecast of a different order of things, a new society"[17] characterized by desire, hope, feasibility, effectiveness, pleasure, and happiness and aiming always toward "the goal of our mujerista utopian project: not only life but fullness of human life-liberation."[18]

For Isasi-Diaz and the *mujerista* theology she advocates, the trickster trope is useful for articulating the task and technique of moral agency from the margins. This agency aims consistently toward liberation from oppression and fullness of life for all. Trickery or mockery is understood as a tool of critique, resistance, and transformation—an act of creative defiance of an unjust status quo that calls that status quo into question, refuses to grant authority to its claims to mastery, and allows the moral agent to imagine new ways of organizing and valuing self and community. Thus, for *mujerista* theology as articulated by its premier spokesperson, the trickster trope effects the last three functions of William Hynes's typology—cultivating the moral agent's creativity, undermining the dominant discourse's claim to authority and universality, and opening up spaces of plenitude out of which new possibilities can emerge.

In contrast, Donna Haraway's appropriations of the trickster gestalt point to a more ambivalent set of effects.[19] Her interpretations of trickster figures, including the biblical figure of the suffering servant, Jesus, and Sojourner Truth, emphasize their multivalent meanings. In one mode, for instance, the self-assured Jesus mocks the establishment, while in another he is despised and brutalized by the powerful. This shape-shifting trickster Jesus, says Haraway, "appears as a mime in many layers; crowned with thorns and in a purple cloak, he is in the mock disguise of a king before his wrongful execution as a criminal. As a criminal, he is counterfeit for a scapegoat, indeed, *the* scapegoat of salvation history. Already, as a carpenter he was in disguise." In yet a different shape, this same figure indicts the Jews of deicide—his death laid squarely at their feet by the gospel writers. While for Haraway the "figure of the Incarnation can never be other than a trickster," she intends by the trickster trope something far more ambiguous than Isasi-Diaz's liberative mockery. For Haraway, the trickster is constitutively "complex and ambiguous," always already "enmeshed in translation, staging, miming, disguises, and evasions."[20]

Haraway reads Sojourner Truth as a trickster figure who is, on the one hand, a figure of humanity who articulates a potentially common language that avoids pretensions to universality, ultimate closure, and the myth of sovereignty. She is "an unruly agent," a truth-speaking sojourner who refuses to "settle down" into the expectations of her racist, sexist context and, yet, who, thanks precisely to her stubborn specificity, figures a new, hopeful humanity.[21] However, in the idealizations of other interpreters, Sojourner Truth takes the shape of the heroically victimized but defiant one who neatly fulfills abolitionist desires. In this incarnation, her speech is not that of a native New Yorker owned by a Dutchman, but rather "the falsely specific, imagined language" of the "supposedly archetypical black plantation slave of the South."[22] In this shape, Truth "adorns posters in women's studies offices and women's centers across the United States"—revered as a unifier of "women" and yet falsified precisely by that coerced universalization.[23] Thus, in the hands of many interpreters, mourns Haraway, the sojourner is immobilized, forced to settle down. But perhaps, Haraway proffers, the interpreter can invoke a fresh unsettling by seeing Truth "as the Afro-Dutch-English New World itinerant preacher whose disruptive and risk-taking practice led her," like Isaiah's suffering servant, "'to leave the house of bondage,' to leave the subject-making (and humanist) dynamics of master and slave, and seek new names in a dangerous world."[24]

In the (never quite) final analysis, says Haraway, trickster figures like Jesus and Sojourner Truth "trouble our notions—all of them: classical, biblical, scientific, modernist, postmodernist, feminist—of 'the human,' while making us remember why we cannot not want this problematic universal." That is to say, tricksters are quintessential shape-shifters, constitutively amenable to multiple interpretations, including those that feign to be self-evidently univocal. As such, concludes Haraway, tricksters are "eccentric subjects"—subjects that call our attention to their own, and our own, contestability; subjects that are perennially under construction; subjects that, thanks to these characteristics, "can call us to account for our imagined humanity."[25]

Haraway's construal of the trickster includes all six functions of Hynes's typology. It recognizes that while shape-shifters may at times aim toward or instantiate freedom or plenitude (recall Isasi-Diaz's liberative *burla*), they are equally amenable to transgressions that unwittingly reaffirm patterns of exclusion, diminishment, and domination. Thus, Haraway underscores our earlier recognition that the trickster, the figuration of ingenuity, is fundamentally amoral. As we noted, ingenuity is itself neither good nor bad. Everything depends on the context within which it is exercised, the purpose toward which it aims, and the means it embraces on its way to that end. We must, ultimately, "account for our imagined humanity," take responsibility for our own Way-Making. It may well be that this is precisely what Isasi-Diaz is doing with her liberative gloss on the trickster—attempting not so much to describe it from afar as to sculpt it intentionally into a gestalt of freedom-seeking agency for her own context. Read in this way, her *mujerista* affirmation of an ethic of ingenuity does not necessarily discard or ignore ambiguity and complexity but rather chooses to dwell elsewhere, to lift up for consideration and strategic embrace the liberative impulses and possibilities of ingenuity.

In her consideration of the trickster trope, ethicist Sharon D. Welch worries that liberation-seeking interpretations may unintentionally sabotage themselves.[26] Welch's concern emerges from her decades-long experience in progressive social justice movements, where the perennial problems of disillusionment, burnout, and despair are prompted not only by the magnitude of the challenge (for example, raising awareness, transforming patterns of behavior, dismantling systems of power, creating new institutions), but also by the naïve expectations and self-righteousness of those who engage in social justice work. The tendency within progressive movements, Welch says, is to eschew ambiguity and limits in favor of certainty and victory. Social justice activists tend to function within a dualistic framework of good versus evil, oppressed versus oppressor, and to aim for total transformation of systems and institutions. However morally reassuring this construal of reality may be, says Welch, it inevitably leads to frustration, cynicism, and a sense of failure. Like "so many of our western myths, our narratives of progress, of freedom, democracy, and prosperity," this view is "predicated on the disavowal of ambiguity and limits." The result is that social justice activists find it extremely difficult "to move from the politics of protest to the very different challenges of building institutions."[27]

What is needed, insists Welch, is the courage and imagination to "shift from a culture of conquest (masked as progress) to an equally vital culture of living with limits, with ambiguity, and with a self-critical recognition of our own abuses of power."[28] Welch suggests the metaphor of jazz to help us consider the shape and aim of moral agency by highlighting the efficacy of improvisation, creativity, fluidity, and teamwork. She also finds the trickster trope useful for thinking about how "to live fully and act creatively in the midst of a world we can never control and can only partially understand."[29] As we have seen, trickster stories are not tales of a morally pure hero who master-fully conquers all foes. They are, rather, ambiguous narratives of struggle and creativity within contexts of considerable constraint. As such, says Welch, they teach us how to live with integrity within the limits of our own world. Trick-sters function, then, not so much as moral exemplars or symbols of freedom but as reminders of how messy and unpredictable moral agency really is: "The trickster shows us the costs of unbalanced power and jolts us back into a prop-erly chastened respect for the fierce and unpredictable power that we and oth-ers can exercise."[30] Moral agency is fraught with ambiguity. It can diminish or enhance, tear down or build up, and it usually manages both at once. Learning to live with this reality, proposes Welch, means understanding morality as "the perilous and at times beautiful human response to the energy and wonder of life." It means embracing "an ethic of risk" whose hallmarks are "creativity and courage"—an ethic motivated by "a passion not for perfection or transgres-sion but for the excess/depth/wonder/possibilities of the everyday"; an ethic whose aim is not "moral certainty" but "ethical integrity."[31]

A CHRISTOMORPHIC ETHIC

Along with Isasi-Diaz, Haraway, and Welch, I appreciate the usefulness of the trickster trope for thinking about the character and aim of moral agency in today's world. Welch reminds me that an ethic of ingenuity for our time must not ignore or deny the complexity and ambiguity of our complicated context. It cannot set itself up as "the" ethical strategy, moral wisdom, or path to justice or faithfulness. To be effective, practitioners of an ethic of ingenuity will need to engage in continual self-critique, never taking ourselves or our projects too seriously, nor assuming we cannot play the fool. From Haraway, I learn to expect that even well-intentioned creative efforts will be diversely inter-preted and (mis)appropriated. Despite its integral dynamism, a Way-Making praxis is yet vulnerable to unintended immobilizations and reifications. Hence, the importance of searching out friends, compatriots, and fellow sojourners whom we can trust to "call us to account for our imagined humanity."[32] Finally, Isasi-Diaz's theologically framed, hopeful interpretation of *burla* reminds me that in spite of complexity, ambiguity, misappropriations, and my own inevi-table missteps and failures, an ethic of ingenuity can and should be directed toward humanizing transformations of individual lives, communities of faith, economic systems, political agendas, and social structures. To aim in this direc-tion is not necessarily to eschew ambiguity, complexity, or self-critique but to refuse to allow these exigencies to impede the work that needs doing.

Surely, it makes a difference that the ethical posture I embrace in this book is not simply an ethic of ingenuity but an ethic of *incarnation* as well. I write as an insider to the Christian tradition and view God's incarnation in Jesus of Nazareth as the central claim of that tradition. Moreover, I interpret that incarnation as an act of audacious Divine Way-Making that reveals God's own preference for confronting evil with the tools of courageous creativity and fierce compassion instead of dominating power or violence. I understand this revelation not as a one-time event in the dusty past but as a persistent truth about who God was in the past, is in the present, and will be in the future. God was, is, and will be ingeniously divine and divinely ingenious—not for the sake of innovation itself or even divinity itself but in order to heal that which is broken, redirect that which has gotten off course, and love into new being that which has lost its vitality.

Without the Incarnation or some such guiding norm, an ethic of ingenuity is amoral. It is not, in other words, an ethic. Co-defined by the Incarnation, however, ingenuity begins to take shape, to have direction—and not just any shape or direction, but a christic one. Thus, I have been interested in this book to explore the historical reality and potential promise of a christomorphic or Christ-shaped ethic, a way of seeing and being that is rooted in a trinitarian sensibility where God is the Ingenious Divine; Jesus as the Christ is Ingenuity Incarnate—humanity reconfigured in the shape of Compassionate Way-Making; and the Spirit is the ongoing vitality and proleptic lure of the Way-Making God who was and is and will be forever.

It is important to note that according to this perspective, God does not embrace the ingenious strategy of incarnation for the sole purpose of surprising and shaming the "principalities and powers" (Ephesians 6:12) of first century Palestine. Rather, this strategy is chosen because it is commensurate with the ultimate divine aim for all time, which includes healing, transformation, reconciliation, and redemption. An ethic of ingenuity contributes to this aim by engendering personal dignity, enabling moral clarity and responsibility, and encouraging repentance, all the while avoiding the destructive methods and consequences of an "ethic" of mastery. By becoming incarnate in Jesus, God embodies and thereby signals divine approval of a way of being aimed at reconciliation and mutual flourishing. This way requires the courageous confrontation of unjust relations, systems, and institutions. Such confrontation is motivated by an impulse toward empathy rather than empire, and it aims at deep transformation over the long haul, not swift but fleeting victory over the so-called enemy. Jesus' third way—the confrontation of evil by blazing a middle path between violence and submission to violence—is ultimately the way of loving one's enemies. To choose not to react violently against the other is to love one's opponent enough to desire their flourishing rather than their destruction. It is to recognize that like them, our lives, too, are marked by long-standing habits of perverted love, and like them, we need forgiveness and grace.

The way of incarnation and ingenuity includes, also, the sober recognition that "successes" will likely be few, far between, and, in this world at least, always partial. After all, incarnation is a slow and fallible process. It depends on finite beings and bodily presence, on the development of relationships, on the assumption of risk, and on the very real possibility of failure. It occurs within and is subject to the vagaries of temporal reality and embodied existence. It has no magic wand to wave, no impenetrable force to impose. Even if it did have such tools at its disposal, it would choose not to use them, for such use would amount to the negation of the aim of mutual flourishing, the destruction of the spirit of compassion that drives this effort. "Imperial power," Sharon Welch notes, "is not only corrosive and destructive, but also profoundly unimaginative."[33] In order to avoid the tools of mastery and keep the spirit of resistance and transformation alive, this way employs ingenuity and imagination—serious play to tackle complex and long-standing problems.

I describe this ethical stance as "christic imagination" based on my conviction that God's incarnation in Jesus constituted, among other things, an impressively imaginative way to bring a word of hope and healing to a world broken by injustice, indifference, and the disease of the love of rule. Using God's act of incarnation and Jesus' life and death as a template, I think of christic imagination as a way of being in the world and of confronting moral challenges that is shaped more profoundly by creativity and "spunk" than fear or anger. Certainly, fear is a natural and sometimes helpful response to exploitation and impending violence. It can generate energy and courage, for instance. Anger, too, can produce constructive results. But both fear and anger can easily become narrowing emotions—emotions that function to reduce one's options, to limit one's vision. When not tempered by other feelings, fear and anger become destructive of self and other. Alternatively, one can respond to entrenched ethical challenges with despair or ennui, feeling powerless or unmoved in their wake. More debilitating than anger and fear, these emotions feed passivity, acquiescence, and self-loathing.

Somewhere between the extremes of fear and despair—between volatile self-destruction and disillusioned passivity—is what we might think of as spunky imagination. This disposition is neither naïvely utopian nor cynical. It does not have time or energy for impractical pipedreams or escapist fantasy. It harbors no illusions of purity, simplicity, or unanimity. It does, however, hold doggedly to narratives of hope and transformation—telling and re-telling the stories about the one who escaped, the few who resisted, the handful who together made a difference. Covetously, hope is kept alive against all odds. In addition to the old tales, the fresh play and perspective of the young are food for the journey, sparks for the imagination. And the imagination needs continual sparking and igniting if it is to have the vibrancy and endurance to fight the good fight, to keep on keepin' on when the odds are overwhelmingly in favor of business as usual. Art, music, dance, theater, literature, and plain old play feed the creative spirit, working the muscles of the imagination as myriad perspectives, angles, emotions, melodies, plot lines, and possibilities are presented and tried on for size.

NEW BEING

Ultimately, what drives and sustains the imagination is a compelling vision—a vision that grasps, a vision that transforms, a vision that enlivens and empowers its bearer to live as if that vision were reality, even when all evidence points in the opposite direction. This kind of compelling, enlivening vision is precisely what Jesus had. His was a vision of the kingdom or kin-dom of God—a place where justice and mercy, peace and abundance would reign supreme; a time when all would be included and no one would go hungry, be imprisoned, or feel unworthy. What a vision this was in his day—so transgressive of the norm, so contrary to the status quo! What a vision this is in *our* day as well! The miracle of Jesus' existence—what sets him apart from others—is that his faithful embodiment of that boundary-breaking, liberative vision was and is made available to others so that we, too, can become grasped by its reality and empowered by its energy. Jesus' way of leaning into that vision through the ordinary details of his living and the extraordinary character of his dying was unprecedented. In fact, he bodied forth that vision so perfectly that he carved out a new space, blazed a new path, and created a whole new option for being.

Jesus' vision and way were challenging, to be sure. They required change, transformation, conversion, and, hence, signaled an end to the status quo. His way was a way without closure, a path permanently open to the winds of the Spirit and to the movement of freedom. The power brokers of his day—those who benefited from the way things were—attempted to squelch the vision by murdering its bearer, but the vision would not die. Rising unexpectedly from the tomb, that vision of a time when and place where God's way of being will prevail and the forces of evil will disappear at last continues to be resurrected even today, in small ways and large, in individual lives and entire communities. The key to its perseverance is imagination. Without imagination, no other order of things is conceivable. There would be no alternatives to the logic of empire and domination, to the beat of market values and commodity culture that pulses through the airwaves and creates the background music of First World existence in a new millennium. Without imagination, there would be only one story to tell, one transcript of events, one all-defining and constraining doxa. Imagination powers the courage and the vision to foster fresh perspectives, devise new strategies, and reinvent ourselves again and again as new challenges and obstacles come our way.

CHRISTIC IMAGINATION

Imagination is "christic" when it is shaped by the vision and way of being in the world embodied by Jesus the Christ, incarnation of God. Thus, where "imagination" has no necessary content, aim, or methodological parameters, *christic* imagination does involve such specifics. Christic imagination is spunk and creativity in service of the kin-dom of God. It is the incarnation or embodiment of reflection and action aimed at mutual flourishing. This aim directs and disciplines the means by which imagination is enacted, requiring that intractable problems, formidable foes, and our own false starts and blunders be confronted with the principle of mercy and without the coercion of violence.[34]

The possibilities for confronting problems in a mode of christic imagination are endless, as expansive as the human mind and the creative spirit. Guided by the life and death of Jesus, the possibilities reach always in the direction of loving, justice-seeking transformation. Inspired by God's Incarnation, they sometimes take surprising shapes and unorthodox avenues. When confronted by the intransigence of evil, christic imagination incarnates ingenuity, looking to the early accounts of God's brilliant overcoming of Satan for inspiration, listening carefully to Jesus' surprising but sage advice about derailing unjust systems of power, and resurrecting these age-old strategies in response to contemporary challenges. Christic imagination is inspired and reinvigorated by stories from throughout history, including those from the early Christian church, medieval Europe, African-American culture, your workplace, and my neighborhood.

To be enlivened with christic imagination is to dare to dream of a more humane world, a more just world, a more merciful world. It is to respond to the inhumanity, injustice, and callousness of present conditions not with despair but with spunky resistance and stubborn creativity. It is to be on the lookout for an interesting wrinkle, unexpected gap in logic, or blind spot that can be used to expose unjust policies, awaken moral sensibilities, and open up constructive dialogue aimed at mutual flourishing. To face the world in the mode of christic imagination is to be armed with the disarming tools of wit and humor. It is to respond to entrenched bigotries, institutionalized inequalities, and long-standing presumptions and habits of mastery with serious playfulness, dead set on transforming those evils but smart enough to realize that their upending will require deep pools of patience and steady waves of inspiration and camaraderie.

Viewed through the lens of christic imagination, the world and its myriad challenges to mutual flourishing look less like insurmountable obstacles than interesting problems ripe for solving. Racism, poverty, environmental destruction, and First World consumerism appear neither as impenetrable conglomerates nor as separable and disconnected phenomena but rather as complex puzzles whose pieces need to be carefully analyzed for distinctive shape, shared features, relationship to larger wholes, and potential interconnections with other pieces. As any die-hard puzzle-worker knows, stubborn persistence and a constantly re-tooled imagination are the key ingredients to eventual success— the tenacity to stay with the task even after the tedium has set in and the big picture is not yet in focus—as well as the agility and daring to try new approaches, make unprecedented connections, and picture a different outcome.

Concrete examples of this kind of creative problem-solving abound and need to be lifted up as signs of hope and cause for celebration. Close to home and on the other side of the world, in multinational companies and small-town churches, imaginations are effectively at work in service of the common good. An example from the corporate context comes from the world of high-end furniture making. Herman Miller, Inc., may be the second-largest office furniture company in the world, but its eighty-year record of world-class, award-winning innovation has been powered not primarily by capitalism's unholy trinity of productivity, efficiency, and profit but by a different trio of values: respect for the dignity and well-being of workers, care for the natural environment, and a desire to make the world a better place. When the company's founder, D. J. DePree, visited the home of his first plant's millwright after the worker's death, he was humbled to encounter for the first time this man's breadth of talent and vision. "God was dealing with me about this whole thing, the attitude toward working people," DePree reflected. "I began to realize that we were either all ordinary or all extraordinary. And by the time I reached the front porch of our house, I had concluded that we are all extraordinary. My whole attitude had changed." Still committed to that 1927 revelation and DePree's subsequent proclamation that a business should be "rightly judged by its humanity," Herman Miller's workers are today shareholders in the company and are regularly "encouraged to think and act like owners."[35] Together, they build workplaces and products that honor the integrity of creation. Specifically, all products and programs are created according to an official "Design for Environment" (DfE) protocol that aims, by the year 2020, "to achieve a range of sustainability targets, including zero landfill and zero hazardous waste generation."[36] As author William Greider notes, "In a business sector notorious for pollution, Herman Miller became a pioneer in assuming responsibility for systematically reducing the ecological consequences of its production."[37] The company's CEO Brian Walker notes unapologetically that Herman Miller, Inc., aims to create not only world-class furniture but "a better world for present and future generations."[38] Toward that end, Walker and the other 7,500 employees embrace ingenuity as a core strategy.

Moving from the multinational, corporate arena to the hot issue in my urban neighborhood these days, the demise of public schools in America is an issue ripe for ingenious response. At stake is not only the caliber of the American workforce and, hence, the nation's economic health in the years ahead, but democracy itself, our nation's "gift" to the world. As we are only slowly coming to realize, an uneducated citizenry is a politically and civically anesthetized citizenry. The failure of public education in America is resulting in masses of essentially disenfranchised people without the means or will to make their voices heard. In communities across the nation, public schools have basically been abandoned by the upper and middle classes. As a result, the segment of the population with the least money, the least education, the lowest voter turnout, the worst housing and healthcare, and the worst jobs is left to populate and care for what has traditionally been a pillar of American democracy and enterprise: K-12 public education. In my urban community of Jackson, Mississippi, the public school demographic is not only overwhelmingly of color but also overwhelmingly poor. Of the children who attend public schools, 98 percent are African American, and an overwhelming majority (more than 80 percent) qualifies for free-lunch programs. In truth, nearly everyone who can find a financial way to leave the system does so. Only the poor kids whose families have no other option, and a tiny handful of others, remain. Not surprisingly, the public schools in Jackson are by and large substandard. Without resources and broadly based community support, buildings and grounds cannot be properly maintained and expanded, teachers cannot be paid competitive salaries, and learning materials cannot be kept up to date or enriched. Is it any wonder that people with means leave the system and that the system is failing to equip the most vulnerable members of our communities for meaningful, productive, and socially responsible lives? Where is the hope for these children and, by extension, for the future of American democracy, industry, and civic life? In a state with the lowest median household income in the nation, the problem will not be solved with money.[39] What shape might a little embodied ingenuity, a dose of christic imagination, take in response to this complex and long-standing problem?

Numerous responses are imaginable. One imagined response that I have seen incarnated began ten years ago, when a handful of people at a mid-sized church in my neighborhood that included a small private Montessori school dreamt of making what they considered to be the wonders of a Montessori education available to more than the forty-five tuition-paying children their school served. The church had a strong commitment to social justice, but amidst all its other outreach ministries, it could not seem to raise enough money for more than one or two tuition scholarships per year to the Montessori school. Was the school destined to serve only the affluent? After much soul searching, an intriguing idea was put on the table: What if the Montessori model of education could be integrated into the struggling public school system? From most directions, the question was treated as an absolute absurdity since the start-up costs for Montessori teacher training and learning materials would be considerable for even a wealthy school district, much less a poor district in the poorest state in the union. However, three years and countless proposals, frustrations, working papers, alliances, and meetings later, the Jackson Public School system unveiled its public Montessori initiative: two elementary "schools within a school"—one in predominantly black South Jackson and one in the more racially integrated North Jackson. The Montessori programs exist side by side with traditional elementary programs, sharing facilities, principals, and also educational philosophies and practices so that the children, teachers, and parents from both the Montessori and the traditional programs benefit from the existence of the Montessori programs. This is a modest experiment, to be sure, but the results to date are encouraging: a rich racial and economic mix of children and families; highly motivated teachers who, while not paid any more than other teachers, are thrilled to be part of "the grand experiment"; academic achievements that rival the best private schools in the area; and high levels of parent and family involvement. Plans for expanding the program into the middle and high school years are underway. There have even been reports of affluent white people wondering if they can get their kids into a public school in Jackson, Mississippi. Wonders never cease! While it may be difficult for those unfamiliar with the unique history, political climate, and economic profile of Mississippi to appreciate it, this small public school experiment, though still in its fledgling stages and struggling with its share of setbacks and challenges, is a dramatic example of the potential for innovative thinking to offer effective solutions to long-standing and complex problems.

These two contemporary stories of ingenuity, one multinational and one local, emerge from different theological traditions (Dutch Reformed and Episcopalian). Although neither of them foregrounds the theological, each is nevertheless pervaded by hopes and convictions forged in and sustained by Christian communities of faith and practice. An ethic of ingenuity is by no means the special province of Christians or of religious people, but it *is* a key part of Christianity's legacy and needs to be claimed as such. Those interested in cultivating christic imagination need not look far for concrete examples of ingenuity incarnate—they exist all over the country and world and are both large-scale and small.

A well-known large-scale example is the enormously successful Jubilee 2000 campaign, named for the biblical concept of Jubilee in which slaves are periodically set free and debts periodically canceled in order to put a check on human tendencies toward overaccumulation and forgetfulness of the poor. Begun as a grassroots movement in Great Britain, this campaign to cancel or significantly reduce the debt of the world's poorest nations eventually played a key role in G7 talks and policy developments at the World Bank and the IMF.[40] What began as an outrageous, ingenious, biblically inspired idea from the margins—that the ancient Jubilee tradition could speak a prophetic word about global poverty to today's political and economic power brokers *and* be heard by them—became incarnate in stunningly effective ways.

A less celebrated but no less remarkable exercise in justice-seeking ingenuity is the Ithaca HOURs movement in Ithaca, New York. Developed in response to the ways that "big-box" stores such as Wal-Mart siphon money and small businesses from local communities, residents of this small city in upstate New York developed their own local currency that works in conjunction with U. S. currency. So in Ithaca, you can pay for your Ben & Jerry's ice cream cone, your doctor's visit, or a new pair of shoes with a combination of Ithaca HOURs and U. S. dollars. While the money spent at national big-box stores heads straight for corporate offices across the country or world, Ithaca HOURs stay in Ithaca, circulating again and again and helping to keep local businesses, and the strong communal ties and civic health they support, alive and thriving.[41] Local currencies like this have now been developed in dozens of communities around the world, all with the intention of keeping local cultures, relationships, businesses, and communities vibrant in today's globalized economy. For those who worry about the corrosive effects of that economy on families, communities, and local environments, local currencies are an ingenious antidote whose circulations of an alternative form of money are not nearly as important as the communal energy, good will, and commitment to the common good they fund.

The challenge of building lives, communities, institutions, and systems that are humane, just, and even pleasurable is ongoing and immense. It is easy to become overwhelmed by the magnitude and complexity of the challenge, which is why it is so important to collect and lift up the ideas and practices that are already working, the incarnations of ingenuity and christic imagination we see around us.[42] Simply knowing about, celebrating, and learning from efforts such as those mentioned above can inspire us to shift our own imaginations into higher gear. Communities of faith can take the lead in this work, searching out and celebrating the ingenious incarnations of hope, solidarity, and healing generated in our communities; proclaiming the "good news" of embodied practices of hospitality and transformation to a world hungry for reasons to hope. In our churches, we can become newly acquainted with the Ingenious Divine of the Incarnation: the One the early church at the margins of power held so dear; the One who challenged systems of individual and communal destruction with wit and ingenuity rather than force and violence; the One who has inspired Christian communities on the underside of power not only to survive with dignity but to resist their oppression and transform their oppressors with defiant creativity and ferocious love.

This dimension of God's being should be especially compelling to children and youth, whose natural passion for imagination and play is still vibrant and who instinctively question the status quo. Introducing our young people to the Way-Making God could be a wonderful gift to them, as well as to the church that struggles to keep them plugged in. It would give them permission to question, to resist, and to unleash their creativity. It would also give them guidance, role models, and a challenging agenda for these quests so their contestations and innovations could contribute to the kin-dom of God. Young people today are *ready* for meaning; they are ready to work hard and creatively for a good thing. Like the rest of us, they are well aware of the emotional and moral emptiness of consumer-focused living. Nevertheless, new product development and communication technologies are today's cutting edge; they are where the energy and creativity are; and that, of course, is where young people will always be. A theological vision highlighting the Ingenious Divine would appeal precisely to the youthful desire to be on the cutting edge, to be creatively engaged in the world around them. It would also channel that desire in genuinely meaningful directions, inviting young people to use their imaginations and deploy their ethical edginess to address today's pressing problems. When religion is less about obedience, authority, and decorum and more about ingenuity, energy, and justice, it will have a chance with today's youth. Reminding our young people that they were created in the image of God the Way-Maker, *imago imaginationis,* and authorizing them to develop life-affirming, justice-seeking disciplines of creativity—in other words, to be disciples of Jesus the Christ, Ingenuity Incarnate—may be the church's best hope for relevance with today's youth.

A Christian ethic of ingenuity might also become a compelling point of dialogue with other religious traditions, most of which have their own indigenous resources for such an ethic. One thinks, for instance, of the Buddha's "skill-in-means," a virtue expounded in the *Lotus Sutra* and exemplified in any number of the morally instructive Jataka tales. Here, we find stories of how the Buddha used "expedient" means to reach a diversity of audiences. Recognizing that what is an effective form of teaching or guidance for one person may not work with another person, the Buddha embraces a wide range of approaches, perspectives, and incarnations in order to guide people toward understanding and awakening. Some of these approaches are quite surprising, unorthodox, and even offensive, given prevailing assumptions of what wisdom ought to look like, how truth comes to be, and who within society has wisdom and truth. For instance, in these narratives the Buddha is typically disguised as someone else in order to teach a lesson. It is also not uncommon for the Buddha to use deception in order to effect the good, as for instance in "The Parable of the Burning House," where he coaxes children out of a burning house with a well-intended untruth.[43] Despite his ethically edgy methods, the Buddha's skill-in-means is at all times an instrument of compassion; it is edginess for the sake of enlightenment. The fact that other religious traditions have resources for an ethic of ingenuity makes it an interesting prospect for dialogue and shared projects. The truth is that interreligious dialogue has often required Christians to put christology on a back burner in order to foreground theological locii that show more dialogic promise. Yet, the theme of ingenuity brings christology front and center. For Christians who appreciate the christological origins and framework of an ethic of ingenuity, Christ would no longer be a stumbling block to dialogue but its main avenue.[44]

CONCLUSION

To live in the mode of christic imagination means that one responds to the world with creativity and flexibility, with a commitment to the nonviolent transformation of systems of violence and domination, and toward the end of participating in the in-breaking of the reign of God that Jesus' life inaugurated. This mode of being, commitment, and aim were enfleshed in a paradigm-shifting, reality-changing way by God's incarnation in Jesus. That surprising, shape-shifting, and morality-exploding divine move found expression in the divine deception motif of the early church fathers. As we look back in order to move forward, sifting through layers of tradition for gems of insight—tools for today's work—it is certainly worth our while to linger over this early Christian trope. It behooves us to reflect on its portrayal of evil and God's ingenious response to it. For us, as for early Christians such as Ireneaus, Gregory of Nyssa, and Augustine, the deception of the devil narrative does not articulate the whole truth or give us the full picture about God, Jesus, or human existence. But it does gesture provocatively toward one set of important truths—a set whose implications for christology, theological ethics, and ecclesiology in our contemporary context are worth serious consideration.

As we have seen, this narrative highlights the presence of a non-normative morality at the very heart of the Christian story. It proposes that God tricks evil into its own undoing. God becomes incarnate, exploding common-sense assumptions about the worth of the material, earthly realm by deeming that realm worthy of divine habitation. Beyond this dramatic revaluation, the act of divine enfleshment constitutes an ingenious strategy aimed at discrediting evil without adopting its methods or aim. The incarnate God functions as a kind of lure, drawing evil out into the open, clarifying its myopic assumptions and aspirations and magnifying its true character as love unhinged, power unbounded, and appetite unlimited. This magnification initiates a new ethical moment—an unprecedented if transitory clarity about good and evil and a compelling vision of a world and a way of mutual flourishing. The vibrancy of vision calls into being a new or renewed moral community, now summoned by the weight of the revelation to choose the good and resist evil, to open ourselves to the reorientation of love, the abdication or limiting of dominating power, and the curbing of appetite.

In a deepening of the commitments and strategies signaled by the sheer fact of the Incarnation, God enfleshes a very particular human praxis—a life (and death) characterized by love of God and neighbor; a life (and death) that resists and rejects, in word and deed, the perversion of love—the love of rule and the logic of empire. In both moments of Divine self-expression— the Incarnation and *this* particular incarnate life—the message is clear: Evil, the love of rule, is to be confronted with fiery compassion, the rule of love. Love perverted can become love redeemed, love recentered. In addition, that confrontation and transformation will demand not only courage and compassion but also, at times, creativity and cunning. Like the Incarnation itself and the defiantly compassionate praxis of Jesus of Nazareth, resisting evil without embracing its insidious logic calls for a combination of defiance, spunk, and creativity. For Christians, living responsibly and faithfully in today's complex world requires christic imagination. It calls, that is, for a Christian ethic of incarnation and ingenuity.

NOTES

Introduction: Child's Play?

1. Ann McGovern, *Stone Soup* (New York: Scholastic, 1968).

2. Nancy Green, *The Bigger Giant* (New York: Scholastic, 1963).

3. For a discussion of how the trickster genre contributes positively to the socialization of the child, see David M. Abrams and Brian Sutton-Smith, "The Development of the Trickster in Children's Narrative," *The Journal of American Folklore* 90 (1977): 29–47.

4. William Bennett, *Book of Virtues* (New York: Simon & Schuster, 1994). For a more recent account that complements Bennett's study, see Vigen Guroian's *Tending the Heart of Virtue: How Classic Stories Awaken a Child's Moral Imagination* (Oxford: Oxford University Press, 2002).

5. McGovern, *Stone Soup*.

6. Claire Huchet Bishop, *The Five Chinese Brothers* (New York: Penguin Putnam Books, 1938).

7. Leo Lionni, *Swimmy* (New York: Scholastic, 1963).

8. Green, *The Bigger Giant*.

9. See the award-winning adaptation of this tale by Janet Stevens, entitled *Tops & Bottoms* (New York: Scholastic, 1995).

10. Darby Kathleen Ray, *Deceiving the Devil: Atonement, Abuse, and Ransom* (Cleveland: The Pilgrim Press, 1998).

11. Margaret Urban Walker, *Moral Understandings: A Feminist Study in Ethics* (New York: Routledge, 1998), 8, 17.

12. Garth Kasimu Baker-Fletcher, *Dirty Hands: Christian Ethics in a Morally Ambiguous World* (Minneapolis: Fortress Press, 2000), 9.

13. Cited by David Batstone, *From Conquest to Struggle* (Albany: State University of New York, 1991), 14.

14. Jeffrey Stout, *Ethics after Babel: The Languages of Morals and Their Discontents* (Boston: Beacon Press, 1988), 86. Stout is undeterred by the reality of multiple moral postures, unlike others who yearn for a return to a golden age of consensus or who despair over the impossibility of genuine dialogue and common projects. See, for example, Alisdair McIntyre's *After Virtue* (Notre Dame, Indiana: University of Notre Dame Press, 1984), x. Stout is also more sanguine about the possibility of ethics than John Caputo, whose critique of ethics as usual is nevertheless quite compelling. See *Against Ethics: Contributions to a Poetics of Obligation with Constant Reference to Deconstruction* (Bloomington: Indiana University Press, 1993).

15. John Caputo, *Against Ethics*, 235–36. I am wary of drawing too sharp a line between Caputo's position and mine because I find his arguments so compelling. I do not want to suggest, for instance, that Caputo is making such patronizing assumptions, though I do think it is possible to read him that way. My more general concern is that postmodern critiques tend to *over*problematize categories such as agency, autonomy, and subjectivity—removing them as goods just when marginalized groups are beginning to claim them.

16. See, for example, Luce Irigaray, *Speculum of the Other Woman* (Ithaca, New York: Cornell University Press, 1985) and *This Sex Which Is Not One* (Ithaca, New York: Cornell University Press, 1985), both English translations. See also Judith Butler, *Bodies That Matter: On the Discursive Limits of "Sex"* (New York: Routledge, 1993).

17. Charles Fishman's fascinating account of what he calls "the Wal-Mart effect" is an excellent example of the vortex-like power of a master narrative or, in this case, corporation. As his study recounts, even those individuals and businesses who eschew Wal-Mart find themselves inevitably shaped by its decisions and practices. In relation to a power of that scale, individual freedom appears neutralized or useless. Charles Fishman, *The Wal-Mart Effect* (New York: Penguin, 2006).

18. According to Irigaray, when women respond to the dominant discourse of patriarchy with liberative mimesis, they imitate the letter of that language but by no means its spirit. They take on the role of the subjugated "other" with an intentionality that turns a deadly serious script into parody, mimicry. When women deliberately play the role of "other," there emerges "some remainder"–something extra that cannot be defined by the character's role, something that resists inscription and that is, consequently, truly Other than the Same. (*This Sex Which Is Not One,* 28). For Butler, performativity is not a single performance or deliberative act but the ongoing process through which cultural, ethical, and religious norms are created and sustained. Performativity is the reiterative practice by which the dominant discourse is inscribed and reinscribed. It is the constant repetition of norms that occurs every hour of every day without necessary intention or forethought. It happens naturally as a part of ordinary existence in a culture in which, for instance, girls are continually "girled" and boys "boyed." Such ordinary repetitions of common sense rules and identities function to stabilize and secure the prevailing norms. They obscure their constructed nature and make them seem second-nature, part of the natural order, "the way things are." In performing one's gender—in embodying or fulfilling cultural expectations of how women or men act and self-identify—one rematerializes the norms that regulate sexuality, hence adding to the authorizing force of the dominant discourse. To become a subject, a person or agent who is culturally intelligible or interpretable, is to reproduce norms. It is to perform and hence reinforce the idealizations that constitute one's culture. See Butler, *Bodies That Matter,* 2–15, 131–37, 231–41.

19. Irigaray, *This Sex Which Is Not One,* 76, 80.

20. Butler, *Bodies That Matter,* 122.

21. Rosi Braidotti, *Nomadic Subjects: Embodiment and Sexual Difference in Contemporary Feminist Theory* (New York: Columbia University Press, 1994), 6.

22. Julian Wolfreys, *The Rhetoric of Affirmative Resistance: Dissonant Identities from Carroll to Derrida* (New York: Palgrave Macmillan, 1997).

23. See especially Pierre Bourdieu, *Outline of a Theory of Practice,* trans. Richard Nice (London: Cambridge University Press, 1977), 164–171.

24. Ibid., 168–69.

25. Sharon Welch offers this basic definition of postcolonialism: "By 'postcolonial' activists and scholars refer to a political situation in which the process of colonization (economic, cultural, and political conquest) is both contested and relatively visible. The term does *not* mean that domination has disappeared. While many of the colonial powers in Africa and the Americas have been defeated, the process of political, economic, cultural, and military domination continues in other forms." *After Empire: The Art and Ethos of Enduring Peace* (Minneapolis: Fortress Press, 2004), xv–xvi.

26. "The discourse of cultural colonialism," says Homi Bhabha, always involves both "the mother culture and its bastards"—both that which is officially authorized and that which is disavowed. Despite its intentions, colonial power creates or produces that which is officially disavowed, where "the trace of what is disavowed is not repressed but repeated as something *different*—a mutation, a hybrid." Homi K. Bhabha, "Signs Taken for Wonders: Questions of Ambivalence and Authority under a Tree outside Delhi, May 1817," *Critical Inquiry* 12 (Autumn 1985): 153.

27. Dube, "Postcoloniality, Feminist Spaces, and Religion" in *Postcolonialism, Feminism and Religious Discourse*, ed. Laura E. Donaldson and Kwok Pui-lan (New York: Routledge, 2002), 115–16.

28. Bhabha, "Signs Taken for Wonders," 155–62.

29. Both Irigaray and Butler have been criticized for constructing what amounts to a "virtual" politics—that is, a radical language that is, in the final analysis, ahistorical, individualistic, and disembodied. Even while they contend that "bodies matter" and spend impressive energies on theories of materiality and embodiment, their critics argue that Irigaray and Butler offer precious few resources for those whose fleshly bodies are daily embattled by systemic poverty and prejudice. At best, they empower individuals to "play" with their subject positions, assuming new self-transformative roles as needed and hence reinscribing, for all their pretensions of subversion, the consumerist tendencies of the master narrative of contemporary capitalism that fetishizes and commodifies change, fluidity, and novelty. See, for example, Jana Sawicki, *Disciplining Foucault: Feminism, Power, and the Body* (New York: Routledge, 1991); and Elisa Glick, "Sex Positive," *Feminist Review* 64, (Spring 2000): 19–45.

30. See James C. Scott's two books, *Weapons of the Weak: Everyday Forms of Peasant Resistance* (New Haven: Yale University Press, 1985); and *Domination and the Arts of Resistance: Hidden Transcripts* (New Haven: Yale University Press, 1990).

31. Scott, *Weapons of the Weak*, 33.

32. Scott's sojourn among the Malay peasants opened his eyes to an alter-world of "everyday resistance" that caused him to question popular analyses of subjugated existence that rely on concepts of "false consciousness" and "hegemony." For more on these two concepts, see Antonio Gramsci, *Selections from the Prison Notebooks*, ed. Quintin Hoare (New York: New York University Press, 1971) and Joseph V. Femia, *Gramsci's Political Thought* (London: Oxford University Press, 1981).

33. Scott, *Weapons of the Weak*, 30.

34. Ibid., 30.

35. Ibid., 30–31.

36. Ibid., 36.

37. Scott, *Domination and the Arts of Resistance*, 18.

38. Ibid., 190–91.

39. It is important to acknowledge the risk involved in such consideration. I do not request a moral reconsideration of deception lightly. From adultery to Enron, the practice of deception usually yields heartache and suffering. It is not to be romanticized. But maybe, just maybe, it has a positive role to play on occasion–specifically, on those occasions characterized by such deep inequalities of power that no other option for self-expression and self-determination among the marginalized is available.

Chapter 1: The Theo-Logic of an Ethic of Ingenuity

1. *Toward a Christian Political Ethics* (Fortress Press, 1983), 80.

2. The ideas explored in this chapter constitute an extension of those presented in the final chapter of my 1998 book, *Deceiving the Devil: Atonement, Abuse, and Ransom*, used by permission of the Pilgrim Press.

3. The resistance is perhaps staunchest among theologians themselves. As Nicholas P. Constas notes based on an extensive review of the question, "Disdain . . . for the theory of divine deception is clearly an established topos within contemporary scholarship." Constas, "The Last Temptation of Satan: Divine Deception in the Greek Patristic Interpretations of the Passion Narrative," *Harvard Theological Review* 97, no. 2 (2004): 146. Among the statements Constas

cites are those that characterize the deception motif as "childish and immoral," "perverted and repulsive," and "unimportant and implausible."

4. Constas, for instance, notes that "a remarkable number of Greek patristic thinkers gave expression to the theory." Ibid., 1. And Kathleen Ashley vouches that in patristic theology, both Greek and Latin, the divine deception motif "enjoyed great popularity and met no serious criticism." Ashley, "The Guiler Beguiled: Christ and Satan as Theological Tricksters in Medieval Religious Literature," *Criticism* 24, no. 2 (1982): 129.

5. For a more thorough discussion of the liabilities of "devil-talk" and the God versus Satan motif, see my *Deceiving the Devil*, 125–29.

6. Says Augustine: "It became clear to me that corruptible things are good; if they were supremely good they could not be corrupted, but also if they were not good at all they could not be corrupted. . . . If they were deprived of all goodness, they would be altogether nothing; therefore as long as they are, they are good. Thus whatsoever things are, are good; and that evil whose origin I sought is not a substance, because if it were a substance it would be good." See *Confessions,* trans. F. J. Sheed (Indianapolis: Hackett, 1942), 118–19.

7. Augustine makes this point repeatedly in his *Confessions.* For example, in Book Four, he reflects: "If material things please you then praise God for them, but turn back your love upon Him who made them. . . . The good that you love is from Him: and insofar as it is likewise *for* Him it is good and lovely; but it will be rightly turned into bitterness, if it is unrightly loved and He deserted by whom it is." Ibid., 60.

8. As Augustine puts it: ". . . when I asked what is iniquity, I realized that it was not a substance but a swerving of the will which is turned toward lower things and away from You, O God, who are the supreme substance; so that it casts away what is most inward to it and swells greedily for outward things." Ibid., 121.

9. From Augustine's powerful articulation of this dynamic of self-imposed bondage: "I was bound, not with the iron of another's chains, but by my own iron will. The enemy held my will; and of it he made a chain and bound me. Because my will was perverse it changed to lust, and lust yielded to become habit, and habit not resisted became necessity. These were like links hanging one on another—which is why I have called it a chain—and their hard bondage held me bound hand and foot." Ibid., 135.

10. Cited by L. W. Grensted, *A Short History of the Doctrine of the Atonement* (Manchester, England: Manchester University Press, 1920), 37–38. Other thinkers who affirmed the notion include Gregory of Nyssa, Ambrose, and Augustine.

11. Augustine, *Confessions,* 40.

12. See Eugene TeSelle, "The Cross as Ransom," *Journal of Early Christian Studies* 4, no. 2 (1996): 151.

13. For instance, it appears prominently in two anonymous, widely distributed histories of salvation written during the later Middle Ages, the *Speculum Humanae Salvationis* and the *Biblia Pauperum,* as well as in drama cycles aimed at religious laypeople. See Ashley, "The Guiler Beguiled": 126–37.

14. I am indebted to Nicholas P. Constas for this discussion of the cultural context of the divine deception motif. Constas, "The Last Temptation of Satan."

15. Cited by Constas; ibid., 140.

16. Ibid., 140.

17. Ibid., 141.

18. Ibid., 142.

19. Ibid., 142–43.

20. Ibid., 147. Constas goes on to explore the image of "Christ the Worm" in the Greek patristic tradition.

21. Ireneaus, *Against Heresies* 5.12.2 in *Ante-Nicene Christian Library*, ed. Alexander Roberts and James Donaldson, vol. 9 (Edinburgh: T. & T. Clark, 1869), 112.

22. *Against Heresies* 5.1.1; ibid., 56. Athanasius also uses a military analogy, asserting that Christ is "just like a general conducting a war, who devised a great and wondrous strategy, and so assumes the appearance of one staggering under Satan's power, so that when the enemy draws near he might completely subdue him." Cited in Constas, "The Last Temptation of Satan," 151.

23. *Against Heresies* 5.1.1; ibid., 56.

24. *Against Heresies* 3.23.2; ibid., 364.

25. See *Against Heresies* 5.21.3; ibid., 113.

26. Origen's rendition of the divine deception trope includes the idea that God is moved by concern for the victims of injustice to create a non-violent response to evil's mastering dynamics: "There was a just and noble king, who was waging a war against an unjust tyrant, but trying to avoid a violent and bloody conflict, because some of his own men were fighting on the tyrant's side, and he wanted to free them, not destroy them. He therefore adopted a uniform of the tyrant's men, until he managed to persuade them to desert and to return to their proper kingdom, and succeeded in 'binding the strong man' in fetters, destroying his 'principalities and powers,' and carrying off those he held captive." Cited in Constas, "The Last Temptation of Satan," 151.

27. Here, I employ ideas from Emmanuel Levinas, especially *Totality and Infinity: An Essay on Exteriority*, trans. Alphonso Lingis (Pittsburgh: Duquesne University Press, 1969).

28. Gregory of Nyssa, *The Great Catechism* 15, in *Nicene and Post-Nicene Fathers of the Christian Church*, ed. Philip Schaff and Henry Wace, vol. 5 (New York: Christian Literature Co., 1893), 487.

29. This view of the body and bodily realm as repulsive extended well into the medieval period and beyond. An example of how pervasive it was can be seen in this excerpt from a classic medieval sermon, *On the Misery of the Human Condition* by Pope Innocent III (d. 1216): "Man was formed of dust, slime, and ashes: what is even more vile, of the filthiest seed. He was conceived from the itch of the flesh, in the heat of passion and the stench of lust, and worse yet, with the stain of sin. . . . He will become food for the worm which forever nibbles and digests; a mass of rottenness which will forever stink and reek." Cited in Gloria Fiero, *The Humanistic Tradition, Book 2: Medieval Europe and the World Beyond* (Boston: McGraw Hill, 2002), 97.

30. Ibid.

31. For a fascinating study of the tenacity of early and medieval Christian affirmations of a *bodily* resurrection in spite of widespread cultural devaluations of the body, see Caroline Walker Bynum's *Resurrection of the Body in Western Christianity, 200-1336* (New York: Columbia University Press, 1995).

32. Gregory of Nyssa, *The Great Catechism* 23, 493.

33. Ibid.

34. *The Great Catechism* 22; ibid., 492.

35. *The Great Catechism* 15; ibid., 487.

36. Ibid.

37. *The Great Catechism* 24; ibid., 494. Constas cites an additional reference to the fishhook image in Gregory's sermon on the resurrection, in which God as "Omnipotent Wisdom" caught "the wise one in his cunning and turn[ed] back upon him his clever devices" so that, "having swallowed the bait of the flesh, he was pierced with the fishhook of deity, and so the dragon was caught with the fishhook, just as it is said in the book of Job, 'You shall catch the dragon with a fishhook' (Job 40:25)." Constas, "The Last Temptation of Satan," 144.

38. *The Great Catechism* 23; ibid., 493.

39. *The Great Catechism* 23; ibid., 494.

40. *The Great Catechism* 24; ibid., 494.

41. Ibid.

42. *The Great Catechism* 25; ibid., 495.

43. *The Great Catechism* 26; ibid.

44. Constas notes that God's deception was seen by many early church fathers as the appropriate response to the devil's deception of Eve in the Garden of Eden, when Satan assumed the camouflage of the serpent: "According to the logic of typological recapitulation," says Constas, "it was only right that an act of deception should be undone by deception. . . . The incarnation of the Logos mirrors and thus reverses the 'incarnation' of Satan in the flesh of the serpent.""The Last Temptation of Satan," 155–56.

45. Constas remarks that in Gregory's treatment, "God's deceit, unlike the devil's, was enacted for therapeutic purposes, thereby classifying it among forms of deception culturally acceptable in late antiquity." Ibid., 145.

46. Gregory of Nyssa, *The Great Catechism* 27, 497.

47. Also like them, Augustine did not endorse the motif as a stand-alone theology; rather, it was combined, often uncomfortably, with other construals of divine identity and agency and with other christologies.

48. Augustine, *The Trinity* 4.14.14, in *The Works of St. Augustine*, trans. Edmund Hill, ed. John E. Rotelle, vol. 5 (Brooklyn: New City Press, 1991), 356.

49. Augustine, *On the Holy Trinity* 3.13.13, in *Nicene and Post-Nicene Fathers*, vol. 3, 176.

50. Augustine, *Confessions*, 119.

51. Ibid., 120.

52. Augustine, *On the Trinity* 3.13.13, in *Nicene and Post-Nicene Fathers*, 176.

53. Ibid.

54. Augustine, *On the Trinity* 3.13.10; ibid., 174.

55. Augustine, *On the Trinity* 3.13.13; ibid., 176.

56. Augustine, *The Trinity* 5.13.19, in *The Works of St. Augustine*, vol. 5, 358.

57. Jon Berquist, *Incarnation* (St. Louis, Missouri: Chalice Press, 1999), 11.

58. Ibid., 10–11.

59. Ibid., 12.

60. My thinking about an incarnational theology is profoundly shaped by the work of Sallie McFague, especially *The Body of God* (Minneapolis: Fortress Press, 1993).

61. Ibid., 88.

62. For classic discussions of the genre of parable and its surprising effects, see Dan Otto Via Jr., *The Parables: Their Literary and Existential Dimension* (Minneapolis: Fortress Press, 1967); John Dominic Crossan, *In Parables: The Challenge of the Historical Jesus* (San Francisco: Harper & Row, 1973); and Sallie McFague, *Speaking in Parables: A Study in Metaphor and Theology* (Minneapolis: Fortress Press, 1975).

63. Walter Wink, *Jesus and Nonviolence* (Minneapolis: Fortress Press, 2003), 10–11.

64. Ibid., 15.

65. Wink argues that the striking of the cheek Jesus talks about in this text involves a superior striking an inferior in an attempt to insult, reprimand, or humiliate. Because Jesus singles out the right cheek as the one receiving the hit, the hitter would typically be using the left hand. But since in first-century Palestine the left hand was used only for unclean tasks, the hitting must have involved instead the back of the right hand, indicating that it was a backhand slap and, hence, not a fistfight among equals but an attempt to punish or insult an inferior. In such a situation, concludes

Wink, "retaliation would be suicidal. The only normal response would be cowering submission."
Ibid., 14–15.

66. Ibid., 16.

67. Ibid., 17.

68. Wink points out that "nakedness was taboo in Judaism, and shame fell not on the naked
party, but on the person viewing or causing one's nakedness (Gen. 9:20-27)." Ibid., 20.

69. See the discussion of Scott's work in the introduction to this book.

Chapter 2: Ingenious Incarnations

1. Dorothee Sölle, *Creative Disobedience*, trans. Lawrence W. Denef (Cleveland, Ohio: The
Pilgrim Press, 1995), xxi.

2. These kinds of questions about the relative possibility and integrity of interpreting the
lives and texts of medieval women from a contemporary angle abound in current scholarship in
religious studies, philosophy, literary studies, history, and psychoanalysis. Christine Neufeld sum-
marizes the challenge succinctly: "Medieval textual practices refract the modern notion of the
Author into a myriad of functions. In addition to the poet 'makers' of texts there are the exegeti-
cal interpreters and glossators, not to mention the scribes, copyists and compilers whose inter-
ventions have simultaneously preserved medieval texts for posterity and frustrated our desire
for access to an 'original' document of a medieval mind. If such 'obstacles' obscure our view of
even the most well-known medieval authors, the challenge of 'reading' conventionally invisible
members of medieval society like women becomes that much more daunting." Christine Neufeld,
review of *The Cambridge Companion to Medieval Women's Writing* in *Arthuriana* 14, no. 2 (2004): 90.

3. There are exceptions to this rule, such as Mechthild of Hackeborn, whose scribe was
Gertrude the Great, but as Dyan Elliott points out, "even this celebrated exception is made to
fit the gendered norm. . . . when the Middle English translator renders Mechtild's reference to
her scribe in the masculine." Elliott, "Dominae or Dominatae? Female Mysticism and the Trauma
of Textuality" in *Women, Marriage, and Family in Medieval Christendom*, ed. Constance M. Rousseau
and Joel T. Rosenthal (Kalamazoo, Mich.: Western Michigan University, 1998). For a recent
interesting if contestable discussion of the relationship between nine medieval female saints and
their male "collaborators," see John W. Coakley, *Women, Men, & Spiritual Power: Female Saints and
Their Male Collaborators* (New York: Columbia University Press, 2006).

4. Amy Hollywood, *Sensible Ecstasy: Mysticism, Sexual Difference, and the Demands of History*
(Chicago: University of Chicago Press, 2002), 247.

5. "The Lady Vanishes: The Problem of Women's Absence in Late Medieval and Renaissance
Texts" in *Seeking the Woman in Late Medieval and Renaissance Writings: Essays in Feminist Contextual
Criticism*, ed. Sheila Fisher and Janet E. Halley, vol. 4 (Knoxville, Tenn.: University of Tennessee
Press, 1989).

6. For example, Catherine Innes-Parker reads medieval texts as palimpsets, using insights
developed by Gilbert and Gubar to describe nineteenth-century women's novels. Innes-Parker,
"Subversion and Conformity in Julian's *Revelation*: Authority, Vision and the Motherhood of
God," *Mystic Quarterly* 23, no. 2 (1997): 7–35.

7. Elizabeth A. Dreyer, "Whose Story Is It? The Appropriation of Medieval Mysticism" in
Spiritus 4/2 (Fall 2004), 166–67.

8. While historians tend to date the medieval period from about 600, scholars of religion
often identify the life and writings of Augustine in the fourth to fifth centuries as its beginning.
The year 1600 is commonly used to signal the end of the period.

9. My former Millsaps College colleague, medieval historian Sanford Zale, proposes that
the pre-modern period is generally characterized by the following: (1) a mythic worldview

with the discourse of religion at its center; (2) a theocratic political system; (3) a hierarchical social system in which inequality is the assumed norm; and (4) group identification rather than individualism as the primary context for self-understanding.

10. Quoted in *Working in America: A Humanities Reader,* ed. Robert Sessions and Jack Wortman (Notre Dame, Ind.: University of Notre Dame Press, 1992), 186.

11. Ibid., 186–87.

12. Woman's "place" was by no means completely devoid of power. Some medieval women ran businesses, managed property, and formed guilds. Others were sought out by powerful men as wise counselors or spiritual authorities. However, such women were the exception to the rule and were still ultimately under male authority. If they were considered by those around them as exceptions to the rule of female weakness, their exceptionality merely reiterated that rule.

13. For a good summary of the evidence, see Rosalynn Voaden, *God's Words, Women's Voices: The Discernment of Spirits in the Writing of Late Medieval Women Visionaries* (York, England: York Medieval Press, 1999), 19–24. Representative quotations include: "The male is by nature superior, and the female inferior; the one rules and the other is ruled" (Aristotle); "Pleasure does not venture to bring her wiles and deceptions to bear on the man, but on the woman, and by her means on him. This is a well made point: for in us mind corresponds to man, the senses to woman; and pleasure encounters and holds parlay with the senses first, and through them cheats with her quackery the sovereign mind itself" (Philo); and "You are the Devil's gateway. You are the unsealer of that forbidden tree. You are the first deserter of the divine Law. You are she who persuaded him whom the Devil was not valiant enough to attack. You destroyed so easily God's image, man. On account of your desert, that is death, even the Son of God had to die" (Tertullian). Cited in Voaden, *God's Words, Women's Voices,* 19–24.

14. Ibid., 19–20.

15. Ibid., 92.1, 466–67. In this view, Thomas reiterates Augustine's earlier insight: "I do not see what other help woman would be to men if the purpose of generating was eliminated." Quoted in Teresa M. Shaw, *The Burden of the Flesh* (Minneapolis: Fortress Press, 1998), 19.

16. James Sprenger and Heinrich Kramer, *The Malleus Maleficarum,* trans. Montague Summers (London, The Pushkin Press, 1948), Part 1, Question 6. Summarizing their argument, Sprenger and Kramer contend that "all witchcraft comes from carnal lust, which is in women insatiable." Thanks to men's more spiritual, rational constitution, they are not nearly so prone to evil—a fact that elicits this enthusiastic benediction from our fifteenth-century authors: "Blessed be the Highest Who has so far preserved the male sex from so great a crime: for since He was willing to be born and to suffer for us, therefore He has granted to men this privilege." Ibid., Part 1, Question 7. As for the ratio of women to men accused of witchcraft during this period, estimates range from 20:1 to 100:1. See Elizabeth Richardson and Herbert Clark, *Women and Religion: A Feminist Sourcebook of Christian Thought* (New York: Harper & Row, 1977).

17. It is important to note that despite the intense and thoroughgoing negativity directed toward most things female, fleshly, and material, medieval people also recognized the importance of this realm. Caroline Walker Bynum's *The Resurrection of the Body in Western Christianity, 200-1336* (New York: Columbia University Press, 1995) is a fascinating study of the apparent refusal of medieval Christians to carry their loathing of the body to its logical conclusion. Again and again, often against all expectation and apparent logic, medieval thinkers held fast to the conviction that at the end of time there would be a general resurrection, and that resurrection would be physical. Despite their association of bodies with change, disease, putrefaction, death, and the concomitant loss of individual identity; despite their continual denigration of bodies and materiality; despite their conviction that God's perfection is enabled by and

reflected in God's absolute immutability—that is, in God's antithesis to the very essence of the bodily realm; despite all these powerful convictions, medieval Christians doggedly insisted that when the last trumpet blows, the physical will be lifted into the spiritual and preserved there forever.

18. Claire Marshall, "The Politics of Self-Mutilation: Forms of Female Devotion in the Late Middle Ages" in *The Body in Late Medieval and Early Modern Culture*, ed. Darryll Grantley and Nina Taunton (Aldershot, England: Ashgate, 2000).

19. Ibid., 11.

20. Martha J. Reineke, "'This Is My Body': Reflections on Abjection, Anorexia, and Medieval Women Mystics," *Journal of the American Academy of Religion* 58, no. 2: Summer 1990, 249.

21. Ibid.

22. The later Middle Ages, when these religious practices were widespread, has been portrayed by scholars as a decadent period characterized by "an excessively world-denying, guilt-ridden, flesh-hating rash of extreme asceticism." Philip A. Mellor, "Self and Suffering: Deconstruction and Reflexive Definition in Buddhism and Christianity," *Religious Studies* 27 (1991): 49–63.

23. See Bynum, *Holy Feast and Holy Fast: The Religious Significance of Food to Medieval Women* (Berkeley, Calif.: University of California Press, 1987); *Fragmentation and Redemption: Essays on Gender and the Human Body in Medieval Religion* (New York: Zone Books, 1992); and *Jesus as Mother: Studies in the Spirituality of the High Middle Ages* (Berkeley, Calif.: University of California Press, 1982).

24. The other three were receiving yearly communion, paying tithes, and baptizing one's children. Reineke, "This Is My Body," 252.

25. Quoted in Shaw, *The Burden of the Flesh*, 51. The following several paragraphs are indebted to Shaw's insightful study.

26. Ibid., 103.

27. Ibid., 105.

28. Ibid., 177.

29. The following discussion of medieval women's food practices is heavily indebted to Caroline Walker Bynum's *Holy Feast and Holy Fast*. My discussion in this chapter is predicated on the assumption that it is possible and useful to set women's experience apart from men's in order to see and analyze its distinctive shape and logic. This assumption of separability must be defended in light of concerns about gender essentialism—a task for which space limitations will not allow full discussion. Bernard McGinn, for one, warns against imposing a contemporary fascination with gender distinctions on medieval texts/realities. He notes that beginning in the thirteenth century, women's visibility rose considerably and "new forms of cooperation between men and women" developed in conjunction with a new vernacular, more holistic theology, so that spurious generalizations about gender differences should be avoided. Bernard McGinn, "The Changing Shape of Late Medieval Mysticism" in *Church History*, vol. 65 (1996), 12, note 19. In full awareness of the dangers of oversimplified generalizations, however, it remains possible to discern important differences in emphasis or intensity between male and female religious expression—for example, that food asceticism and sexual purity, while certainly present in medieval men's religiosity, were at the very *center* of and embraced with unparalleled intensity in women's spiritual practice. It is also important not to overstate the democratizing impulses that began in the thirteenth century. For example, this negative appraisal of women's spiritual and intellectual capacities, authored by influential churchman Jean Gerson in the fifteenth century, could easily be confused with sentiments typical of earlier ages: "First, every teaching of women . . . is to be held suspect. . . . Why? The reason is clear;

because not only ordinary but divine law forbids such things. Why? Because women are too easily seduced, because they are too obstinately seducers, because it is not fitting that they should be knowers of divine wisdom." Jean Gerson, *Ouevres complete*; cited by Rosalynn Voaden, *God's Words,Women's Voices*, 7.

30. Bynum, *Holy Feast and Holy Fast*, 119.

31. Ibid.

32. Ibid., 119–120.

33. Ibid., plate 25.

34. See this book's introduction for discussions of Irigaray and Butler.

35. Donald Weinstein and Rudolph Bell, *Saints and Society:The TwoWorlds ofWestern Christendom, 1000-1700* (Chicago: University of Chicago Press, 1982), 235.

36. Bynum, "'. . . AndWoman His Humanity': Female Imagery in the ReligiousWriting of the Later Middle Ages" in *Gender and Religion: On the Complexity of Symbols*, ed. Caroline Walker Bynum, Stevan Harrell, and Paula Richman (Boston: Beacon Press, 1986), 276.

37. Julian of Norwich, *Showings*, trans. Edmund Colledge, O.S.A., and James Walsh, S.J. (NewYork: Paulist Press, 1978), 127–28.

38. Elizabeth Alvilda Petroff, ed., *MedievalWomen'sVisionary Literature* (Oxford: Oxford University Press, 1986), 239.

39. See Elizabeth Petroff's commentary on the "benefits" of illness for medieval women; ibid., 37ff.

40. Quoted in ibid., 43–44.

41. Bynum, *Holy Feast and Holy Fast,* 296.

42. Quoted by Petroff, *MedievalWomen'sVisionary Literature,* 190–191.

43. Hadewijch as quoted by Petroff, ibid., 194.

44. Ruth Evans, "Virginities" in *The Cambridge Companion to MedievalWomen'sWriting*, ed. Carolyn Dinshaw and DavidWallace (Cambridge: Cambridge University Press, 2003), 22.

45. Ibid., 23.

46. Ibid., 23–24. Evans recounts that in the *AncreneWisse*, "virginity is famously described . . . as 'a precious liquor, a valuable liquid like balm, in a fragile vessel.' The vessel represents 'women's flesh' and the balm 'is maidenhood held within it (or chaste purity once maidenhood is lost).' And 'this brittle vessel is nonetheless as brittle as any glass; for if it is once broken, it is never mended to the wholeness it had, any more than glass. But it breaks more easily than brittle glass does.'" Ibid., 26.

47. Ibid., 31.

48. "As St. Jerome says, 'to live in the flesh without the action that the nature of flesh asks is not earthly life but angel's life and heavenly.'" Ibid., 25.

49. According to her autobiography, *The Book of Margery Kempe*, she and her husband agreed that if she would pay off his debts before she left on pilgrimage to Jerusalem and agree to eat meat and drink with him on Fridays instead of fasting, then he would free her from her conjugal duties to him so that she could give her body to God.

50. Evans, "Virginities," 22–23.

51. Ibid., 32. According to Evans, the most popular version of the tale involves a Jew who "obtains the host and tests its much-vaunted properties by subjecting it to abuse and torture: striking it, piercing it until it bleeds, burning and boiling it. The host's miraculous intactness brings about the conversion of onlooking Jews."

52. The scholarly term for the medieval phenomenon of betrothing oneself to Christ is "bridal mysticism," which Ulrike Wiethaus defines as "a particular type of devotion in which the human soul, envisioned as feminine, aspires to a union experience with her bridegroom, the human Christ."

According to Wiethaus, the phenomenon is reported to have been propagated by Bernard of Clairvaux in the early twelfth century and to have involved a noteworthy emphasis on sexuality: "Although the proponents of *bridal mysticism* rejected physical sexuality as sinful or at least highly fraught with ambiguity, they accepted spiritual reality as fully sexual. Whereas the courtly lover is destined to remain eternally titillated yet sexually frustrated, the Cistercian follower of Bernard may, or is even expected to, revel in orgiastic abandon—spiritually." Wiethaus, "Christian Piety and the Legacy of Medieval Masculinity," in *Redeeming Men: Religion and Masculinities*, ed. Stephen B. Boyd, W. Merle Longwood, and Mark W. Muesse (Louisville, Ky: Westminster John Knox Press, 1996), 49, 52. Although bridal mysticism had numerous male practitioners, it was apparently more popular among women, and its adoption by women certainly had distinctive implications for their self-understanding. Where men's involvement meant a reversal of gender roles as they assumed the female subject position vis-à-vis Christ, women bridal mystics dove even more deeply into their femaleness in order to enjoy the ultimate union with the Divine.

53. *Hadewijch: The Complete Works,* ed. Mother Columbia Hart, O.S.B. (New York: Paulist Press, 1980), 281.

54. Ulrike Wiethaus, "Sexuality, Gender, and the Body in Late Medieval Women's Spirituality: Cases from Germany and the Netherlands," *Journal of Feminist Studies in Religion* 7, no. 1 (1991): 35–52.

55. Ibid., 51.

56. Ibid., 50.

57. Petroff, *Medieval Women's Visionary Literature*, 33–34.

58. This discussion of Hildegard is based on Anne L. Clark's excellent essay, "The Priesthood of the Virgin Mary: Gender Trouble in the Twelfth Century," *Journal of Feminist Studies in Religion* 18, no. 1 (2002): 5–24.

59. Quoted in Clark, ibid., 14.

60. Ibid., 15.

61. McGinn, "The Changing Shape of Late Medieval Mysticism," 205.

62. Ibid., p. 9.

63. Ibid., 198–199.

64. Ibid., 206.

65. For a succinct discussion of the differences between medieval scholastic theology and affective piety, see Rosalynn Voaden, *God's Words, Women's Voices*, 7–14.

66. Nicholas Watson, "The Composition of Julian of Norwich's Revelation of Love" in *Speculum* 68 (1993): 643.

67. Ibid., 647.

68. Elliott, "Dominae or Dominatae?", 54.

69. Cited by Elliott, ibid., 65, 66.

70. Aquinas articulates the widely held assumption this way: "Now it is clear that a manifestation of divine truth which derives from a bare contemplation of the truth itself is more effective than that which derives from images of bodily things. Sheer contemplation is, in fact, nearer to the vision of heaven, according to which truth is gazed upon in the essence of God." Quoted in Voaden, *God's Words, Women's Voices*, 16.

71. Quoted in ibid.

72. Ibid., 19.

73. Ibid.

74. Ibid., 102.

75. By contrast, women whose comportment as visionaries did not abide by the standards of *discretio spirituum* suffered rejection and hostility. Margery Kempe, for instance, was continually

rebuffed and maligned by church officials and her visionary text widely discredited. More dramatically, Marguerite Porete and Joan of Arc were put to death because their visionary accounts were of purportedly demonic origin. Ibid, 40.

76. Petroff, *Medieval Women's Visionary Literature,* 46.

Chapter 3: Making a Way Out of No Way

1. *Domination and the Arts of Resistance* (New Haven: Yale University Press, 1990), 192.

2. An excerpt from a song sung by generations of African Americans. Cited by Lawrence Levine in *Black Culture and Black Consciousness* (New York: Oxford University Press, 1977), xiii.

3. These four "moments" are representative of countless instantiations of liberative creativity in African-American history, including those stemming from Africana, diasporic, and non-Christian experiences.

4. Among the numerous articulations of this perspective were the influential presentations made by U. B. Phillips in his *American Negro Slavery* (New York: D. Appleton and Company, 1918) and Stanley M. Elkins in his *Slavery: A Problem in American Institutional and Intellectual Life* (Chicago: University of Chicago Press, 1959). Some scholars argued that the extreme brutalities of the Middle Passage, combined with the family-destroying, language-replacing, ego-diminishing practices of the American slave system, functioned to strip slaves of the resources of their African identity and traditions, turning them into morally and ideologically pliable creatures poised for imprinting by the new dominant culture and its religion. (For the classic articulation of this "tabula rasa" view, as well as its classic refutation, see E. Franklin Frazier's *The Negro Church in America* [New York: Schocken Books, 1964]; and Meville J. Herskovits, *The Myth of the Negro Past* [Boston: Beacon Press, 1958].) Others suggested that most slaves felt no compulsion to question or defy their enslavement because American slavery was an essentially benevolent institution. According to historian Herbert Aptheker, this popular line of reasoning allowed members and ancestors of the slaveholding class not only to rationalize slavery but "to feel absolutely philanthropic" about it (Aptheker, *American Negro Slave Revolts* [New York: International Publishers Co., 1974], 2). It also fueled the powerful and long-lasting stereotype of black people as inherently passive, gullible, and manipulable—too dumb, defenseless, lazy, or resourceless to recognize and resist their own exploitation, and hence constitutionally incapable of genuine moral agency.

5. See, for example, the work of Herbert Aptheker, Eugene Genovese, Kenneth Stampp, Lawrence Levine, Albert Raboteau, Gayraud Wilmore, James Cone, and Dwight Hopkins.

6. Dwight N. Hopkins, *Down, Up, and Over: Slave Religion and Black Theology* (Minneapolis: Fortress Press, 2000), 108.

7. Ibid., 256.

8. My discussion of the trickster in slave culture is informed in particular by these studies: Alan Dundes, *Mother Wit from the Laughing Barrel: Readings in the Interpretation of Afro-American Folklore* (New York: Garland Publishing, Inc., 1981), especially the essays by Bernard Wolfe and Zora Neale Hurston; Lawrence W. Levine, "'Some Go Up and Some Go Down': The Meaning of the Slave Trickster" in *The Hofstadter Aegis: A Memorial,* ed. Stanley Elkins and Eric McKitrick, (New York: Alfred A. Knopf, 1974), 94–124; Riggins R. Earl Jr., *Dark Symbols, Obscure Signs: God, Self, & Community in the Slave Mind* (Maryknoll, N.Y.: Orbis Books, 1993); and Dwight N. Hopkins, *Shoes That Fit Our Feet: Sources for a Constructive Black Theology* (Maryknoll, N.Y.: Orbis Books, 1993), 84–130.

9. Trickster tales were by no means limited to Rabbit or even to animals. For the sake of brevity, however, I will limit my consideration here to Rabbit. Most contemporary Americans know of Brer Rabbit through the collection of Uncle Remus stories presented by journalist Joel Chandler Harris, but few recognize the problematic nature of the narrative convention and

interpretive angle Harris creates, which portrays plantation slavery as a benevolent institution. As Bernard Wolfe notes, in Harris's collections the stories of Brer Rabbit are told to an adorable white boy, son of the plantation owners, by a doting "Uncle Tom" Negro whose "beaming countenance" and "cheerful and good-humored" voice reveal not a hint of critique of slavery. Reflecting on the potentially subversive character of the Brer Rabbit tales, Harris insisted that the stories depict only the "roaring comedy of animal life" rather than any insight into slave discontent or strategic resistance. Harris's narrative frame and intention notwithstanding, Wolfe and others highlight the pointedly critical content of the tales he recounts. Wolfe, "Uncle Remus and the Malevolent Rabbit" in *Mother Wit*, 528.

10. Quoted in Levine, "Some Go Up," 105.

11. It may be that this self-critical approach to their own moral system, combined with their keen awareness of its departure from the dominant system, kept slaves and their descendants from trumpeting its merits. This might help explain why scholars as brilliant as Eugene Genovese have assumed that while slaves were quite good at challenging the dominant moral code, they "could not readily counterpose a coherent alternative." *Roll, Jordan, Roll: The World the Slaves Made* (New York: Vintage Books, 1972), 608. In this chapter, I am suggesting that, in fact, they and their ancestors *did* counterpose a coherent, though by no means inflexible, alternative.

12. For an interesting discussion of negative portrayals of Rabbit, and a fascinating interpretation of the Tar Baby tale, see Wolfe, "Uncle Remus and the Malevolent Rabbit" in *Mother Wit*.

13. Levine, "Some Go Up," 115–16.

14. Ibid., 106.

15. Ibid., 105.

16. Earl, *Dark Symbols, Obscure Signs*, 132.

17. There were, of course, other ways of interpreting Christianity even among the master class, but the dominant interpretation sanctioned slavery.

18. Peter Randolph, "Plantation Churches: Visible and Invisible" in *Afro-American Religious History: A Documentary Witness*, ed. Milton Sernett (Durham, NC: Duke University Press, 1985), 64, 66.

19. As Albert Raboteau suggests, "slavery was not only accepted as an economic fact of life, but defended as a positive social good, sanctioned by Scripture and capable of producing a Christian social order based on the observance of mutual duty, slave to master and master to slave. It was the ideal of the antebellum plantation mission to create such a rule of gospel order by convincing slaves and masters that their salvation depended upon it." *Slave Religion: The "Invisible Institution" in the Antebellum South* (New York: Oxford University Press, 1978), 152. Eugene Genovese makes a different but related point about slaveholders' religiously-based rationalization of slavery: "Southern ideologues repeatedly retreated into the view, to which their racism lent plausibility, that the slaves could not take care of themselves and that their masters had a Christian duty to do it for them. They thereby turned aside abolitionists' religious attack and mounted a powerful counterattack by interpreting the demand for abolition as a call for unchristian irresponsibility toward the fate of one's fellow man." *Roll, Jordan, Roll*, 76.

20. Cited in Gilbert Osofsky, *Puttin' On Ole Massa* (New York: Harper and Row, 1969), 32.

21. James H. Cone, *The Spirituals and the Blues* (Maryknoll, N.Y.: Orbis Books, 1972), 23.

22. As ex-slave Peter Randolph put it, "He who will lisp one word in favor of a system which will send blood-hounds through the forests of Virginia, the Carolinas, Georgia, Kentucky, and all the South, chasing human beings (who are seeking the inalienable rights of all men, 'life, liberty, and the pursuit if happiness,') possesses no heart; and that minister of religion who will do it is unworthy of his trust, knows not what the Gospel teaches, and had better turn to the heathen for a religion to guide him nearer the right; for the heathen in their

blindness have some regard for the rights of others, and seldom will they invade the honor and
virtue of their neighbors, or cause them to be torn in pieces by infuriated beasts." "Plantation
Churches," 65.

23. The term is doubly apt, describing not only the secret or "invisible" nature of the slaves'
religion but also the fact that generations of historians neglected slave sources and hence rendered them invisible.

24. Raboteau, *Slave Religion*, 212.

25. Randolph describes his own experience: "Not being allowed to hold meetings on the plantation, the slaves assemble in the swamps, out of reach of the patrols. They have an understanding
among themselves as to the time and place of getting together. This is often done by the first
one arriving breaking boughs from trees, and bending them in the direction of the selected spot
. . . . Sometimes the slaves meet in an old log-cabin, when they find it necessary to keep watch.
If discovered, they escape, if possible; but those who are caught often get whipped. Some are
willing to be punished thus for Jesus' sake." Randolph, "Plantation Churches," 67.

26. Cited by Dwight N. Hopkins, *Shoes That Fit Our Feet*, 19.

27. Ibid., 18.

28. Osofsky, *Puttin' On Ole Massa*, 35.

29. Raboteau, *Slave Religion*, 59.

30. Hopkins, *Shoes That Fit Our Feet*, 19–20.

31. Genovese goes so far as to suggest that the slaves "conquered the religion of those who
had conquered them." *Roll, Jordan, Roll*, 212.

32. My understanding of the interplay between African and American religious worldviews
and practices during the slave period has been especially informed by the works of Peter Paris,
Albert Raboteau, Lawrence Levine, James Cone, and Dwight Hopkins.

33. Hopkins, *Shoes that Fit Our Feet*, 84.

34. Ibid., 85.

35. Jesus was viewed, says Raboteau, as "an everpresent and intimate friend" with whom
slaves easily identified due to the hardships and sufferings he, like the slaves, had to endure. *Slave
Religion*, 259.

36. Levine, *Black Culture and Black Consciousness*, 6.

37. John Lovell Jr., "The Social Implications of the Negro Spiritual," in Alan Dundes, *Mother
Wit from the Laughing Barrel*, 457.

38. Levine, *Black Culture and Black Consciousness*, 33.

39. Ibid.

40. Ibid. White Christians, too, sang songs with similar images, and yet as Levine points out,
"for this same message to be expressed by Negro slaves who were told endlessly that they were
members of the lowliest race *is* significant." Ibid., 34.

41. As ex-slave Frederick Douglass asserted, songs such as "O Canaan, sweet Canaan, I
am bound for the land of Canaan," meant "something more than a hope of reaching heaven.
We meant to reach the North, and the North was our Canaan." Other spirituals whose double
meaning is not difficult to discern include, "Steal away to Jesus," which many contend was used
to signal the convening of a secret prayer meeting, and "Run to Jesus, shun the danger, / I don't
expect to stay much longer here," which may have signaled an imminent attempt at escape.
Levine, *Black Culture and Black Consciousness*, 51. Such secret communication tactics did not
always go unnoticed by whites. Frightened of the possibility of slave revolts, some developed
a sensitive ear to slave double-speak and were even known to jail slaves for singing songs sus-
pected of having subversive intent. See Raboteau, *Slave Religion*, 248.

42. Hopkins, *Shoes that Fit Our Feet*, 26–32.

43. Anthony Pinn, "Sweaty Bodies in a Circle: Thoughts on the Subtle Dimensions of Black Religion as Protest," *Black Theology: An International Journal* 4, no. 1 (2006), 18.

44. Cone, *The Spirituals and the Blues,* 16–17.

45. It should be noted that not all slaves rejected the master class's moral system. Some, says Raboteau, embraced white notions of virtue with such devotion that they developed "an attitude of moral superiority to their masters—an attitude that could simultaneously support compliance to the system of slavery and buttress the slave's own self-esteem." Raboteau, *Slave Religion,* 301.

46. Based on their comprehensive study of "slave flight" between 1790 and 1860, John Hope Franklin and Loren Schweninger conclude that "a significant number of slaves challenged the system and . . . the great majority of them struggled to attain their freedom even if they failed." *Runaway Slaves: Rebels on the Plantation* (New York: Oxford University Press, 1999), xiv.

47. The classic study of slave revolts is Herbert Aptheker's *American Negro Slave Revolts* (New York: International Publishers, 1974; originally published in 1943).

48. Due to space restrictions, my discussion takes up only a few of the many forms of "micro" resistance employed by slaves. Other forms I would like to have addressed include humor, architecture, and communication. For discussions of these topics, see Levine, *Black Culture and Black Consciousness*; Osofsky, *Puttin' On Ole Massa*; Hopkins, *Down, Up, and Over*, and—discovered just before this book was going to press—Jacqueline Bussie, *The Laughter of the Oppressed* (T & T Clark, 2007).

49. The phrase is Aptheker's, *American Negro Slave Revolts*, 3. Dwight Hopkins refers to this kind of protest as "micro resistance" in *Down, Up, and Over*, 254ff.

50. My summary of the impact of slavery on parenting and parent-child relations is based on Marie Jenkins Schwartz's informative book, *Born in Bondage: Growing Up Enslaved in the Antebellum South* (Cambridge, Mass.: Harvard University Press, 2000).

51. Cited by Schwartz, ibid., 1.

52. As Marie Jenkins Schwartz concludes in her study of slavery's impact on children and parenting, "Through their attempts to shape childhood according to their own ideals, slaves created a world of their own making and refuted the slaveholder's belief that the babies slave women bore in bondage belonged to no one but the owners." Ibid., 4.

53. Ibid.

54. Ibid., 164.

55. Ibid., 101, 123, 132.

56. The reasons for this are multiple, says Schwartz, including "a relatively healthy climate and the absence of tropical disease"; work regimens that "appear to have been less demanding than those for crops [such as sugar, coffee, and cocoa] cultivated in other parts of the Americas"; and a plantation system and geography that made escape more difficult than in other places. *Born in Bondage*, 6.

57. Ibid.

58. As Schwartz documents in her study, "Slave parents were determined that their children would endure and a people persist. When southern planters boasted that they treated their slaves better than any other working people, slave or free, slaves demanded that they live up to the claim." Ibid., 6.

59. Eugene Genovese's classic thesis is that paternalism was the main force behind plantation slavery, binding master and slave together in a mutually reinforcing relationship that provided slaves with protection and basic necessities in exchange for labor. According to Genovese, this arrangement gave slaves certain amounts of leverage vis-à-vis slaveholders, but it also required that they accommodate to the overall structure of white domination. One point on which

Genovese has been criticized is the relatively sanguine picture he paints of the master-slave child relationship, which many argue discounts the economic or materialist motivations of slaveowners as well as the hardships slave children endured. See *Roll, Jordan, Roll.*

60. Schwartz, *Born in Bondage,* 8.

61. Ibid., 163.

62. Osofsky, *Puttin' On Ole Massa,* 25.

63. For analysis of the stealing versus taking differentiation, see Hopkins, *Down, Up, and Over,* and Raboteau, "Slave Autonomy and Religion" in *The Journal of Religious Thought* (2001), 61.

64. Letter dated March 28, 1860, from fugitive slave, the Rev. J. W. Loguen of Syracuse, New York, to slave owner, Mrs. Sarah Logue of Tennessee, as it appears in Aptheker, *A Documentary History of the Negro People,* Volume 1, 451.

65. Cited by Genovese, *Roll, Jordan, Roll,* 602.

66. Of course, slaves' thieving did not always have such noble motivations or intentions. Sometimes it was undertaken not for survival, protest, or freedom but for revenge or self-aggrandizement. In such cases, it merely mirrored the moral bankruptcy of slaveholders and could claim no moral legitimacy.

67. My understanding of this phenomenon is primarily indebted to John Hope Franklin and Loren Schweninger's comprehensive study, *Runaway Slaves,* and to Osofsky's *Puttin' On Ole Massa.* The quote is from Genovese, *Roll, Jordan, Roll,* 648.

68. Osofsky explains that escapes to the North were difficult for several reason: Slaves had few resources to support long journeys through a dangerous and heavily monitored land; most had no geographical education or awareness and hence no conception of where "North" really was or how one could reach it; most lived in the deep South, far away from free states; the consequences for getting caught were dire; and many slaves had been frightened by white-generated rumors that "Yankees were cannibals who looked upon them as tasty morsels." *Puttin' On Ole Massa,* 18.

69. Ibid., 15, 28.

70. Franklin and Schweninger, *Runaway Slaves,* 90.

71. Ibid., 20.

72. Ibid., 30.

73. Genovese makes a provocative claim relevant to this point. He begins by recognizing that slaves "developed their own values as a force for community cohesion and survival." Then he contends that "in so doing they widened the cultural gap and exposed themselves to even harder blows from a white nation that could neither understand their behavior nor respect its moral foundations." *Roll, Jordan, Roll,* 294.

74. Genovese seems unaware of the deep theological warrants within Christianity for the slaves' ethic of ingenuity. He suggests, for instance, that "the doctrine of the legitimacy of taking from Ole Massa could not arise simply as an alternative morality, securely rooted in the slaves' autonomous world-view," because slaves' "religiously formed sensibility could not offer adequate justification" for such behavior. *Roll, Jordan, Roll,* 607–08.

75. This invisibility can be attributed to three main causes: (1) racist assumptions that slaves were incapable of anything other than brutish submission or revolt, which created an unintentional layer of camouflage for all but the most overt reactions; (2) the deliberate cloaking strategies used by slaves; and (3) slaves' focus on the primary good of survival, which was a precondition of other, more visible goods such as group mobilization and structural change.

76. In order, these phrases belong to E. Franklin Frazier, *The Negro Church in America,* 44; Lawrence Levine, *Black Culture and Black Consciousness,* 78; and Eric C. Lincoln and Lawrence H. Mamiya, *The Black Church in African American Experience* (Durham, N.C.: Duke University Press, 1990), 8.

77. Additional indignities include "refusing to christen black babies, serving blacks communion only after all whites were served, and denying blacks access to church burial grounds." Eddie S. Glaude Jr., "Of the Black Church and the Making of a Black Public" in *African American Religious Thought*, ed. Cornel West and Eddie S. Glaude Jr. (Louisville, Ky.: Westminister John Knox, 2003), 343.

78. See Rayford W. Logan, *The Negro in American Life and Thought: The Nadir, 1877-1901* (New York: Dial Press, 1954).

79. Evelyn Brooks Higginbotham, *Righteous Discontent: The Women's Movement in the Black Baptist Church, 1880-1920* (Cambridge, Mass.: Harvard University Press, 1993), 4–5.

80. Ibid., 5.

81. Ibid., 4.

82. Glaude, "Of the Black Church," 347.

83. Benjamin E. Mays and Joseph W. Nicholson, "The Genius of the Negro Church," in Sernett, *Afro-American Religious History*, 340.

84. Peter Paris, *The Social Teaching of the Black Churches* (Philadelphia: Fortress Press, 1985).

85. From the preamble to the Free African Society in Philadelphia, founded in 1787 by Richard Allen and Absalom Jones. Quoted in Glaude, "Of the Black Church," 345.

86. Frazier, *The Negro Church in America*, 44.

87. Quoted in Lincoln and Mamiya, ed., *The Black Church in the African American Experience*, 8.

88. Quoted in Mays and Nicholson, "The Genius of the Negro Church," 343.

89. Higginbotham, *Righteous Discontent*, 7.

90. Ibid.

91. Glaude, "Of the Black Church," 341.

92. Paris, *The Social Teaching of the Black Churches*, 108.

93. Reflecting on the popularity of eschatological themes in black preaching and music, Gayraud Wilmore reminds us that this so-called otherworldliness may be best interpreted as "an interim strategy" in the face of overwhelming opposition. It developed an alternative vision for the future and cultivated hope, courage, and other resources for the struggles at hand. Thus, black religion's eschatology was "not otherworldly-quietistic but other otherworldly-disruptive." In the independent black church movement, it infused present-day struggles with transcendent meaning and possibility, and it nurtured an awareness of a radically different future that was "already breaking in upon this world in many hidden and deceptive ways." Wilmore, *Black Religion and Black Radicalism: An Interpretation of the Religious History of African Americans* (Maryknoll, N.Y.: Orbis, 1973), 51.

94. Gayraud Wilmore, *Last Things First* (Philadelphia: Westminster Press, 1982), 88.

95. Wilmore, *Black Religion and Black Radicalism*, 52.

96. W. E. B. Du Bois is among those who worried about the norm of ingenuity in black culture. While recognizing that "deception is the natural defence of the weak against the strong" and "the only method by which undeveloped races have gained the right to share modern culture," he nevertheless mourned the fact that "the price of culture is a Lie" ("Of the Faith of the Fathers" in Sernett, *Afro-American Religious History*, 318). In an ideal world, equality and justice would reign, and there would be no need for subversive strategies. But in our less than ideal world, one searches for strategies of resistance to injustice among the options at hand. Certainly, one would prefer to resist in forthright ways, as with negotiation or democratic dialogue, but when such ways are foreclosed by the prevailing power relations, one is left with three choices: acquiesce to the injustice; resist it violently; or resist it nonviolently. Ingenuity as a tool of resistance can be both violent and nonviolent, but when co-defined by what I am calling incarnational norms and aims, then, I argue, it becomes a viable form of nonviolent resistance.

97. For a helpful discussion of these and other positions, see Lincoln and Mamiya, *The Black Church in the African American Experience*, ch. 1. See also Peter Paris's thoughtful reflections in *The Social Teaching of the Black Churches*, 27ff.

98. See Peter Paris's excellent discussion of the complex character of African-American morality in *The Social Teaching of the Black Churches*, ch. 3.

99. There is a range of opinion about the causes and character of the black church's relative quiescence during the early 1900s, ranging from Gayraud Wlimore's contention that black churches were thoroughly "deradicalized" to more moderate proposals that they were simply overwhelmed by the mass migrations and precipitating economic depressions, which depleted the membership rolls and leadership ranks of many southern and rural churches while flooding northern and urban churches with unprecedented numbers and needs. Still, few scholars contest that the black church's moral authority and agenda for transformation were in crisis during these decades.

100. See James M. Washington's editor's introduction to *A Testament of Hope: The Essential Writings of Martin Luther King, Jr.* (San Francisco: Harper & Row, 1986), xiv–xv.

101. The Civil Rights movement and King's own life and ideas certainly included more than the strategy of nonviolent resistance, but for the purposes of my discussion in this book, it is that element that is of most interest and, hence, my focus in this section. An additional thing to note is that while I focus here on King's embrace of nonviolent resistance, I am well aware that this embrace was prefigured in important ways by generations of black predecessors, including key family members, teachers, and mentors, and that it would not have been possible, moreover, without the shared commitment of his movement colleagues.

102. King, "Love, Law, and Civil Disobedience" in Washington, ed., *A Testament of Hope*, 45.

103. King, "Nonviolence and Racial Justice," ibid., 7.

104. King, "Pilgrimage to Nonviolence," ibid., 39.

105. King, "Nonviolence and Racial Justice," ibid., 7.

106. Ibid., 8.

107. Ibid.

108. Of course, the transformative effects of this strategy of moral suasion should also not be *over*stated, as King himself seemed to learn as the struggle wore on.

109. King, "The Social Organization of Nonviolence" in Washington, ed., *A Testament of Hope*, 33.

110. King, "Nonviolence and Racial Justice," ibid., 9.

111. King, "I See the Promised Land," ibid., 282.

112. King, "The Most Durable Power," ibid., 11.

113. King, "Pilgrimage to Nonviolence," ibid., 38.

114. King, "Love, Law, and Civil Disobedience," ibid., 49.

115. Ibid., 48–49.

116. King, "My Trip to the Land of Gandhi," ibid., 26.

117. Eugene TeSelle, "The Cross as Ransom," *Journal of Early Christian Studies* 4, no. 2 (1996): 169.

118. An additional point of notable ingenuity was King's creative synthesizing of African-American and European-American religious traditions. See Clayborne Carson, "Martin Luther King, Jr., and the African-American Social Gospel" in West and Glaude, ed., *African American Religious Thought*, 696–714.

119. Robert Michael Franklin, *Liberating Visions: Human Fulfillment and Social Justice in African American Thought* (Minneapolis: Fortress Press, 1990), 103.

120. This quote is the title of their important edited volume (Old Westbury, NY: Feminist Press, 1982).

121. Alice Walker, *In Search of Our Mothers' Gardens:Womanist Prose* (San Diego: Harcourt Brace Jovanovich, 1983). Here is Walker's definition of womanist in full: "1. From womanish (Opp. of 'girlish,' i.e., frivolous, irresponsible, not serious.). A black feminist or feminist of color. From the black folk expression of mothers to female children, 'You acting womanish,' i.e., like a woman. Usually referring to outrageous, audacious, courageous, or willful behavior. Wanting to know more and in greater depth than is considered 'good' for one. Interested in grown-up doings. Acting grown up. Being grown up. Interchangeable with another black folk expression: 'You trying to be grown.' Responsible. In charge. Serious. 2. Also: A woman who loves other women, sexually and/or nonsexually. Appreciates and prefers women's culture, women's emotional flexibility (values tears as natural counter-balance of laughter) and women's strength. Sometimes loves individual men, sexually and/or nonsexually. Committed to survival and wholeness of entire people, male and female. Not a separatist, except periodically for health. Traditionally universalist, as in: 'Mama, why are we brown, pink, and yellow, and our cousins are white, beige, and black?' Ans.: 'Well, you know the colored race is just like a flower garden, with every color represented.' Traditionally capable, as in: 'Mama, I'm walking to Canada and I'm taking you and a bunch of other slaves with me.' Reply: 'It wouldn't be the first time.' 3. Loves music. Loves dance. Loves struggle. Loves the Folk. Loves herself. Regardless. 4. Womanist is to feminist as purple to lavender." *In Search of Our Mothers' Gardens*, xi.

122. Katie Geneva Cannon, a leading womanist ethicist, remarks: "The structure of the capitalist political economy in which Black people are commodities combined with patriarchal contempt for women has caused the Black woman to experience oppression that knows no ethical or physical bounds." *Black Womanist Ethics* (Atlanta: Scholars Press, 1988), 4.

123. Emilie M. Townes, *In a Blaze of Glory:Womanist Spirituality As Social Witness* (Nashville: Abingdon, 1995), 10.

124. Cannon, *Black Womanist Ethics*, 2.

125. Ibid., 3.

126. Ibid., 3–4.

127. Ibid., 75.

128. Ibid., 104–05.

129. Ibid., 125–27, 134.

130. Ibid., 144.

131. Joan M. Martin, *More than Chains and Toil: A Christian Work Ethic of Enslaved Women* (Louisville, Ky.: Westminster John Knox, 2000).

132. Ibid., 152.

133. Ibid., 151–52.

134. Ibid., 80. The emphasis is Martin's.

135. Ibid., 111.

136. Higginbotham, *Righteous Discontent*.

137. Another interesting manifestation of this ethic is articulated by Carla L. Peterson in her impressive analysis of the liberative liminality achieved by nineteenth-century black women public speakers and writers such as Sojourner Truth, Jarena Lee, Nancy Prince, Mary Ann Shadd Cary, and Sarah Parker Remond. These women, argues Peterson, gained entry into the forbidden (for black women) arena of public civic debate "by 'achieving' an additional 'oppression,' by consciously adopting a self-marginalization that became superimposed upon the already ascribed oppressions of race and gender and that paradoxically allowed empowerment." *"Doers of the Word":African-American Women Speakers and Writers in the North (1830-1880)* (New York: Oxford University Press, 1998).

138. Higginbotham, *Righteous Discontent*, 190.

139. Ibid., 191–92.

140. Pierre Bourdieu, *Outline of a Theory of Practice*, trans. Richard Nice (London: Cambridge University Press, 1977), 169.

141. Higginbotham, *Righteous Discontent*, 193.

142. Ibid., 197. As Higginbotham says, "By insisting upon nonconformity to society's norms and established rules, black Baptist women subverted the cultural logic of white superiority and condemned white America for failing to live up to its own rhetoric of equality and justice as found in the Constitution." *Righteous Discontent*, 222.

143. Ibid., 227.

144. Westfield quotes Katie Cannon here. N. Lynne Westfield, *Dear Sisters: A Womanist Practice of Hospitality* (Cleveland, Ohio: The Pilgrim Press, 2001), 2.

145. Westfield, *Dear Sisters*, 64.

146. Ibid., 65.

147. Ibid., 11–12.

148. Ibid., 91.

149. Quoted by Westfield. Ibid., 33.

150. Ibid., 99.

151. Quoted by Westfield. Ibid., 100–101.

152. Ibid., 102–03.

153. See, for example, Levine's discussion of the trickster motif in slave culture. He insightfully thematizes the complex ethical stance symbolized by the trickster and embodied by slaves and ex-slaves, but then he refuses to grant this stance genuine status as a moral posture, arguing that while it constituted a distinctive "practical set of values and norms of behavior," it should not be viewed as a "counter-morality" of its own. Levine views the ethical stance of cunning and ingenuity as a kind of secular survival strategy that is fundamentally at odds with the slaves' "African heritage and their new religion" of Christianity. *Black Culture and Black Consciousness*, 123–24. My guess is that African Americans may hesitate to embrace an ethic of ingenuity as a viable and long-standing moral tradition for several reasons. If their long subjugation has been justified by whites at least in part on the basis of blacks' purported immorality, then blacks' hesitation to embrace a non-normative morality should come as no surprise. In addition, the fact that ingenuity has tended to be associated with the "secular" realm (as per Levine) and has been viewed as absent from the key theological warrants of scripture and tradition may also contribute to the tendency within African-American communities to downplay it as a central virtue.

Chapter 4: Incarnating Imagination

1. Joerg Rieger uses the experience of pain or hurting to frame his constructive theology, arguing that those with relative privilege who wish to work toward the common good cannot rely only on their own perspective of the world but must learn to see things from the perspective of the oppressed, of those in greatest pain. Only through this contextual lens can they see the common good and develop genuinely common interests and shared projects of liberation. "Developing a Common Interest Theology," in Joerg Rieger, ed., *Liberating the Future* (Minneapolis: Fortress Press, 1998), 124–41.

2. Paula M. Cooey, *Willing the Good: Jesus, Dissent, and Desire* (Minneapolis: Fortress Press, 2006), 9.

3. I offer an analysis of 24/7 temporality and its attendant theological and ethical challenges and possibilities in "It's About Time: Reflections on a Theology of Rest," in Darby Kathleen

Ray, ed., *Theology That Matters: Ecology, Economy, and God* (Minneapolis: Fortress Press, 2006), 154–71.

4. While I appreciate Anthony Pinn's distinction of fantasy from imagination and agree with him that imagination can function to reiterate rather than resist the unjust status quo, I am not convinced that imagination necessarily or essentially lacks genuine prophetic intention or effect. I am intrigued by Pinn's contention that imagination mitigates eros and irreverence, but I will need to hear more from him on this subject before abandoning imagination for fantasy. As I understand it, fantasy is an ingredient of imagination rather than a rival concept. See Anthony B. Pinn, "Embracing Nimrod's Legacy: The Erotic, the Irreverence of Fantasy, and the Redemption of Black Theology," in *Loving the Body: Black Religious Studies and the Erotic*, edited by Anthony B. Pinn and Dwight M. Hopkins (New York: Palgrave Macmillan, 2004), 157–78.

5. Gandhi expressed some sympathy for violence as a response to oppression, proposing that it was a better alternative than cowardice, and yet he was unequivocal in his conviction that nonviolence was the morally superior response.

6. Walter Wink, *Jesus and Nonviolence* (Minneapolis: Fortress Press, 2003), 72–73.

7. Jim Wallis, *God's Politics: Why the Right Gets It Wrong and the Left Doesn't Get It* (New York: HarperSanFrancisco, 2005), 211.

8. See, for example, William J. Hynes and William G. Doty, eds., *Mythical Trickster Figures* (Tuscaloosa: University of Alabama Press, 1993); Susan Niditch, *Underdogs and Tricksters* (San Francisco: HarperCollins, 1987); the work of Gerald Vizenor and Mac Linscott Ricketts; Henry Louis Gates, *The Signifying Monkey* (New York: Oxford University Press, 1988); Ellen Basso, *In Favor of Deceit* (Tucson: University of Arizona Press, 1987); Barbara Babcock-Abrahams, ed., *The Reversible World* (Ithaca: Cornell University Press, 1978); Cheryl Exum and Johanna Bos, eds., "Reasoning with the Foxes," *Semeia: An Experimental Journal for Biblical Criticism* 42 (1988); Lewis Hyde, *Trickster Makes This World* (New York: North Point Press, 1998); Mathias Guenther, *Tricksters & Trancers* (Bloomington: Indiana University Press, 1999); as well as those to be considered in what follows.

9. William J. Hynes, "Inconclusive Conclusions: Tricksters—Metaplayers and Revealers" in William J. Hynes and William G. Doty, *Mythical Trickster Figures*, 202–217.

10. For a nice summary of *mujerista* theology, see Isasi-Diaz's website: http://users.drew.edu/aisasidi/Definition1.html.

11. Ada María Isasi-Díaz, "Burlando Al Opresor: Mocking/Tricking the Oppressor: Dreams and Hopes of Hispanas/Latinas and Mujeristas," *Theological Studies* 65, no. 2 (June 2004): 340.

12. Ibid., 344.

13. Ibid., 344–46.

14. Ibid., 344.

15. Ibid., 346–47.

16. Ibid., 349.

17. Isasi-Díaz quotes Gustavo Gutierrez here. Ibid., 350.

18. Ibid., 356.

19. Donna J. Haraway, *Simians, Cyborgs, and Women: The Reinvention of Nature* (New York: Routledge, 1991), and "Ecce Homo, Ain't (Ar'n't) I a Woman, and Inappropriate/d Others: The Human in a Post-Humanist Landscape" in *Feminists Theorize the Political*, ed. Judith Butler and Joan Scott (New York: Routledge, 1992), 86–100. I originally intended to offer a biographical descriptor of Haraway (for example, Donna Haraway, historian of science), but as a scholar she plays the trickster and is nearly impossible to pin down.

20. Ibid., 90.

21. Ibid., 97, 92.

22. Ibid., 97.

23. Ibid., 92.

24. Ibid., 98.

25. Ibid., 98.

26. Sharon D. Welch, *Communities of Resistance and Solidarity* (Maryknoll, NY: Orbis Books, 1985); *A Feminist Ethic of Risk* (Minneapolis: Fortress Press, 2000); *Sweet Dreams in America: Making Ethics and Spirituality Work* (New York: Routledge, 1999); *After Empire: The Art and Ethos of Enduring Peace* (Minneapolis: Fortress Press, 2004).

27. Welch, *Sweet Dreams in America*, 4, xxi.

28. Ibid., xviii.

29. Ibid., 51.

30. Welch, *After Empire*, 64, 66.

31. Ibid., 32, 156, 25, 157.

32. Haraway, *Simians, Cyborgs, and Women*, 98.

33. Welch, *After Empire*, 178.

34. The phrase, "the principle of mercy," is from Jon Sobrino's book, *The Principle of Mercy: Taking the Crucified People from the Cross* (Maryknoll, NY: Orbis, 1994).

35. Quoted in William Greider, *The Soul of Capitalism: Opening Paths to a Moral Economy* (New York: Simon & Schuster, 2003), 248.

36. Brian Walker (Herman Miller CEO), "A Better World Together," http://www.hermanmiller.com/CDA/SSA/Category/0,1564,a10-c382,00.html.

37. Greider, *The Soul of Capitalism*, 245.

38. Walker, "A Better World Together."

39. According to the Economic Research Service of the U. S. Department of Agriculture, the median household income in Mississippi in 2004 was $34,278. (http://www.ers.usda.gov/Data/Unemployment/RDList2.asp?ST=MS). The median income in over half the counties in Mississippi is less than $30,000.

40. Wallis, *God's Politics*, 272ff.

41. www.ithacahours.com.

42. Jim Wallis compellingly makes this point throughout *God's Politics*.

43. This story and others can be accessed via www.buddhanet.net, gakkaionline.net, or any number of other sites featuring Buddhist traditions and texts.

44. David Jensen's *In the Company of Others: A Dialogical Christology* (Cleveland: Pilgrim, 2001) is a recent example of the possibilities for christology-focused dialogue with other traditions.

INDEX

purity, 34, 58, 65, 67, 158;
moral, 11, 24, 51, 94, 146–147;
sexual, 63, 75–78, 81, 84, 177 n. 29, 178 n. 46

Quirizio da Murano, 69

Raboteau, Albert, 97–98, 180 n. 5, 181 n. 19, 182 n. 24, n. 29, n. 32, n. 35, n. 41, 183 n. 45, 184 n. 63
racism, vii, 101, 109–110, 114, 120, 122–123, 127, 131–132, 141, 145, 147, 153, 160, 181 n. 19, 184 n. 75
Randolph, Peter, 96, 181 n. 18, n. 22, n. 25
reconciliation, 112, 123, 156
redemption, 10, 27–29, 42, 44, 74, 77, 87, 119, 124, 146, 156, 177 n. 23, 189 n. 4;
salvation, 23, 27, 34, 74, 87, 136, 152, 172 n. 13, 181 n. 19
reign of God.
See kingdom of God
Reineke, Martha, 60–61, 177 n. 20, n. 24
religion, 60, 88, 113, 141, 165
resistance, 110, 115, 121, 124, 136, 141, 149, 152, 157;
everyday, 18–19, 48, 102;
to evil, 33, 134, 143;
to injustice, 2, 9, 15–18, 21, 46–47, 64, 92, 96, 98, 102, 108;
nonviolent, 32, 46, 116, 118–24, 142, 145;
parenting as, 102–04, 183 n. 50;
politics of, 17, 20;
running away as, 106–08;
stealing as, 106;
working as, 105–06, 129–30
Rieger, Joerg, x, 188 n. 1

salvation.
See redemption.
Satan/the devil, 23–31, 36, 38–39, 57, 85, 96–97, 117, 141–42, 159, 166, 171 n. 2, 172 n. 5, 173 n. 22, 174 n. 44, 176 n. 13
Schwartz, Marie Jenkins, 103, 105, 183 n. 50, n. 51, n. 52, n. 56, n. 58, 184 n. 60
Schweninger, Loren, 107–108, 183 n. 46, 184 n. 67, n. 70
Scott, James C., 17–20, 48, 91, 171 n. 30–n. 32, n. 37, 175 n. 69,
Scott, Patricia Bell, 125, 189 n. 19
Shaw, Teresa, 65, 176 n. 15, 177 n. 25
slavery, viii, 14–15, 17, 35, 48, 91–108, 129–131, 136, 150, 180 n. 4 and 9, 181 n. 19, 183 n. 45 and 59
Smith, Barbara, 125
Sölle, Dorothee, 51, 175 n. 1
spirituals, 100, 181 n. 21, 182 n. 41, 183 n. 44
Sprenger, James, 176 n. 16
Stevens, Janet, 169 n. 9
Stout, Jeffrey, 12, 169 n. 14
subversion, 2, 4, 9–10, 15–17, 20, 54, 70–71, 83, 86, 91–92, 101, 117, 123–124, 130, 132, 134, 136–137, 150, 171 n. 29, 181 n. 9, 182 n. 41, 185 n. 96, 188 n. 142
suffering, 19, 21, 29, 32, 37, 42, 45, 53, 63, 67–69, 87, 89, 99–100, 105, 109, 111, 123, 128, 136, 140, 147–149, 151–153, 171 n. 39, 176 n. 16, 177 n. 22, 179 n. 75, 182 n. 35;
self-inflicted, 71–75
Sutton-Smith, Brian, 169 n. 3

Tertullian, 57
TeSelle, Eugene, ix, 123, 172 n. 12, 186 n. 117
Townes, Emilie, 126, 187 n. 123
trickster, 8, 10, 19, 93–96, 108, 150–55, 169 n. 3, 180 n. 8–9, 188 n. 153, 189 n. 8
Truth, Sojourner, 152–153, 187 n. 137

vernacular theology, 69, 82–83
Via, Dan Otto, 174 n. 62